*The Collected Clinical Works
Volume 11*

Education for Prevention

Individual Psychology in the Schools

The Education of Children

Alfred Adler

New Translation by Gerald L. Liebenau
Edited by Henry T. Stein, Ph.D.

Classical Adlerian Translation Project

© 2006 by Henry T. Stein, Ph.D.

All rights reserved under International and Pan-American Copyright Conventions. No part of this book may be reproduced or transmitted in any form or by any means, electronic or mechanical, including photocopy, recording, or any information storage and retrieval system, without prior permission in writing from the editor. All inquiries should be sent to Henry T. Stein, Ph.D., Classical Adlerian Translation Project, 2565 Mayflower Lane, Bellingham, WA 98226. Tel (360) 647-5670 or e-mail to HTStein@att.net .

Published 2006 by The Classical Adlerian Translation Project.

Printed in the United States of America

0-9770186-1-X

Table of Contents

Table of Contents

Editor's Preface 2006... ii
Part 1: Individual Psychology in the Schools 1
    Preface by Alfred Adler..2
    Introduction 3
    Chapter I: The First Five Years 5
    Chapter II: On the History of Problem Children 14
    Chapter III: Children's Lifestyles 22
    Chapter IV: Children in Difficult Situations 28
    Chapter V: Real and Imagined Childhood Memories 35
    Chapter VI: Childhood Memories and Dreams 43
    Chapter VII: On the Meaning of Recollections,
        Fantasies, and Dreams 51
    Chapter VIII: On the Theory of Dreams 59
    Chapter IX: Overview: Social Feeling 66
    Chapter X: Four Case Histories 71
Part 2: The Education of Children 99
    Chapter I: Introduction 100
    Chapter II: The Unity of Personality 109
    Chapter III: The Striving for Superiority and its
        Educational Significance 115
    Chapter IV: Directing the Superiority Striving 126
    Chapter V: The Inferiority Complex 133
    Chapter VI: The Development of the Child:
        Preventing the Inferiority Complex 141
    Chapter VII: Social Feeling and the Obstacles
        to its Development 150
    Chapter VIII: The Child's Position in the Family:
        The Psychology of the Situation and its Remedy 159
    Chapter IX: The New Situation as a Test
        of Preparation 164
    Chapter X: The Child at School 172
    Chapter XI: Influences From Outside 183
    Chapter XII: Adolescence and Sex Education 191
    Chapter XIII: Pedagogical Mistakes 199
    Chapter XIV: Educating the Parent 205
    Appendix I: Individual Psychology Questionnaire 210
    Appendix II: Five Case Histories With Commentaries 215
Index.. 242
Appendix A: Basic Principles of Adlerian Psychology 258

Editor's Preface - 2006

Volume eleven features two essential classics on child guidance for educators and psychotherapists. Part One contains the first English translation of Adler's book *Individual Psychology in the Schools*, initially published in 1929 in German, then in 1933 into Dutch, and later in 1936 into Spanish and Hebrew. Part Two contains *The Education of Children*, originally published in English in 1930, and newly edited for improved readability.

Individual Psychology in the Schools represents Adler's first attempt to introduce Individual Psychology into the schools at the Pedagogical Institute in Vienna. Although he addressed teachers in his lectures, he also hoped to gain the cooperation of psychiatrists, psychologists, and parents in the process of "improving the lot of children, teachers, and families." Between 1924-1927, Adler attracted more than six hundred Viennese teachers to his course; these lectures became the basis for his book. By 1927, the city of Vienna would hire only elementary, secondary, and special education teachers who had graduated from the Pedgogical Institute. During this period, "anyone can learn anything" became his famous educational motto.

The Education of Children also consists of lecture material. Presenting abundant and detailed insight into personality development, the book was apparently daunting to parents but appealed to a wider range of professionals. Adler emphasized the influence of exaggerated, early feelings of inferiority that can trigger an unhealthy striving for power in a child, often resulting in overt or covert warfare with adults. He illuminated the range of weapons that the weaker or fearful child may employ, such as bed-wetting and eating problems. Adler encouraged parents to be empathic, understanding, and encouraging, suggesting that threats and punishment are useless and antagonizing. He offered advice on sex education, recommending that it be tailored to a child's interest and intellectual level. His primary advice to educators was to avoid discouraging any child at school. Typical of Adler's constant efforts to educate parents, teachers, and professionals, he attempted to democratize his contribution to psychology.

For readers unfamiliar with Adler's ideas, a brief overview, titled "Basic Principles of Classical Adlerian Psychology," is included in the appendix.

Part 1

Individual Psychology in the Schools

Lectures for Teacher and Educators

---

[1] Originally published as *Individualpsychologie in der Schule: Vorlesungen für Lehrer und Erzieher*. Leipzig: Hirzel, 1929. Initially translated into Dutch (1933), Hebrew (n.d.a.), and Spanish (1936 & 1941). Translated into English by Gerald L. Liebenau, 2004.

Preface

This is a first attempt to introduce Individual Psychology into the schools and to participate in the development of the schools as centers for raising children. This book contains the lectures which I presented to teachers as a docent at the Pädagogische Institute of the city of Vienna. My subject was "Problem children in School."

The reader will recognize at first glance that I aimed at cooperation among psychiatrists, teachers, and the families. This work represents a small picture of what I and my friends had tried to do for many years in school counseling centers: to improve the lot of children, teachers and families. For those inexperienced in this matter this may seem like much too slow a process.

We, the Individual Psychologists, teachers, and parents who have worked with us, as well as knowledgeable pedagogues around the world believe differently. If our work continues as it has to date, if we continue to succeed in winning and maintaining the confidence and trust of teachers, then the educational system will rest on better principles and will adapt itself to the work of those who labor for the benefit of the people.

Vienna, 31 August 1929   Dr. Alfred Adler

Introduction

The following work represents a collection of lectures that I presented as a docent to teachers at the Pedagogical Institute in Vienna. The purpose of these talks was to facilitate the introduction of the basic principles of Individual Psychology in the school system. They thus represent a complement to the practical work that was provided for many years by those who started Individual Psychology counseling centers in Vienna and in other cities abroad. The reader can find a brief summary of these centers' achievements in the "Educational Counseling Booklet" published in the 7th annual edition of the Internationale Zeitschrift für Individualpsychologie.

If the material in that booklet seems to some readers somewhat simplistic then I must remind them that outside the circle of Individual Psychologists there existed only a skeletal knowledge on this subject. Over the years of concerted effort we popularized that knowledge so that it had become familiar even to those who could not differentiate between a scientific theoretical exposition and an artistic performance. At the same time we have every reason to believe that those who think they have greater insight into human nature, as well as those to whom Individual Psychology appears superficial, are incapable of working with such skeletal knowledge.

For that reason I have endeavored over the course of many years to develop Individual Psychology not only along purely theoretical lines but also by working directly with physicians schooled in psychology, with educators, and with parents to develop the ability to deal with problem as well as with nervous children. We watched with astonishment as some of our critical readers tried to render particular concepts out of their organic context and to interpret them from their own quite different viewpoints. This approach was applied to the starting point for our views on the feeling of inferiority. In our opinion the suffering that results from tensions growing out of life's demands is a positive outcome. Our critics fail to see this suffering as only relative to other concerns that stem from growing up. Another fallacy, of course, is the malicious statement by some that the ability to postulate that we have practiced, and in which we have been carefully trained, is "unscientific." They seem to believe that new results can be fathomed by any means other than by postulating!

But we cannot complain. The more we understand Individual Psychology the greater becomes the awareness of an immense inner connectivity, the iron network that we employ to discover psychic connections and that is so useful for preventing and dealing with problem children, and for remedying neuroses.

We are constantly making progress. Teachers, parents, physicians and psychologists in ever increasing numbers turn to the study of Individual Psychology. In our school counseling centers we have successfully created the means for contributing to the flawless development of school children. Teachers, physicians, parents as well as children happily devote themselves to this endeavor with increasing effort and love. The significance of the school counseling centers gains increasing recognition.

This brief booklet contains, in addition to theoretical and practical advice for schools, a questionnaire to assist in understanding and treating problem children. There is also an Individual Psychology sketch for what is normal and abnormal regarding the inability to cooperate, and an investigation into its causes and consequences.

The Author

Chapter I

The First Five Years

All of you engaged in the field of education need to hear about both theory and practice. Consequently, we shall discuss cases of problem children, or you may present specific cases which we can then discuss in terms of finding ways to help such children. First, we must connect the child with the school and increase his interest in it. We also need to know the role of the school in his life and the school's expectations for all students. We must recognize that we are dealing here with an extension of the family. If the family were able to bring up their child properly, the school would be superfluous. We know from the history of schools that when they did not exist, an education by the family was quite sufficient. However, even in those times children from the upper ranks of society attended, for example, schools for princes which prepared them for the business of governing and administrating. Later, the church in its own interest established schools that furthered knowledge to satisfy the needs of church and state. Growing organically in accordance with the needs of the people, schools responded to the needs of society at times when trade and technology made education a necessity. This led to the need for a public school. Over time, the public school has taken various forms responsive to the demands of the governing authorities.

Today, we face the additional problem of how a school should function. Clearly, school must be regarded as fundamental for a well-rounded education of the public.

The task for the school is how to develop individuals able to meet the needs of life and regard the demands made on them not as something for others to fulfill, but as concerning them directly, and as something in which they must become involved. The ideals of a nation reach into the heart of the family. Therefore, the means must be developed in the family and in the schools to ensure that education prepares an individual for society.

We constantly look for interrelationships; we understand human nature in terms of the individual's attitude toward others, as the development of a person's regard for others. The personality does not begin developing in the school; it begins in the family. The first impressions made on a person already have significance. The family shapes the way a child enters school. At the beginning of school the child faces a new task, as does the teacher. The better a child is prepared to accept the need for schooling, the fewer problems he will face. The poorer a child is prepared, the greater his problems will be. The school is an experiment, a test that will show his level of preparation for the social demands of school. To be well prepared means to be able to adjust, not only to join in with others, but to have regard for others, to be interested in them, not only to accept the pleasant aspects of school as a personal favor, but to consider difficulties encountered as one's own and to make the effort to overcome them.

The school is not the first social challenge that a child faces. The first social task is the child's relationship to his mother. We can observe how the mother has prepared the child to develop proper relationships. What is a healthy relationship of a child to his mother? To be interested in her, to feel that she is a genuine fellow human being. However, many mistakes are made that result in the child never becoming a true fellow human being.

The mother captivates the entire interest of the child. She creates comfortable situations for him that often are so extreme that he can hardly function independently, expecting everything from the mother. Such behavior by the mother, who is present every minute of the day, creates automatic behavioral responses in the child. Because the child is not given the opportunity to practice overcoming difficulties, he is poorly prepared to face life.

Another result occurs when the mother fails to convey to her child the feeling that he is a fellow human being. Children who are resented, orphaned, illegitimate, unwanted, ugly, or adopted often cannot conceive that fellow human beings exist. Their ignorance of love shapes their attitudes. They feel as if they live among enemies and pattern their lives accordingly.

The first type of child cannot function independently; he constantly looks for support from another person. The other type holds onto the idea of being persecuted and demeaned. Such children for the most part do not trust others and fear failure. In both cases a problem is created that will dominate their entire life. Both types of children will always believe that they must be pampered, must avoid difficult situations, must attempt to escape, and must guard against anyone harming them.

The first four or five years in a child's life create an attitude that becomes automatic. He will no longer be open to new experiences.

When a pampered child enters school and instead of pampering finds unfamiliar situations, he will feel bad, but will continue striving to be pampered and become the center of attention. Constantly on the lookout for someone who will take an interest in him, he will want to be the center of attention. He can achieve this goal in two ways. He may exert a considerable effort to do well, and by behaving extremely well, draw attention to himself. In this way, he will almost have reestablished his former comfortable and familiar situation. Such a child abhors difficulties. On the other hand, he may try to be extremely conspicuous, become lazy, or behave badly. He may act up and be defiant in order to draw the teacher's or his classmates' attention to himself so that they occupy themselves with him. We can now observe a process in these children who will follow a psychological direction in which everything becomes a means toward an end. In most cases, these children are not well prepared. They lack concentration and are unable to make friends, which they regard as difficult because they are always busy with themselves. They have no confidence in themselves and become increasingly disaffected from school. Such children always believe they are right. They favor situations that are familiar from home rather than accept new situations in school. They regard schoolwork with disdain and reject it. Obviously, faulty preparation lays the foundation for such an attitude, which cannot be changed simply with warnings and punishment.

We find the same phenomenon in children who feel hated. They feel neglected and increasingly encounter problems. We must first investigate and try to understand what occurs in such a child. Teachers must examine all psychological directions. When they notice failures, they must consider that the mother might have pampered the child when he was four or five years old. Because the child thinks that at home with his mother everything was better, he now will try to avoid doing anything because nothing can substitute for his lost paradise. This child is unprepared to cooperate, to have any understanding for others and to play with them. He has never considered whether he could get along if he had to.

We must be grateful that the teacher who works in this area finds it exceedingly satisfying and interesting, because he has an opportunity to prevent difficulties. If an overburdened teacher must work with 30 to 40 students, then only one solution can help him ease his burden: He must be experienced and practiced in understanding the type of child he faces. Unfortunately, we cannot easily use rules to turn this task into an artistic accomplishment. However, by applying Individual Psychology, we run little risk of making a mistake. We can maximize human nature not only by opening the right path for a child, but also by persuading the parents not to hinder their child from taking that path.

I would now like to focus on a crucial issue. The quality of home training is too often quite inadequate in that the challenges of life are made much too easy for children. For parents their greatest gift is their children for whom they have always desired a position of prominence. The children feel this desire and wish to exploit the preferential treatment they are given. This situation leads to an unusually large number of pampered children.

These children, as well as the second type mentioned above, lack social feeling; they have no interest in others. Having been pampered, their interests lie only in themselves and in their own well-being. Once having been pampered, they become unaware that other kinds of people exist because they have never encountered them. Their egotistical interest grows and becomes hardened. Such feelings are never inborn, but are created out of the experiences during their first years of life. The damage done to a child results from a feeling of not belonging anywhere and of being unacceptable. Such a child will never develop the feeling of being part of a community. He will lack courage and be unable to engage in various activities, which can take many forms. Every new task becomes a test and is viewed as an experiment. We must understand how a child behaves when confronted by a new task, by developing keener insights and recognizing the nuances of this process.

There is no such thing as a unique occurrence. A person will follow the same lifestyle for his entire life. The flaws in an individual become apparent only when he must face a task. As long as no one expects anything from a child, and as long as he confronts no difficulties, we have nothing to observe. How well a child functions can be established only when he faces a new situation. At that point, we can see how well he is prepared. We cannot wait until we have taught all the parents how to prepare a child correctly; we cannot wait until a child gets into minor or major difficulties. We must focus on prevention. A teacher with a realistic and effective grasp of psychology can do a great deal. It is not enough to be able to recognize a failing that developed during a child's developmental phase and to describe it as having been caused by pampering or a lack of affection. We can describe how a painting is done, but that does not mean we know how to paint. An individual must develop the skill that this process requires. Anyone can learn and practice the art of educating, which requires an understanding and consistent striving to reconcile the facts of life with the ideal of a social existence and preparing a child toward that end.

From whom do we expect the first preparation for a social existence? My understanding of society entails an unattainable ideal that we can only imagine since the totality of all human efforts would not suffice to attain it. Our most important task is to practice the art of motivating a child to reach for that social ideal. Only moving in this direction can avoid the mistakes that lead to a problem child, to neuroses, suicide, alcoholism, sexual perversion, criminality, etc. Who has the initial task of fulfilling this objective? The mother. We must remember what the mother should have done. We can see the results of following a wrong course. We must compensate for what a mother has not done and correct her mistakes. A mother has two functions: 1. To win over the child to herself; to direct the child's interest toward her; to become in the child's mind a fellow human being. 2. To direct the interest of that child toward others and toward the father as another fellow human being. The father should make his contribution by seeing that the child takes an interest in siblings and outsiders. The task of the school is grounded in these two functions of the mother, which are often neglected to some degree. Every task becomes a social problem. When a sibling arrives, the manner in which the first child relates to the sibling also becomes a social problem for which the child must be properly prepared.

Speech is a social problem. How does a child connect through language? Children whose social feelings have not been sufficiently developed usually have language problems. How can we become useful to society? A concern for others, developing an interest in them, becoming a friend, acquiring a religious or political viewpoint, love, and marriage all represent social problems that answer the question whether or not a person has an interest in the welfare of others. Those considered problem children have no interest in the welfare of others. They lack social feeling, optimism, and courage. Just as we can establish whether a mosaic has been laid correctly, so can we judge the correctness of the Individual Psychology process by our ability to foresee how a child will act when he confronts a social problem.

The following report concerns a five-year old pre-school child whose history enables us to predict how well he will behave in school. I will explain how, in a short period of time, the case can be made clear and we can confirm our judgment.

"This child is difficult to deal with."

The child obviously is hostile. He is constantly aggressive and probably lived in a benign environment in which he was pampered. The question arises why the child is still aggressive; does he now feel he is no longer pampered? Clearly, his situation is not as favorable as before. We can easily make that conjecture.

"He is hyperactive."

This is not new to us. Can we imagine an aggressive person who is not hyperactive? Were the child not active, we would think him not intelligent.

"He loves to break things."

That is the nature of an aggressive person.

"Occasionally, he has fits of anger."

This is a natural reaction. It means that he must be an intelligent child. We must establish whether any child is mentally retarded and should, therefore, be treated quite differently. Such children have no lifestyle. This child has a goal to fight and conquer for. He likes being victorious.

"The mother claims that the child is healthy and full of life.. He always wants someone to be occupied with him."

Families struggle when parents give in to a child who will do anything to irritate others.

"He climbs with his dirty shoes on top of the best table. He gets great pleasure from playing with the lamp while the mother is busy elsewhere."

The child knows exactly where to attack.

"When the mother plays the piano or starts to read, the child begins to play with the lights... He is always restless at the table and demands constant attention..."

The child wants to win so that he can maintain his position at the center of attention. The following thought comes to mind: If the child is so eager to be at the center of attention, then at one time he was in that position and seeks to regain that familiar situation. What is it that could have forced him out of that position? A younger brother or sister?

"He is always punching his father and demanding that he play with him."

We can see that he finds ways to be aggressive and annoying.

"He is used to sticking his hand into a cake and stuffing his mouth with it."

The child could make the same point of being aggressive by not eating.

"When the mother has company, the boy pushes the guest from the chair and occupies it himself."

We can see in this act that he does not like other people and he lacks social feeling, which also makes him behave aggressively toward his brother.

"When the father and mother sing and play the piano, the child yells that he dislikes the song."

The child does not like being ignored. When we observe bad behavior, we must not punish the child. Punishment does not help. We must recognize where we can intercede. The child in this case feels bad, offended, and neglected.

"The father is a singer and performs at a concert. The mother accompanies him on the piano. The boy yells out: "Dad, come to me..."

He constantly strives to have his parents occupy themselves with him.

"The boy has fits of anger when he wants something and does not get it..."

He demonstrates his aggressive attitude.

"He breaks everything. He removes all the screws from his bed with a screwdriver..."

Again, he displays his anti-social behavior. He does what he can to hurt his parents and show his displeasure.

"Occasionally, he makes cynical remarks to people, especially when he has done something and knows that he can get away with it."

People think he is an intelligent person because of his critical remarks. He cannot keep himself busy with anything for any length of time. The mother tries to distract him (in which she obviously does not succeed).

"When the mother slaps him, he laughs and stays quiet for maybe two minutes... The mother thinks that the grandparents pampered him excessively. Now he no longer is really pampered."

That is the reason he developed as he did. His social feeling was never developed since he clung only to his mother and father.

"The mother and father are always exhausted; the boy, never..."

Obviously he does not tire because he enjoys what he does. The mother and father do not enjoy being with the boy which is why they are exhausted. Force will not help in this case. He would seek revenge were he forced to behave.

"He does not think or concentrate."

His lifestyle does not require thinking and he is also unprepared. By now he should be able to function on his own, but cannot do it.

"He never attended a kindergarten..."

Apparently, the mother's task was to keep the boy for herself. We must recognize how all these factors interrelate. We can claim to understand this boy when we know that we are dealing with a part of the total individual. Understanding means seeing things in their context, not as a sum of fragments.

Individual Psychology in the Schools

Chapter II

On the History of Problem Children

At the last lecture, I spoke of a five-year old boy who was forced out of his comfortable central position by a younger brother. He now strives to regain that position. At this point, we should ask several questions that arise when we have to deal with a problem child in school. Can an innate hereditary instinct exist, tracing back to the time when humans still ran wild? Modern theories of psychology hold that such a concept still exists. In this case, that hypothesis cannot be advanced. Grasping at such a theory is tempting, if not satisfying. However, we shall not allow ourselves to consent to this idea. We want to reestablish the child's equilibrium. Our point of view is very important: What happens to the child if he fails the test when still with his family at home and then arrives at school, where a new test awaits him? He arrives as a complete individual who will not seek to adjust because he has already set his own goals. He strives to be the center of attention, hoping to regain his earlier comfortable situation. He will show his intention in various ways by following his habitual behavior. He demonstrates how much we should depend on the school to assume responsibility for his re-education. We get these children already completed and we are expected to correct what parents failed to achieve. We must begin by doing the right thing, because society expects us to do better than the parents have done at an earlier stage.

I don't need to recite the many ways that problem children display in school what they have learned at home, and the impulse that drives them to continue their ways. We would be foolish to presume that after four or five years of becoming used to a particular behavior or situation, and adopting an attitude that can already be categorized, a child will not appear that way whatever the circumstances. Because each student represents a particular type, we can guess how he will behave in any given situation, and how his social behavior will consistently fall into the same role. When such a child faces a problem that does not suit his role, we will clearly see how much he can accomplish. This situation is similar to the theater where an actor who had always played comic roles suddenly has to play a tragedy, and the audience starts to laugh. Every child enters life with an awareness of playing a particular role and will act accordingly. Recognizing this fact is most important when our goal is to understand a child's attitude toward his tasks, and particularly when we want to predict his conduct. Our task is to discover faulty adjustments made in such a life plan, and to correct them.

In this case, the punishment meted out by the mother was totally ineffectual because the boy had attained his goal to his satisfaction, such as when he turned off the light and his mother had to occupy herself with him. He had the feeling that he was right, that he is in the right place, which is the one owed to him. He will also occupy the center of attention in school and he cannot be deterred from playing a central role. This behavior is typical for children who were extensively pampered while growing up. Where does pampering begin and where does it end? Because of his weakness, a child naturally requires help in the beginning. The individual is a social creature who, because of weakness, frailty, and insecurity in his early years, must depend on another person to relate to him and care for him.

In all problems relating to the development of a person's inner life, the causes and impetus are in the context of other problems. This contextual importance applies not only to the child, but to all of us. This framework encompasses a child's entire development, regardless of drives and instincts. Without our being aware of it, the social context always becomes a prerequisite. Human beings are not born with directed drives. However, some people successfully detach their drives from the social connection. For that reason, most psychologists have assumed that human beings are bad by nature and from necessity train and change their drives so that they are not directed against the well-being of society. The opposite is true. Whatever a child brings with him into the world will be integrated with all inborn possibilities into a social framework which he will consider primary. This process is essential because of the individual's weakness and inferiority. We can see this tendency also in the animal world where animals not well suited by nature to fend for themselves have a tendency to herd. The weak gather together, thereby gaining new strength that ensures their existence. Because of the nature of weakness, human beings live inseparably in communities. What the individual brings with him into the community is not important, but what he makes of it.

In the case under discussion, we can see a healthy boy from a well-to-do family. We determined the reason for his problem behavior, which became apparent when he faced a social function for which he was unprepared. When he was born, he had everything he wanted. Before his brother arrived, he operated over a far more extensive field which he dominated fully. He does not take well to a diminution of the gratification of his needs and defends himself against it by seeking other ways to satisfy his needs through power. We are now searching for a way to adjust him as he should have been adjusted after birth. We must increase his sphere of action, by opening to him those directions in which he can become useful and which also benefit others. As a pampered boy, he had never learned this lesson because all his interests centered on himself, and because it was not necessary, he never took an interest in anyone else.

We can understand all the activity and accomplishments of the sensory organs only as a coordinated whole. When we look at someone, we connect with that person; when we speak, we make a further connection. These factors become very meaningful if we understand them in terms of what they represent. We can gather from a child's look the extent of his social feeling. Children who are unable to look someone in the eyes provide us with obvious evidence that they have reasons to avoid contact. The ability of a child to speak proves his ability to establish contact. We cannot connect with another person if we have no desire to do so, if we are not prepared for it, if our life plan lacks the tendency to establish a connection. These factors provide superb guideposts for understanding an individual. While we should not grasp at singular forms of expression or single pieces of evidence, we have the obligation to find new confirmation for our perceptions. Observing merely individual psychological observations leads us to overlook complications.

We must test individual manifestations for a decrease in social feeling. When I speak of drives, I am not sure where that leads. However, if I know that all drives are caught in this social net that surrounds us, then I know what they signify. Humaneness should be regarded as a social ideal; it is the individual expression of social feeling that comprehends and senses humanity as a unity. Such a society has not yet been developed. Measured in terms of social growth, humankind is in a constant state of development. Because nature regards humans as orphans, people cannot conceivably develop other than as social beings. Everyone must be a part of the whole and must contribute his part. We have the task of shaping children into instruments for social progress, which is the essence of Individual Psychology as a philosophy of life. Examining only particular parts has no value. We must look for the personal goal guiding each of someone's decisions, which he cannot escape without insight. Awareness of this goal allows us to recognize a direction in the chaos we encounter in individual symptoms.

Without a goal, we are unable to think, act, or feel. We cannot avoid setting a goal in whatever we do. When we draw a line, we can draw it to its end only when we think of a goal. We cannot draw a line with regard to drives; we cannot possibly act before setting a goal because we can follow a path only when we can see ahead. We set goals because the individual is a living being capable of action. If we were flowers or plants, goal-setting would have no meaning. The inner life is movement; it exists only in freely acting life forms. If a plant had an inner life, if it could think, feel, and understand to any extent, it could make no use of such capabilities because it is firmly rooted and cannot move. The situation is quite different with life forms able to act. Because of their ability to act, they must prepare what they intend to do: to escape danger or to satisfy some need. They must see ahead. What we understand by inner life is something that foresees, which develops as a unity. What we regard as the ability to think is seeing ahead, reasoning how something can take shape, and planning for a responding action. Since our needs are embedded in a social framework, our actions show whether the way we set our goals properly includes society.

Problem children follow a goal that does not conform to the rules of society. However, the goal can conform to the individual's striving to be greater, to find a place for himself that conflicts with the demands of society. He seeks a place where he feels superior to others, but where he will be a useless rather than a useful member of society. With this principle, we find the starting point for applying Individual Psychology.

First, we must establish the truth of the complaints we hear because this child is not a part of the social framework, but lives outside of it as a useless person. We now face the challenge of raising an ideal fellow human being. We have no false illusions that such a feeling of fellowship develops by itself. However, we must creatively attempt to further this effort and, by asserting our own creative powers, develop the child toward that end. Friendship, love, marriage, school, political beliefs, all life situations require preparing the child to be useful. His attitude toward these tasks reveals his level of preparation for dealing with them.

Our assignment is to investigate. When we see that a child seems to have lived a positive life until a sibling appears and then begins to strive negatively for attention and excessive recognition, then we can understand how this is not the goal for useful superiority which a healthy upbringing can establish. We want to know why so many children facing difficulties display a lack of preparation. We also want to know how they display this lack of preparation. What has occurred that results in being unprepared for life? When a child is transferred from a school where he learned nothing to one where the other students are ahead of him, we want to know whether he was lacking in preparation, and how this happened. This importance of preparation applies also to children who for years were taught by the mother, father, uncle or a sister and who then enter a public school. How do we deal with such children? To establish simply that a child cannot perform as expected does not suffice. The teacher needs to determine what the child lacks and find a way to bring him to the level of the others. Every teacher accomplishes this task instinctively, but we seek to establish its value scientifically. An experienced clinical psychologist can help us in such situations. We psychologists treat cases where such shortcomings manifest themselves not only as problem children, but also as neurosis, mental retardation, criminality, suicidal tendencies, alcoholism, sexual aberrations, tendencies toward prostitution, etc. We can recognize these cases as if looking through a microscope and can often see ahead, predicting that if a particular child gets into difficult situations, he will be unable to deal with them. Time and again, with problem children, we see a failure of courage when confronted by problems. We can presume that a problem child does not have the courage to regain his former preferential situation by striving to become a useful member of society. He tries to accomplish this task by easier ways which make him feel powerful, but which do not require courage.

When we look closer into this particular child's history, we find that he was afraid at night and jumped out of bed, running to his mother for protection. We also read that he approached strangers with downcast eyes. Someone who leads a useless life is discouraged. Not trusting himself to have the strength to deal with his tasks, he looks for easy ways out. A person who fails in life has no courage. A criminal has no courage. He tries to be stronger than another person and gain the upper hand by using cunning. A thief breaks into a house only when no one is in it, when he can be the more powerful from the outset. A murderer kills only when he believes the other person is weaker. Nevertheless, I am a little optimistic about criminals because we could change a great deal if people understood that a criminal can only become one after losing his courage. Evading our country's laws represents no triumph. More people must recognize that criminality is an expression of cowardice.

I once heard about a thief who entered a room in which two teachers were sleeping. One of the teachers berated him for engaging in such an activity and asked why he did not try to make his living with honest work. Holding a revolver in his hand, the thief answered: "Are you aware of the problems involved in our kind of work?" His response revealed his lack of courage. Transgressing social feeling never shows courage.

The reasons for the lack of preparation lie in earliest childhood, characterized by situations where the child at the initial stage of life seems to have been overly burdened. An overly burdened child cannot develop like one who grows up under average circumstances. What causes a child to be overburdened? Some children are weaker than others, born with inferior organs, or afflicted with illnesses early in life which rob them of happiness. Some children who suffer from a weak digestive system that cannot digest mother's milk, vomit, have cramps, and feel uncomfortable day and night. The need for nourishment in such children can only be satisfied carefully in order not to harm them.

Such situations often last long periods of time, so we can easily understand how these children do not think they live in a paradise. A child in such a situation begins life suffering and with problems, which explains why he lacks an interest in others. Tormented, depressed, and burdened, this type of child does not take an interest in others. Everything that interests such a child revolves around nourishment. Many children grow up being mainly interested in satisfying their need for food. Such concerns preoccupy them. Later in life, they will also have dreams related to eating. Their interest lies mainly in what they will eat next. Even such interests can be guided toward useful endeavors, for example, by developing a refined taste. They can become good cooks; they will feel comfortable with food. We find that such a heightened interest lasts to the end of their lives and in whatever circumstances occur, they will look for anything related to food.

Physical weaknesses closely relate to structuring the inner life. Although organs may not be entirely weak, tensions arise in a child resulting from an organ inferiority. When we expose a healthy child to poor conditions, tensions occur not unlike those in a child with weak organs. We have noted that the sensory organs in those children become particularly significant. Children with poor eyesight cannot stand not being able to see and will, in fact, seek situations where they must see. These children want to do better, to get into situations where they can be victorious. Their interest in eyesight becomes increasingly greater. With the exception of the blind, the interest of those with poor eyesight is much stronger than would be expected. They are much more attentive and alert, seeing colors, shades, nuances, and perspectives much better than others. Often such a child becomes an artist. I do not believe that a child with normal eyesight could ever become a good painter. Instead, we find poor eyesight among painters, who suffer form near- or far-sightedness, astigmatism, are color blind or poor in distinguishing colors, have only one eye, etc. This compensation for weak vision can be understood only in terms of the creative powers that force a child to grow beyond his difficulties.

We also often encounter another deficiency that distracts children from the beginning, causing many to lose courage and believe they are inferior. We find this reaction in left-handed children. Individual Psychologists have found that 35 to 50% of people are left-handed, although barely 10% are aware of it, but they all experience it. Our culture usually demands right-handedness. When a left-handed child enters school, he shows that he is not properly prepared and is clumsy, which earns him reprimands or punishment. Such children initially are unable to work as well as others. However, they must be trained to use the weaker, right hand, in order not to feel that they cannot achieve as much as others. This training requires a considerable investment in time and the proper method.

Centuries ago the methods employed for teaching to read and write were inadequate. Einhart wrote about how Charles the Great tried very hard to learn the art of writing and reading. However, the great ruler never acquired those skills "because he had no talent for it." Clearly, the method for teaching these subjects was poor. Since Pestalozzi, this method has improved greatly. Even the mentally retarded can learn. The teaching method is always important. We engage in some activities without knowing how extensively we trained to become skilled in them and don't even understand the context in which we learned those skills, unless someone points this out to us (for example, training how to box). To train the right hand in the case of left-handedness is a very special undertaking. Some children instinctively find a method or, when they are encouraged, a better method to get over their difficulty. They will feel good having been successful. They will tend to develop excellent handwriting, learn to draw particularly well, etc. A noticeably large percentage of left-handed people have beautiful handwriting.

A simple test will uncover the secret of left-handedness. Simply have a person fold his fingers, and the left thumb of a left-landed person will lie above his right thumb. Many naturally left-handed people are particularly skillful because they exercised and have overcome their deficiency. Whoever overcomes, succeeds. The majority of left-handed people, however, do not get over their problem, remaining clumsy and manually inept. Unable to wrestle with difficulties, they cannot deal with life's tasks. Therefore, many left-handed people become problem children, criminals, suicides, etc. A child has two choices, to either become discouraged or fight. By fighting, he will discover a good method for developing himself and strive to overcome his problem. Being unaware of a child's left-handedness can lead to believing that he is untalented or lazy. The only explanation for laziness is that a child no longer expects to be successful. When people expect to be successful, they are never lazy. Laziness expresses a feeling of inferiority, which becomes apparent as soon as a lazy person faces a problem in life.

We can make the same observations in other aspects of development. The explanation for an unwillingness to persist in a struggle to overcome difficulties is always the same: a lack of courage, a lack of interest in others, and self-centeredness. Because problem children always take evasive steps, we want to observe what steps they take to avoid useful activities.

Chapter III

Children's Lifestyles

What we have covered so far concerns two basic questions: Since when in a child's life have deficiencies existed, leading to his lack of preparation; and what peculiarities existed before these deficiencies occurred.

I have shown how we can identify early childhood situations that allow us to establish in a child the presence of a serious feeling of inferiority. I have also touched on what constitutes a feeling of inferiority. Such a feeling of inferiority cannot be ascertained through questioning. This condition appears only when a child faces a particular task which reveals it. As long as he has not been challenged, as long as he has everything he desires, self-assessment will never take place. Only in situations where a child faces a task will we learn whether he believes he is capable of dealing with that task. Eventually, we can uncover what lies behind his belief. The way a child walks and moves in the most basic sense expresses an emotional reaction we must seek to understand. If he sets out to deal with a problem confident of being able to do it well, a clearly apparent optimistic impact will recur time and again during all phases of his life. We will see action, a creative force, confidence, and a belief in his accomplishments that will become explicit and be reflected in the way he expresses himself.

Understanding these early signs will also clarify for us when a child hesitates, walks haltingly, looks around unsure of himself, becomes doubtful, perhaps is even brought to a halt, or is at a loss. Such a child lacks self-confidence. We will gain a better understanding if we don't localize our test, but examine the individual in several places. We have to conduct a horizontal examination in various places to determine how this self-evaluation is expressed, and how it changes into action. We should establish whether the child feels secure or insecure under various conditions, and whether he regards himself as an equal or feels inferior. We should also begin a vertical examination. We should compare present manifestations with peculiarities in the child's past. We will then have a line that shows us the genetic structure of the child's lifestyle. This line enables us to investigate, compare and confirm and, because of the unity of human inner life, we will then be confident that all the points along the way, all the ways in which the child expressed himself then and now, will agree. We can ask about the child's earliest memories and, if we understand those, if we have gained some experience in reading old memories, we can easily find the focal point that reveals his system. At the same time, we will have a gauge to measure his self-assessment, which has become an unconscious habit.

Let me speak specifically about unconscious habits. Every experience a child has in early life affects him. It forces him to assume a position with regard to that situation which includes a goal of superiority, and how to attain it. This constant striving to strengthen his personality feeling will manifest itself in different ways. A process of training develops in the child a growing, conscious or unconscious, sense of role-playing. After some time, an unconscious guideline emerges which allows him to make his way in life consistent with his habitual movements and forms of expression, as if he had learned a poem by heart. He does not have to look for words; everything has become automatic. The poem is not in his consciousness, but runs on by itself; it lies, as they say, on his tongue. A pianist who has learned a piece of music plays it by heart. He no longer has to think about notes; the piece plays itself.

In the current literature on psychology, we find the theory of the unconscious as postulated by Eduard Hartmann. Psychoanalysis, and those following other schools of psychology, accept to some degree that in this unconsciousness we find an expression of drives (sexual drives) which, from the standpoint of our culture, we must regard adversely. This unconsciousness is viewed as bad because, in order to improve life, a controlling cultural guideline is superimposed upon it to facilitate the morality of our striving to get along. We find, to the contrary, that the human being developed despite his inadequate physical condition under the ameliorating influence of the community, the most important compensating factor, which, after he has been won over to do good, directs his mistaken drives toward usefulness for the common good.

A child's lifestyle, as well as his self-esteem, remains constant as long as he lacks self-knowledge. We expect his upbringing to awaken that self-knowledge, which is not enough. Self-knowledge must become active so that the connection between that self-knowledge and correct behavior is clear to the child and to us. Certain types of recollections prove what a child has suspected and felt and which, at a later stage in life, he will be able to understand. I have never encountered a child who did not understand an explanation of his lifestyle.

I will present an example demonstrating that even very young children recognize the lifestyle so clearly that they themselves can have an effect on it. A two-year old girl was dancing on a table to the great dismay of her mother who yelled at her: "Get down, you'll fall!" The girl calmly continued dancing. The three-year old brother, who had looked on, yelled to her: "Stay there!" The little girl immediately climbed down from the table. The boy understood his sister's lifestyle. Clearly, a child can be taught to feel important by doing the opposite of what she is told.

We are interested in deficiencies and we want to observe how far away a child moves from problems, whether instead of acting he shows us merely a will, which does not help. A superstition, also found in the literature of psychology, says that an expression of will proves that action is about to begin. This effort at deception hides great divergence between will and deed. When we find merely a will, we can be quite sure that nothing happens. Some children offer good will as their price for being left alone. Yet, they cannot change because their lifestyle has become a habit and their will is attuned to that lifestyle.

I would like to describe a case I regard as a model because it neatly fits everything together. In order to track down traces of an unconscious habit, we must collect a number of details from a child's earliest years of life, facts that contributed to his habitual attitude.

The information given to us is not always trustworthy, but when we ask a child or adult to look back into his earliest childhood and tell us anything that comes to mind, we are collecting fragments of his lifestyle. When that person tries to come up with a recollection, he will select what was important then, but what now has become mostly inscrutable. These focal points are imprinted on his automatic lifestyle. We are dealing here with an unconscious guideline that is active and creative, but can move in only one direction.

The case I am presenting concerns a thirteen-year old boy who manifested a number of deficiencies that were so extensive that he was expelled from the fifth grade of his public school. He was the worst student, and he was believed to have committed a number of thefts. He often disappeared for several days from home and from school until, wretched, he either found his way back alone, or was returned by the police. He presented the picture of a neglected child and everyone who knew him was sure that his was a hopeless case. He was transferred to a reform school where improvement was expected. In this institution, he was assigned a teacher who had worked with me. Given the boy's habitual attitude, the teacher was not satisfied merely punishing him and making him feel hopeless. Before beginning to work with him, he first wanted to know his lifestyle. He followed what we regard as the right path. He thought: At whatever point I start my investigation, I must arrive at something that represents completeness. The ways he expresses himself cannot be broken down into separate parts, but must all fit the unity of the whole person. Beginning with an examination of his report cards, he discovered that the boy was a good student in the first three grades. His grades turned poor only in the fourth grade and also in the fifth.

The teacher now faced the following question: Since when had these deficiencies become so intrusive that they caused him to perform poorly in his tests? He concluded that after having the same teacher in his first three grades, the boy had a different teacher in the fourth grade. He knew that such deficiencies occur only if the first teacher was friendly, and the second was unfriendly and strict. The boy confirmed the teacher's assumption. He said: "The teacher in the fourth grade did not like me," causing the boy to feel that his difficulties were the teacher's fault. His comment helps us understand this case. What had occurred does not even have to be true, because what the boy feels is just as effective as if it were true. Whether I believe there is a tiger outside my door or there actually is one makes no difference. The facts are not important, only how we see them. The teacher concluded from this information that the boy would progress only when encouraged and when he felt liked. He wanted to be pampered. Obviously a pampered child, he grew up in a poor but indulgent family in which his mother prevented him from becoming independent. He approached every task demanding that he must first be treated kindly. We recognize here his lack of self-esteem. If someone says: I go along only conditionally, it means he lacks courage. We know that pampered children lack courage which, when all goes well, does not necessarily become obvious.

The teacher continued to question the boy: "What did you do with the things you stole?" The boy responded: "Because I was such a poor student, I thought that if I gave gifts to my schoolmates, they would be more friendly toward me."

This is a frequent motive for children to steal. If this boy did all that in order to be treated more kindly, then we see again the same form of expression, the same attitude toward life. He wanted to be treated kindly and had found no other way than to steal. Sadly, this boy acted as if he were in the right and had no other choice. It is an insolvable problem: How to win friends when lacking the means to do that.

Another question: "Why did you run away?" We can anticipate his answer: "When we were assigned homework, I knew how I would do. I always received the poorest grades." Many students do not want to go to school because they are constantly punished and receive poor grades. Then the parents are informed, the father comes to school, and continues the boy's punishment at home. This boy had faced the same situation. He said: "My father found out what I had done, that I had skipped school again, and then he whipped me. My mother, who liked me very much, became very sad, cried, and was very nice to me." In other words, he wanted warmth, he wanted to be liked; consequently, he avoided all situations preventing him from reaching his goal. Part of the child's deficiencies we call skipping school or running away from home. But if someone likes where he is, then he does not run away.

We may ask: How does this boy strive for significance? He knew exactly how to achieve it. He knew that when he returned home, his mother would be full of concern and receive him with kisses and embraces. Thus, he succeeded in being pampered and liked. Every act of his moves toward the same goal: to be loved. When he came home, he gathered wood, stealthily placing it at night outside his mother's door. We can recognize the same line of movement that he followed when he stole in order to bribe someone at school. While this may appear different, it still is the same expression of his habitual lifestyle. Everything moves toward the same goal: to be someone, to be more than what he is now.

I want to make some additional observations about how this boy came to steal and how, by doing so, he was closely tied to his mother. Two early memories help us find the answer. He related that he had once seen a stranger carrying home a deer that had drowned in the Donau River after it had flooded. He also recalled seeing a burning railroad car from which people were retrieving balls and taking them home. We see here two focal points that must have had a considerable impact on the boy. They indicate a line in his lifestyle that points to the possibility of acquiring someone else's property by stealing.

About being so closely tied to his mother since early childhood, he tells the following: "When I was four years old, my father sent me out to buy a newspaper, but...." The boy already said enough to provide a clue to the Individual Psychologist. He started out mentioning his father, but then cut his sentence short with a "but." From what followed, we recognize the exclusory action - "I went to my uncle who accompanied me to my mother." In other words, he ended up being with his mother.

Because this boy will constantly strive to find a pleasant situation, his lifestyle automatically leads to low self-esteem. This kind of child does not trust himself, cannot stand alone, and will always look for support. The mother, to be sure, had performed her first function in an exceptional manner. She conveyed to her boy the feeling of being a fellow human being. That, however, is not enough. She should have provided him with opportunities to establish relationships with others, beginning with his father. We can see that she failed to establish a friendly relationship between the child and his father because she did not want to relinquish him, wanted to make his life easy, and had constantly been there to support him. Now, he faces problems that he cannot solve. We know what we must do: We must perform this second function of the mother, which is to expand the boy's social feeling. We have recognized the line of his social feeling. He can steal, run away, and skip school, whereby he harms another's interests. Can you see the lack of courage in his behavior? He gives up the fight because he was reprimanded and expects to be given poor grades. His striving for personal standing becomes apparent, revealing that he is not prepared for a social life. We can carry out the mother's second function only if we also perform the first. Our treatment, all pedagogical healing, is based on fulfilling the mother's two functions. There is no other way.

We must uncover his shortcomings and show him that he demands things that someone might expect to obtain after having been successful, but not at the outset. We must show him that he has unsuccessfully tried to be appreciated, liked, and honored before he has achieved anything. He will understand the connection when we show him by example. We can point out that he has been caught in his lifestyle, and that his discouragement closely relates to this useless, unconscious guideline. We can discern the level of a child's self-esteem from his actions, and when we compare these with other forms of self-expression, the picture becomes quite clear. We will often get into awkward situations if we fail to fully elicit these focal points. We will also find that the more experience we have, the deeper we delve into this subject, the easier the task becomes. I have attached a questionnaire, which should help in establishing the lifestyle and degree of self-esteem that can be found in these children.

Chapter IV

Children in Difficult Situations

We have now come far enough for you to become a collaborator with me; that is, you can report cases that we will then discuss together. We will practice the art of reading and understanding reports on problem children. We will also attempt to discover how a lifestyle, a habitual and restrictive attitude toward life, can be changed.

The two most important questions are: When did complaints about a child's behavior begin? In what situations does a child demonstrate conspicuous behavior? To behave appropriately, to address problems in life properly, and to solve them in useful, commonly acceptable ways are all social tasks requiring understanding and experience. We also know the tests schooling imposes on a child. First of all, the school represents an experiment in establishing the extent to which a child is prepared for its demands and rules; however, the atmosphere of the school also matters. In some schools, more children than we would expect are poorly prepared, particularly in schools with little understanding for the uniqueness of children, and where authoritarianism rules. We know that many children are not trained at home to obey blindly because our society does not advocate blind obedience. A school following a regimen of strict discipline would pose too difficult a test for children from more lenient families and would precipitate more deficiencies than would otherwise be the case. Starting school brings on new situations both in the school and outside, such as changes in teachers or the need to transfer to another school, the possibility that the child's standing in class might change, and various influences on a child from classmates. Outside influences can also change a child's attitude significantly. Encouragement from the family is extremely important for a child as the following example will show.

A ten-year old girl came to me with her mother, both crying and sobbing. The mother explained that only a few months earlier she had taken the child back from foster parents who had raised her. The mother had given up her daughter because she had divorced the father shortly before the child was born. While with her foster parents, the daughter had developed quite well, had made good progress in school, and was about to enter the fourth grade.

I subsequently spoke with the mother who told me that her husband had been an alcoholic, that it had been impossible to live with him, and that she feared the child could have inherited something of her husband's flawed nature. She now pledged herself to raise the child in a model fashion, although I was not clear on what she meant by "a model fashion." The child started school in the fourth grade, but was put back into the third grade for lacking maturity. Even there, she was unable to keep up with her class and failed in a number of subjects. The teacher told her that she was not suitable for the third grade and that if her performance continued along the same line, she would have to be transferred to the second grade.

The girl seemed perfectly normal. I said to myself that if a girl living in the country can advance successfully to the fourth grade, she cannot possibly be dim-witted. When the mother told me that her child was bright, I concluded that other factors had to come into play. I delved deeply into the difficult circumstances surrounding this child. I knew that she had been brought up by foster parents and was now back with her mother. Further questioning showed she was inattentive when reading a book, or when engaged in other activities. She had frequent daydreams and acted very sad. The mother said: "I cannot understand this. I am very strict with her in order to avoid what happened to my husband, and yet she fails to make progress."

When I thought further about the child's situation, I concluded that living with her foster parents must have been a good experience for her. So I asked how the foster parents had treated her, and whether she was still in touch with them, exchanging letters, etc. Since she had lived for nine years with her foster parents, then another story was possible. As she explained, she had had a very pleasant life with them. I thought how I would behave were I in the same situation and had been taken from a good life with foster parents to my mother who was strict. This child's mother had ideas about a model upbringing that she tried to apply to her daughter. I gathered that this child recalled the good times with her foster parents and now despaired. If she had wanted to leave the foster parents, she could have gone to her mother, but now that she was with her mother, there was no way out. Probably many times this girl would say to herself: "If I fail completely, then mother will throw me out and I can go back to my foster parents." She feels trapped and cannot escape.

The answers to the questions I asked were as I expected. Given her upbringing, I could understand how this child could be absolutely devastated. She told me how happy she was living with her foster parents and that she also liked school, where she had made good progress. I had to talk to the mother again. I told her that I knew what had to be done, but did not think that she was capable of going through with it. The mother asked for my advice. I told her that in her place, I would speak pleasantly with the child and admit that I had made a mistake. I suggested she tell her daughter that she now realized it would be far better for the two of them to live together merely as good friends. The mother agreed to follow my advice. I advised her to practice this new relationship and let her daughter feel that her situation was not hopeless, but caused by a mistake. I also asked that she visit me again in two weeks.

After two weeks, the mother and daughter appeared smiling and full of joy. The mother also brought greetings from the teacher. He said he was very glad to see that the girl, who had been the worst student just two weeks ago, was now doing quite well.

In this situation, the key influence did not come from school, similar to other cases where adverse conditions contribute to a child's discouragement. These conditions include poverty and deteriorating family situations forcing children to go to work, leaving them with little energy for schoolwork. Life for these children is dismal and friendless. When we identify problem children, we must look into their early history.

Children in the upper grades may experience adverse conditions which are neither in school nor outside. These matters concern the health of the child. Children suffering from epilepsy, for example, eventually fail completely. High school children between the ages of 15 and 16, and often those as old as 16 and 17, may show signs of juvenile mental illness. Such children often are unjustly criticized and mistreated, even though their deficiencies do not result from ill will.

In any case, ill will is never the beginning, but always the result of discouragement. We have no reason to become upset with ill will, because it is a last effort to gain esteem with unpleasantness, and to aim for recognition even by useless means. We should never fight children, merely investigate and uncover the mistakes in their lifestyle.

The child of which I spoke earlier was pampered, then suddenly confronted by a situation for which she was not prepared. A better prepared child may have succeeded where this girl failed. Often, we will find some illness may cause a child's failure. For example, some cases of influenza can cause serious brain damage, leaving a child unable to perform as well as before. In cases of impaired hearing, a child might try at first to perform as well as previously. We must consider a child's hearing impairment, until an adjustment has been made allowing him to deal with that problem. Students who become sick from anemia cannot succeed as well as others because the illness keeps them in a constant state of fatigue. We can also understand how children afflicted with tuberculosis or similar diseases and who suffer from fever, unbeknown to anyone, will lag behind in their work.

We also should try to understand why some children, after having recovered from an illness, regress in their work. In the course of a lengthy illness, a child will lose technical skills, show gaps in learning, and require tutoring.

Another important point is frequently overlooked. Ill children are often pampered excessively, a situation which, after having recovered, they will not easily want to relinquish. Yearning for the warmth they had enjoyed, they will change their behavior. Many behavior problems following an illness, which some physicians attribute to damaged internally secreting glands, result from pampering during an illness, such as scarlet fever and whooping cough. We often find in reports on problem children that they had started behaving badly while ill with scarlet fever. We can well understand how parents will make a seriously ill child feel immensely valued. Such a child might want to be ill again. Children may also make a minor illness seem major and act as if they suffer from a serious illness in order to impress parents. They may also want to draw out illnesses for long periods of time. For some children, an illness is a state of bliss. A hypochondriac will present suffering in the strongest light to achieve a favorable situation; no demands will be made of him, he will gain greater recognition, and someone will take care of him. His suffering makes him the center of attention.

In some cases, after an illness, a child changes for the better and his work improves. The following is a case in point. It concerns the second child of a teacher. We know that a second child departs from the usual pattern for child development. He seems as if in a race, trying to overtake the firstborn and seeking to attain everything as quickly as possible. When such a child encounters a strong sibling, a difficult situation can then ensue. The father in this case was at his wit's end and decided to enter the child in a juvenile disciplinary institution. The boy fell ill with hip tuberculosis and spent one year in bed. When he recovered, he returned to school. He was completely changed and became the most pleasant, industrious child. How can we explain his change? This boy, the second child, while ill felt that he was at the top and that everyone was constantly concerned with him. He was told that he was not mentally behind and he certainly felt loved by his parents because of all the care they gave him. This experience taught him a lesson and made him see the error of his ways. This case gives us a clue how we can achieve a successful resolution by demonstrating with deeds and not with words that a child is not mentally impaired.

Once we have learned how children can undergo a transformation while in school, we come to the second question: What had occurred while a child's lifestyle was formed, when the child was four or five years of age and when habitual, mistaken attitudes were formed? Whatever happed then eventually led the child to fail completely or become more or less unsuitable when his lifestyle was being tested. We have established that whatever the circumstances, a lack of social feeling was apparent. We found that during the first four or five years, these children were overburdened and experienced harmful situations that marked them indelibly. They developed an erroneous apperception which put the world in a different light, causing them to set goals that were not appropriate for social interaction. When challenged, these children tend to engage in useless activities. This applies to three types of children, all of whom lack courage: children with inferior organs, pampered children, and neglected children.

Children in these categories are under extreme pressure because of the circumstances under which they live and, thus burdened, must form their lifestyle. These children cannot deal with their problems, or solve them only partly. They never accomplish anything and would prefer to avoid everything. Some want to take on problems by storm, but tire quickly and never reach their goal. Many seek ways by which they can eliminate having to deal with life's problems. We cannot get over the impression that they behave as if something were too much for them to bear. They are pessimists and cowards. We can observe these characteristics throughout their lives, whatever the circumstances, except when they find themselves in favorable situations. When under certain circumstances things go well for them, they even seem to have courage. If they follow another path, however, they will become discouraged. These children tend to avoid all duties and have their own ideas about how to gain esteem. They look for satisfaction by their own standards.

Some do not play well with others, or do so only when they can be in charge. They make a great fuss and by detaching themselves, try to eliminate school altogether, i.e. by running away. Over time, this detachment manifests itself in various ways. We see it most clearly in children who do not want to go to school at all. When a child has come so far as to give up all hope, the next step is not to go to school. However, because a child cannot stay out of school, he will lie and start training himself to avoid school by falsifying signatures and committing other deceptions. Of course, not every child succeeds in such tactics, but if a child does not go to school, he will hide somewhere to remain undetected. These children are mostly found in large cities. Some are more adept in avoiding school, and others are only too happy to learn how to do it. The ways that a child can pursue a useless life, to steal, victimize other children, perform sexual perversities, rob, etc. can easily be taught. These children mostly have not been caught. Probably every thief or liar has escaped punishment, and every forger has succeeded in his pursuit at some time. To a child, success in doing something wrong, and being able to boast about it to others becomes very meaningful. Eventually a gang of neglected children organizes, which is stronger than the individual member. Members of such gangs grow up at the peril of society. When caught, they rationalize their dilemma by believing they were merely not smart enough, and insisting that had they been smarter, they would not have been caught. They think they can dare anything without getting caught. Their goal for superiority is to be cunning, crafty, and deceptive.

We must now consider prevention. If teachers could only be persuaded not to discourage a child. If a child were confident of succeeding in school, then the childish tendency toward criminality and gangs would be subdued. Every expert in juvenile delinquency agrees that discouraged children no longer believe they can do useful work; lacking courage, they fear ghosts, fear being alone, being in the dark, etc. This does not surprise us since we know that such children started out by expecting others to take up their burden. They confess: "I turned out this way because my mother spoiled me, or, because as a child I was always rejected." We don't even want to mention the many ugly and crippled children among criminals. The teacher's task is to raise the confidence of these children so that they can meet life's demands in useful ways.

Individual Psychology has an optimistic outlook and does not consider talent and ability innate. To anyone who insists that talent is acquired at birth because everyone believes this, and then swears by all kinds of other foolishness to support that position, I would point out that the last time a woman was burned at the stake as a witch was 150 years ago. Until then, a great many women suffered unbelievable tortures and were sent to their deaths as witches. All the learned authorities, judges, priests, and women themselves believed in witchcraft. Who can say today that a commonly held belief must be valid for that reason alone and that it cannot be challenged? It is wrong and impedes progress to insist that not everyone can accomplish whatever life demands. Obviously, the mentally retarded and others afflicted with illnesses are not included here.

From the very beginning, the human psyche had to deal with the demands of society. Our physical make-up is proof of our dependency on others. Our sensory organs speak a social language and the highest law by which we exist concerns our contact with others, relationships, and our attitude toward fellow human beings. Actually, the whole world is reflected in our bodies. We are part of the whole and exist in an invisible alliance with society; our ideals develop in a social context. The physical frailty of our organism would have brought about the eradication of humankind had society not prevented it. Everything that is socially useful has universal validity. Morality sets the standards for social life. Beauty is what society regards as beautiful. Everything we find valuable is also universally regarded as valuable. Science seeks to elevate people to better conditions. From religion springs commonly valid rules for living. Every worthwhile political position endeavors to further humankind. Individual Psychology has the task of pointing the way toward discovering the underlying interrelationships that realize the sense of community.

Individual Psychology in the Schools

Chapter V

Real and Imagined Childhood Memories

I will present a case that recently came to my attention. It concerns a boy, an only child, about 12 years old. We know that an only child grows up under circumstances quite different from children with siblings. Always at the center of attention, he is difficult to raise as an independent person because adults are so ready to do things for him. Surrounded by adults, he is the smallest and grows up feeling weak. On the one hand, he has increased incentive to develop himself, but on the other hand, he has the convenience of a life that presents no trouble and that he can lead without exerting any effort. Not surprisingly, these children regard work as something unpleasant. The ideal that was, in fact, forced on them, to be the center of attention and be pampered, holds them back from all kinds of work and accomplishments. Added to this unfortunate dynamic are the mistakes made by those close to the child. The parents are constantly fearful because this is their only child. They are also fearful because they had settled on only one child for whatever the circumstances, whether illness, their economic situation, differences in their marriage, etc. Consequently, their home life gives a somewhat misleading impression. Our task is not only to identify the child's faults, similar to selecting a sour note from a melody, but also to recognize the broader perspective.

The mother in this case is widowed. She had previously lived in good circumstances, but her situation worsened and now she is poor. Although she was able to save paintings, jewelry, and other valuables, she has spent all her cash.

Aside from being an only, pampered child, the boy had a very pleasant childhood during which he was given whatever his heart desired. This situation changed after his mother became poor.

Three years ago, the boy's father died leaving only the mother to bring him up. Possibly, the father's care had a certain influence on the child's development. If the father had imposed discipline on him, that could explain why the boy's deficiencies surfaced only after his father's death.

He was doing poorly in school. This child, who had become used to being in the limelight and having someone pave the way for him, began to fail as soon as he experienced unpleasantness and bitterness, something to which he had not been accustomed. This only child was pampered, lacked independence, and had an ideal goal of finding someone to take care of him.

He was transferred into a new school where he made no progress. Every new situation is an intelligence test, a test of character telling us whether that person has become a true fellow human being, and whether he was well prepared. Pampered children are not ready for such a test; because their focus is strictly on themselves, they have no need to take an interest in others. They are always on the receiving end and never give. We can say that in this case mistakes obviously were made.

The boy stayed away from school. He began to steal, which he did with great vehemence. He denied everything, even when directly confronted with his larceny. He stubbornly maintained his innocence, against his mother's entreaties and in spite of being threatened with harsh punishment. His uncle once presented the boy with a good idea, but his response showed again that his lifestyle is inflexible even under favorable circumstances. The uncle had promised to take him on a three day hike, something the boy had long desired. The boy admitted to him that he had stolen a piece of jewelry and then pawned it through someone else.

This case is becoming perfectly clear to us. What should we do now? We must agree on the mistake that was made. Although the parents had succeeded in getting the boy interested in his immediate environment, he could not extend his interest beyond that narrow circle. He enjoyed private tutoring, was given everything he desired, and developed well both physically and mentally. His attitude, however, was always to receive and never to give He spent the money he received from stolen goods in meaningless ways, such as on candy, the movies, and going to the beach.

When confronted, he said something that seemed quite normal and not at all strange: "If you give me so little allowance (the attitude of a receiver), then I must take something."

These expressions give us insight into his lifestyle. Everything must fit that lifestyle. He was pampered and suddenly feels robbed. He has no other way of expressing himself whether at home, because of poverty, or in school with his schoolwork. He functions intelligently. If we ignore morality, compassion, and social feeling, we can see nothing wrong with his behavior. Only when we measure his behavior against social feeling can we judge him. Social feeling is our gauge according to which we find his behavior unacceptable, dilatory, and irrational. On the other hand, feeling robbed, what alternative does he have other than enriching himself? How and why does this child feel robbed? This question may have various answers, but we must continue to investigate until we are able to answer it. I would like to briefly clarify again the whole system of Individual Psychology. In this case, we already know the two most important questions and presume that the particular situation which contains a mistake may seem insoluble to this child. If he had hopes of being able to accomplish schoolwork, he would have gone to school. All situations demand a developed social feeling. When we look back at his early childhood, we recognize and understand how he was unable to develop an interest in others. We are left only with uncovering the specific shortcomings that developed in the structure of his lifestyle, and examining them in order to understand their significance.

We mentioned the three types of children:
1. Children with inferior organs.
2. Pampered children who only take and never give.
3. Neglected children who do not know about the existence of social feelings and lack an interest in others.

When we examine the lives of these children more closely, we can establish the reason they failed at a certain point in their life. We can recognize from the meager but meaningful fragments provided to us the reason these children are not well suited for the world, and why they lost their social feeling. The answer lies in the conditions which existed in their early childhood and under which they grew up. The firstborn who is followed by a sibling always looks backward toward the lost Paradise. The second, on the other hand, boldly looks forward and wants to overtake the firstborn. However, the firstborn may be stronger, frustrating the second child in his efforts and leading him to go astray. I should also point to the unusual development of an only girl growing up among boys, or of an only boy among girls.

Earliest childhood memories are meaningful fragments. Individual Psychology discovered a rich store in such recollections which almost fall into our laps because of our theory concerning the unity of the individual whereby every singe aspect is a part of the whole. From an earliest recollection, we can grasp the entire structure of a lifestyle, or a portion thereof, even if it is meaningless to others. When we uncover situations in a person's life familiar to us, we recognize immediately that they have significance and can be related to and give meaning to specific, early childhood memories. We can often predict what kind of childhood memories we will encounter. Recognizing the connections is most important for us. In these earliest childhood memories, we find signs indicating organ inferiorities or illness, pampering or neglect. We can measure these categories of childhood memories. When children in the past related a dream about: "a Christmas tree full aglow," it was not regarded as significant. We now know that a person who holds such a memory is particularly interested in visual effects and has a keen visual sense. Such a strong desire to see will leave a permanent imprint on his psyche. If someone tells about having been ill in childhood and having suffered greatly, we have a fragment indicating that this person was strongly affected by a childhood illness. Persons with such memories frequently take a major interest in illness and death. Possibly, the first of these two children would become the visual type, exhibiting a tendency for colors and drawing; the second child might be more interested in the sciences, becoming a physician in order to associate more closely with death.

Biographies of prominent people time and again describe how they remember having pursued a career they had desired in earliest childhood. When we hear childhood memories such as: "I remember having gone somewhere with my mother," we can easily establish that this was a pampered child who could not forsake memories of having been with his mother. Sometimes such memories can be predicted when people tell stories in which the figure of their mother constantly appears. These are not always obvious and predictable phenomena and cannot be encompassed with rules or formulas to understand them. In such cases, we must allow our imagination to roam. What could be the meaning of a child's recollection as follows: "I recall having lived in the country with my mother while my father resided in the city?" In this situation, the mother devoted herself fully to the child while the father was excluded from the circle of those who pampered him. We make a serious mistake in cases of pampered children to recommend that the father apply strict discipline and to counsel that he not pamper the child. This path would lead to ostracizing the father even further. The teacher in such cases should also avoid disciplining since the child would soon reject him either openly or covertly.

Sometimes we find double fragments, particularly in cases of pampered children, showing a changed situation in which a child was cut off from pampering. We then get recollections that speak loudly to us with phrases such as: "I remember when my younger brother was born." We understand such memories and can draw conclusions from them about the particular tragedy this child experienced. Not only a firstborn, but also other children may encounter conditions that seem unbearable forming character traits such as strong jealousy, etc. of which every child is capable when brought into such a situation. These character traits carry over into advanced age. People who as children had realized how easy it is to experience sudden failure and how quickly powers can dissipate will later often harbor beliefs such as: "Do what you like, it makes no difference anyhow."

In neglected children we encounter childhood memories such as: "I remember when I was beaten." Obviously, the recollection of these memories is no accident. We realize the significance for a person when, speaking of his developing years, he tells: "Basically, I was treated awful; I was tortured." It is not even necessary that he had to be beaten.

I remember the case of a person who came to me for treatment who had no self-confidence and, therefore, associated with men and women who were far below his social standing. He told the following childhood memory: "I remember sitting in a room looking out the window. My parents went out of the house with my older brother and left me alone." He was very reticent and saw others as enemies. Intellectually, he had developed well and progressed well in school. He was depressed, however, because he was short, homely, and weak. His brother, on the other hand, was tall and handsome. He was also bothered that his mother was fonder of the oldest brother than of him. At least, that was his impression. After many years, he once spoke to his mother about that. She told him that she did not love the older boy more, but because of his pleasant nature felt closer to him, while he was constantly critical, argumentative, and cynical.

The same person told of another childhood memory as follows: "I remember flinging myself at my mother in a fit of rage and pulling her hair." Four years later, she bore a girl. She seemed to favor the new baby, leaving him feeling that he was hemmed in between siblings whom the mother preferred over him. He also had strict governesses, which soon led him to give up the fight. We can understand how he grew closer to his father, which is the second phase in a child's development. It indicates that the mother was unable to win over eh child and that something had happened which caused a distancing between mother and child. When a father picks up on the love a mother fails to show to a child, the next step is for the child to develop a closer relationship with the father. We learned that this particular boy was not tolerant toward the female sex. When we delve a little further in such cases, we understand how far such intolerance can lead once a child has matured and an attitude toward the other sex is being formed. This boy did not take his masculine role seriously, since he had few expectations for his part. He fell in love late in life with a girl who was being courted by several other men, and who had difficulties deciding whom to marry. He told me that he was happy that she decided not to marry him, a decision he greeted as liberating. In this case, again, he failed to take his masculine role seriously. Eventually, he fell in with a young vagabond with whom he entered into a homosexual relationship.

These developments are of the greatest importance, which is why we need to inquire about a person's earliest memories and dreams. Most of the time these seem so clear that doubting them seems impossible. For example, when a child tells of being pursued by a tiger, it shows an attitude that sees the whole world as beastly. As a result, they behave like hunted animals. When we are told that a child dreamed of running around naked, we should understand that such a dream can be helpful to us. It tells us that this child dislikes being exposed and would like to remain a mystery to other from whom he wants to hide his true self.

We shall find hints under all kinds of conditions that point the way along which a child has developed and indicate to us the strength of his social feeling. When we consider how heavily a child was burdened from earliest childhood, we will understand the problems these burdens entail. We will then not be surprised when such a child later fails to be cooperative and is unable to work with others. Even the physical bearing expresses a degree of courage, optimism, and energy.

Childhood memories do not have to be genuine in order to be meaningful, but can also be fantasies. I have a childhood memory that is pure fantasy, but to which I have been closely drawn for all my life. I harbored this memory, of which I was very proud, until I was 35 years old. I was five years old when I entered first grade at Penzing public school on Diesterweggasse. I recall that my schoolmates and I routinely had to cross a cemetery. This was never a pleasant experience for me and while it depressed me, my comrades happily went their way. The problem of death concerned me very early in life. I was three years old when I was present when my brother died. When I was four, I contracted pneumonia and the doctor gave up on me. I had an early interest in death. When the father of one of my friends asked me what I planned to be I said, as a five year old, that I wanted to become a doctor. His response was: "They should hang you from the first street light." I thought that this poor opinion of physicians applied only to those who were incompetent and stuck to my decision. It was during that time period that I found walking across the cemetery to be a heavy burden. I then decided to free myself of that fear. The next time I had to cross the cemetery, I decided to hand back and let my comrades go ahead. I placed my school bag on the fence and started walking back and forth across the cemetery, first slowly and then faster, until I was no longer afraid.

I retained this memory until I was 35 years old. Then I met a man with whom I had attended the first grade. I asked him: "What ever happened to the cemetery? He thought for a few moments and then answered: "There was never a cemetery!" Yet, that image was firmly implanted in my memory. I then asked a number of other people about it and was always given the same negative answer. I had in fact fantasized the whole story. It is evidence of courage in a child by which problems with training can be overcome. We will always discover the importance of training and the application of an appropriate method for overcoming problems. This fantasy of mine was not useless, but belonged to my spiritual training. It contributed to my ability in real situations to face more squarely problems that relate to death and it kept me from being fearful.

We see what may seem a new problem, but one suitable for providing us with more fragments. Fantasies and daydreams also allow us to uncover the burdens a person may carry, revealing the same tendency in a child to seek a goal that will free and relieve him from the pressures under which he lives. We can understand that many children will describe fantasies, such as being wealthy, in order to be able to buy anything they desire. Here, again, we can find clues to the extent of the person's social feeling. In some fantasies, we find that one child wants to buy everything for himself, while a second may also want to buy something, like a castle, for parents or siblings. A third child may want to give to the poor, while a fourth may want to relieve the world of all misery. These fantasies appear to poor children who are seriously worried about money.

Many children fantasize about being heroes, or dream of conquering a large army with smaller forces and taking prisoners. This is a daydream of cowards. Children who have such dreams can overcome their cowardice only in a fantasy. The source that gives the impulse to such dreams is a feeling of physical weakness.

Some fantasies reach for the supernatural. These are desires to enter the heavens, Paradise, etc., which aim at a better goal and conditions better than humanly attainable. These are fantasies of children who like to think they are not the product of their parents, and had come to them only by accident. They hope that eventually this mistake will be discovered and they will be taken to where they really belong, a wealthy home. Such fantasies can take other forms, such as believing a certain other person is their true parent. I have encountered such fantasies in children whose fathers were employed as gardeners or coachmen on the estates of titled persons (earls and princes). These children were convinced that they were born to the earls or princes and believed that one day this fact would become known. One boy had at one time created a considerable uproar with such a fantasy. The boy vehemently believed he was not the son of his father, thereby causing considerable problems for his mother.

In Vienna, a frequent childhood fantasy concerned ways of saving the emperor from a disaster, such as from run-away horses, and being richly rewarded in return. I don't know whether these days such fantasies are transferred to the chancellor.

Another fantasy entails saving a very beautiful and wealthy girl from drowning. In this fantasy, we can see a striving for esteem. Much credence must be given to such fantasies since these are fragments out of which a lifestyle is structured.

Childhood fantasies and daydreams allow us to measure the degree to which a child has the courage to live. I recommend that we assign children to write essays on subjects such as: "What I Fear." From these and similar reports, we can discern the individual's lifestyle.

Chapter VI

Childhood Memories and Dreams

A boy of six and one-half years remembered the following incident: "I fell into the water when I was four years old." We can see from this memory that his entire perspective focuses on the dangers people may encounter. When children are asked to look back into their past, what conclusions they draw, what incidents they select, and what interests they express are all very important. This child's interest focuses primarily on how easily a person can be hurt. Who knows what this accident, given its force, unleashed in his thinking. He clings to this unpleasant memory. Consequently, he grew up guarding against all dangers. The accident became a guidepost for his life. Most children already grow up feeling discouraged, sensing danger, and with a special interest in the dangers of life, which is probably in some ways necessary. Fear is meant to act as a preventive measure. However, in most cases fear is exaggerated.

Everything is open to exaggeration, even cleanliness, for example, which certainly is a good habit. However, to dwell on cleanliness day and night destroys the harmony of life. Caution must also be reasonably incorporated within a person's total life sphere and experiences. Otherwise, the individual will see danger in its extreme everywhere and as a result, hesitation, anxiety, and doubt will play far too great a role and keep him from accomplishing anything in life. A child's recollection of such experiences shows us someone with a great interest in danger, which becomes a guidepost for his entire life. When we delve further, he will undoubtedly recall many dangerous situations he experienced. We must not overlook the nuances in a recollection. When we question a person further about a particular recollection, we can gather important clues. Our conclusion would be different if the boy finished his statement with: "I survived." He would then be a different type of person, who would clearly know that dangers exist, but would not fear them, and would know that strength can overcome danger. We should practice discovering and combining related phenomena in order to recognize that the life of a six-year old is a distinct unity.

Another child remembered what transpired when he was two years old: "Dad took away the pacifier and I cried." That is a harsh way to stop a child from using something to which he has become accustomed. The boy now expects someone to take something from him and will constantly be on guard against having anything taken from him. However, he thinks only of himself.

Another child recalled the following: "I alerted my parents to the need to change my sister's diapers when she cries." The boy knew that his sister had soiled her diaper and tried to help his parents by alerting them. He played the big protector as a substitute for his parents. We shall find that later in life, he will tend to act fatherly. He will also show a concern for others. We can see the difference in this boy as opposed to the other two children described earlier. The first two think only about themselves and show very little social feeling. In the third child, we can see the impact of social feeling in that he does not think only about himself. We can also see a striving for significance. However, we cannot object to that since he relates in useful ways to others.

Another child said: "When I was two years old, I rode in a car for the first time." We can derive from this memory only that the boy felt good in that situation and that he has an interest in action. He is possibly the second child in his family and has been in a race, because he chose to remember an incident that would speed up movement. He may also be a striving firstborn. Furthermore, this recollection has a detrimental aspect, which is racing to achieve a goal quickly and wanting to be first. To arrive at that conclusion will require further confirmation or adjustments.

Another child's memory: "I remember my grandmother's funeral, the coffin, and the hearse." This incident may contain the seeds of an aspiring physician who wants to wrestle with death and overcome it. We encounter this particular memory with many physicians.

One child responded to being asked what he wanted to be with: "a gravedigger." When asked why he made that choice, he replied: "I want to be the one who buries others and not the one being buried."

When we compare the last two recollections, we can see the difference in social feeling. The second boy thinks only of himself and also seeks superiority as a way of overcoming death. Because he thinks only of being personally superior, superiority is applied in a totally useless way.

"I recall the visit of my aunt, who brought me strawberries." This boy obviously expects something and is not prepared to give. He is interested in only those situations where he receives something.

Another recollection: "I remember that when I was two years old, I went to the Prater (Note: Vienna amusement park) for the first time." I cannot see anything here other than a preference for fast action.

If he had added that he had gone with his mother, it would mean something different to us.

Recollection of a student in the third grade of public school. She is between eight and nine years old: "When I was four years old, I could draw well." This statement did not surprise us, but we are curious about something else. We are interested in why this girl had selected drawing from her memory. It raises the question whether she was left-handed. We know how to discover a left-handed person. We ask him to fold hands and if the thumb of the left hand is on top, it means that he is left-handed. Children are not aware of this phenomenon and neither are most parents. However, such children suffer the problems associated with left-handedness because they are trained to use their right hand. Out of this struggle, which we can discern from the girl's recollection, we can see that her right hand was not quite suitable at first. We may conclude that her interests bore fruit. From what I can see here, her handwriting is beautiful. We would not be surprised if this child initially struggled with problems, but has successfully overcome them.

Her recollection continues: "I often wanted to draw this little man when my mother said: 'You draw his nose like a pickle.' I did not let that bother me and continued to draw." Here we have confirmation that she had struggled and succeeded. That has become her guidepost for life: One has to struggle with difficulties and then can succeed. "When I finished my drawing, I showed it to my mother. She said: 'Now you don't draw his nose like a pickle.' From then on, I could draw handsome little men. I always remember that."

Another recollection: "When I was two years old, we went to Neuwaldegg."

We can see little more here than a love of being in the country and taking pleasure in fast action, which can have various meanings.

"Suddenly, I heard music."

This child has a particular interest in music and sounds. We might learn what she made of that.

"I started to dance."

This has to do with rhythm and a physical engagement with rhythm.

"Some people who were passing stopped."

She likes making an impression. She would like to be admired, to be stared at. She has a particular bent in that direction. We suspect that she has other traits from which we can draw the same conclusion.

"A woman came along with a child. When I saw the child, I ran to it."

She seems to have a tendency to connect with others, a sign of having social feeling.

"Feeling full of joy, I bit the child's hand."

At this point, we become a little uncertain about her social feeling. I should point out that another person may make a judgment about an incident that differs greatly from ours. This child tends to put a favorable light on something bad that she does, relating to her desire to be admired. When she does something bad, it must look as if it were good.

"The child cried."

Here we see that she reacts to what is audible.

"Her mother scolded."

Again, she shows her audible perception.

"I ran to my mother."

This girl is obviously pampered and wants to exclude others. She likes being at the center of attention. Probably an oldest or an only child, she wants to appear to be good.

Recollections of a pupil in the fourth grade:

"I can still remember that when I was two and one-half-years-old, I rode with my parents on a train."

This child probably has an interest in seeing different places, possibly also enjoys fast action. We shall not speculate further about this statement, but move on.

"After two months, I returned home and saw a little sister lying in a bed."

This becomes a tragedy. Probably an only child, she rides away from home, is sent by her parents to some strange place, and when she returns home, finds trouble. Such a child will feel she can find no security in life, and someone will always do her in. In school as a girl and later as a wife, she will look around to see if someone overtakes her. She will constantly be pursued by the same fate and be jealous.

"I was not happy...."

This further confirms our conclusion. No other science can work with greater certainty than ours. Most of the time we know in advance what will happen and most of the time we get confirmation, albeit not in so many words, but in a sense that conforms to our expectations.

"...because I believed that my mother loved my little sister more than me..."

We can already see jealousy in the future. This girl will constantly be on the lookout for someone who loves another more than her.

"I was angry with my sister and hit her. Then she started to cry and mother came with a trinket for her."

We have a child here who is not exactly a winner today, or someone who will rank with the best. Her fear that someone will overshadow her inhibits her. We can see the power we have to free this girl from her erroneous belief by looking for the motives I have previously mentioned.

"Then she went to sleep and I did not look at her."

Any commentary is superfluous.

The following are the recollections of a nine-year old girl:

"When I was three years old, I was frightened by my mother because she wore a black hat. She looked scary. I went to my sister whom I liked better."

We can see that at the early age of three, this girl had distanced herself from her mother. Something obviously must have happened and we can only guess that the mother was unable to retain the child's affection. The girl's statement contains something similar to an accusation. She is being critical. Why does her mother not wear a beautiful hat? We can conclude that she was well practiced in her critical attitude toward her mother. This criticism of the mother is followed in the next phase when the child turns to her father, provided he can give her the warmth she cannot find in her mother. How did this child arrive at her critical attitude? Here again we shall probably find the birth of a sibling which may well be the starting point of the tragedy she experienced. She feels that her mother had cheated her, had turned away from her, and began to be critical of her. Possibly, the mother badgered her so that as the child matured this kind of treatment took on harsher proportions. As long as a baby is confined to a crib, a nagging mother can do little damage. However, as soon as a child begins to understand, her mother's behavior will turn her off. Possibly, the mother had become ill and unable to care for the child, so that she was tended to by an aunt, her grandmother, a housekeeper, or a sister. Perhaps the mother had fallen gravely ill, which may explain the child's fear of her (for example, she may be mentally retarded, have epilepsy, etc.). We shall also investigate whether the child is critical by nature.

Another recollection of the same child:

"When my brother was born, he cried so much that I said: "Give him back. I don't need him; he cries too much!"

It sounds like the continuation of a predictable novel. Our suspicion is confirmed.

A third recollection of the same child:

"My sister once said to me: 'Look, a hay wagon is passing. If you don't behave, the driver will take you and hide you under the straw.' I was afraid."

We can compare these recollections for any contradictions. Even the sister was able to cause the child to be afraid, showing that she also reproaches her sister. If we had only this one recollection, we might not be able to see as clearly that this child feels imposed upon. Her recollection sounds like an accusation against the sister. Others cannot easily do right by her; she likes to complain and pointedly find fault with others.

A fourth recollection:

"My sister once dressed up like a fine lady. I really thought she was a fine lady, but then she took off her hat and I recognized her immediately."

Here again, we can see the girl's critical disposition: One can't trust people. They get dressed up to look like fine ladies and in the end, they are not that at all. We can recognize the critical attitude and a pessimism regarding the worth of other people. She begins with her mother. We can clearly see from her reaction the power of first impressions transmitted by the mother, and their impact on the child. Coincidentally, we suspect that she is a visual type.

I have already spoken of the significance of childhood fantasies, such as, when a child is fearful. Fear is a good way to draw attention to oneself and exploit another person. We can recognize that this child expresses fear in order to attract someone to serve her. I have no doubt that for her, fear is like a whip that she applies for her own purposes.

I once knew a lady who had such great fear that she never went anywhere alone. Finally, she was persuaded to visit the theater by herself. She returned home alone, was about to open the door, and suddenly saw a strange man standing in the doorway. She yelled out: "Go away. Don't you see how frightened I am?" Fear is the shabby power of the weak who lack courage.

Fantasies about work are extremely valuable, showing us a child's interest and how he wants to express himself.[2] However, some children between the ages of fourteen and fifteen have no idea what they want to become, which is significant. A fourteen-year-old who has not yet decided what he would like to be, probably does not believe he can find his way in life. He has shut his eyes to the future because it seems to him to be an insolvable puzzle. I recommended years ago a writing assignment for children in school on the topic "What I Would Like to

---

[2] See Kramer in *Heilen und Bilden*.

Be." Such an assignment forces a child to make some decision, to think, or, at least, to write: "I don't know." The child's attention will be drawn to this uncertainty and it allows for ways to help him. I have never seen negative answers to this topic and I believe children in the third and fourth grades should have this assignment. For psychological purposes, this topic can also be posed as follows: "The many things that I wanted to be."[3] When we examine the various occupations named, we will find strong indications of how children arrive at gaining superiority, how they want to develop themselves. The only exceptions are those children who had lost their courage long before. Those children will write, for example: "When I was little, I wanted to become a general, later a policeman, and then what my father is, a coachman."

During puberty girls will write: "I wanted to become a dancer, and then an actress, a singer, or a teacher. Then I wanted to go into films, but in the end, I shall dedicate myself to housework." We often find thinking in this direction when we propose writing on this subject.

Children's Dreams

A thorough psychological examination requires an inquiry into the dream world. The ancient problem of dreams has had enormous significance in history. Books from ancient times focus on dream analysis, regarding the interpretation of dreams as a way of viewing the future. Many have regarded dream analysis as a science. We should add that during the last decades two scholars contributed significantly to dream interpretation: Schubert, who is almost unknown, recognized in dreams a reflection of the individual. We find similar indications in the works of older writers, for example, Lichtenberg, who lived in Goethe's time, and who expressed that a person's character can be more easily understood from his dreams than from his behavior. Freud contributed much to our understanding of dreams, but his conception has gaps in that he relates everything to sexual infantile desires. I have consistently fought against this belief. Later, Freud dropped this one-sided perception and tried to apply the "death wish" to his dream interpretation.

For me, the significant point has always been: Why do people dream without understanding their dreams? Why can't we do something with our dreams? A person awakens feeling: Today, I had a dumb dream and don't understand anything about it. People give no credence to their dreams because they have no idea what to do with them.

---
[3] See Furtmueller in *Heilen und Bilden*.

Individual Psychology has solved that problem and thereby taken the most important step toward understanding dreams. The purpose of a dream is not to be understood, but to awaken moods and feelings from which the dreamer cannot escape. If we keep in mind that we retain these moods, feelings, and emotions, then we will understand the reason we are dreaming: In order to put us in a state of mind, or mood, in which we can accomplish something that we cannot do with logic alone. We cannot deny that even if we do not understand a dream, the mood it creates stays with us and moves us. For example, someone who has a fearful dream will not feel encouraged the following day. Because his waking was accompanied by such a negative mood, the dreamer will be motivated and moved in a direction that reflects his dream. Someone who faces a test and has little confidence in passing it, dreams of falling from the edge of a mountain into an abyss. That person's fearful mood then increases to the point where he loses all courage, failing to show up for his test the following day. On the other hand, someone with self-confidence would be fortified by his mood to reach his goal were he to dream, for instance, that while walking through a sunny lane, he suddenly found a magnificent castle that filled him with joy. This person will awaken refreshed and happy, in a mood encouraging him to face his test.

Individual Psychology in the Schools

Chapter VII

On the Meaning of Recollections, Fantasies, and Dreams

Today, I would like to discuss several childhood memories with you. Here we have the recollection of a nine-year-old girl in the third grade.

"When I was little, our neighbor came and pulled me out of the stroller. Then she put a dress on me that belonged to her daughter. I ran out of the hallway and up the steps, but then could go no further. My mother came for me."

When we examine this recollection for its deeper meaning, we find that this child needs another person who will do something for her.

The neighbor pulled me out of the stroller; she put a dress on me; mother came for me."

We have here a lifestyle, or fragments of a lifestyle, structured so that she always feels weak and needs support. These are expressions of a serious feeling of inferiority and we can conclude that we are dealing with a pampered child.

"From then on, I did not dare go down the steps alone."

Here we have another confirmation that this child does not trust herself to do anything alone. We can gather from her lifestyle that she feels insecure and has no confidence in herself.
We are fortunate in having other childhood recollections from her and can, therefore, further confirm our findings.

"We went for a walk along Ottakringer Street. I wanted to push my little cousin in the stroller. She fell out of the stroller along with all the cushions. I really got it then."

Here she wanted to do something on her own and look, she failed! Even the greatest skeptic would say at this point that we are correct in our assessment.

> *"When my mother traveled to Karlsbad for the first time, I cried very hard. However, when my father told me that she would soon return, I consoled myself."*

What can such a child do when her support is no longer there? She can console herself only when her support returns.

> *"When she then came into the house, I yelled: 'Mommy!' She was very happy to learn that I could already speak."*

These are small indications of the child's relationship to her mother.

> *"The first time I was given a banana I wanted to eat it with the skin."*

This is how badly a child can fare when left to depend on herself.

> *"My father then peeled the banana. I spit it out and rubbed my face with it. Only then did I eat it."*

We don't know the significance of that recollection other than when she is on her own, she does not know how to deal with a given situation.

> *"We went to Sulz for a summer vacation. I had a small goat in a stall. One time the goat got out and I started to cry."*

Now someone must come for help, right?

> *"Then a girl from next door came by and caught the goat for me."*

She is helpless when left alone. Someone must always come to help. She will act according to her lifestyle, which is to look for support. At home she will keep her mother busy with her, and in school she will demonstrate her helplessness so that the teacher must be especially considerate of her. We are in that favorable situation where we can draw the most far-reaching conclusions. The facade can change, outward appearances can change, but the structure will remain the same. The feeling of inferiority can seem to disappear under pleasant conditions, but will reappear when those conditions change.

We can also find this structure in dreams, with some experience and the application of techniques, which can easily be acquired through the network of Individual Psychology. The pedagogue has a great advantage when he can draw conclusion from small incidents. He has the entire life of a child before him like a detailed biography. He knows what can be expected from a child and what must be done in order to avoid making mistakes. A child has no idea what goes on inside of him. If a child were to know this and could understand what we can see, and if he could recognize what faults are contained in the structure of his lifestyle, and that these failings arise from mistakes that will lead to harm, then the following would occur: He would behave as before, would look around helplessly and seek support, but would also know that his behavior is a mistake resulting from faulty training. In the second phase, the child will make mistakes, but recognize them and even try to demonstrate with those mistakes how weak he is and how much he needs help. In the third phase, he will start to repair his mistakes. After gaining this insight, he will constantly train and strive to turn in a better direction to make himself independent. He will then realize that this new directions offers a much better way to live. From then on, he will do well with his family, in school, and in life.

We must investigate the unconscious nature of the lifestyle, a task in which we are assisted by various fragments, such as: the manner in which a person speaks, how he shakes hands, his posture, changes in face color; in short, every slight movement he makes can reveal something of his lifestyle. All this movement occurs as if the individual played a role without any controlling forces, and we cannot reasonably expect a child to guard over the ways he expresses himself. Clearly, when a child recognizes this process, the habitual behavior can be interrupted. Every person has a unique way of expressing himself which never leaves him. That is his internal, repetitive pattern. When he pays attention to it, he interrupts this automatic process and when he begins to think about it, the automatic process no longer functions. Darwin said, for example, that when the lining of the nose is irritated, we sneeze automatically. However, when we begin to contemplate how this process takes place, we will not sneeze.

A patient can be advised to contemplate the process of sneezing and he will not sneeze.[4]

If a person takes a casual stroll, he does not think about the way he moves. However, when he suddenly encounters an icy patch in the

---

[4] A marvelous example can be found in Meyerink's *Der Fluch der Krote* (The Curse of the Toad).

road, he becomes afraid and watches his movements. He will not longer be walking "unconsciously." This example is similar to a person's automatic lifestyle. As long as the automatic activity works adequately well, as long as the person faces no problems, he does not think and everything progresses in ways that he has been trained to expect. Only when he faces difficulties, does he start to think. If his thinking at that point were in accordance with common sense, it would be fine. The goal of a child is to act in accordance with his automatic behavior. His conscious thinking will follow that same line of thought. If we were to apply the automatic lifestyle in place of what the other psychologists call the "unconscious," we would discover that the conscious and the unconscious aim for the same goal and are not distinguishable. We strongly disagree with those who proclaim that malevolent forces play a significant role in the unconscious.

We can find additional fragments of a lifestyle in children's daydreams and in fantasies concerning what they would like to become. I will now present such a daydream in which we can recognize what is most often found in daydreams and fantasies, that is, a reflection of what a particular child is really missing.

"The Child Obsessed with Money"

"A mother who had very little money once told her children: You can wish every day for as much money as you like."

Based on our experience, this daydream points to a child with a keen interest in money, which could have occurred only if that child experienced some problem concerning money. Were this not so, the child would not have arrived at this particular fantasy.

"Olly then responded by saying: 'I would like to have a house. Can you get me a builder?' 'Yes,' the mother answered and there came a builder who built me the most beautiful family home in the world."

This child must have had some experience with the idea of having a family home built. She had possibly once lived under better circumstances which suddenly changed, causing this issue to become a particularly important one.

"When the house was finished, I bought the most beautiful furniture in the world. Then I placed an ad in the newspaper for a maid

who would clean and who would also love children. Many applicants came and we finally hired a girl named Lotte. We had rooms filled with toys. When we started to live in the house, I went to Gerngro[5] where I bought myself a silk dress."

This child must have once lived in more prosperous times. She must have had wealthy neighbors with expensive homes.

"I also bought a lovely coat and a straw hat. I then went home and asked for 140 billion."

With such a sum, the child clearly expressed how much she exaggerates money. She suffers from a strong feeling of inferiority and believes that life cannot go on without money, which she needs for support.

"Then I went to buy lunch. The next day I invited every child I knew to a children's party."

Here we see emphasized how strongly a child without any possessions feels, and how in contrast she arrives at such extravagant wishes. This movement goes from below to above. She asks for billions and then goes out to buy lunch with it. She has no idea what to do with money.

"When the children came, I first gave them a very good meal, then we played games, and then they all went home."

She wants to connect with other children. We cannot say she has only egotistical feelings, because she does not want money only for herself. Of course, this tendency to spend money for other is also a feeling of superiority. She gains in esteem by doing something useful and by leaving some of her riches to others.

We shall also encounter these fragments in dreams. Individual Psychology is not satisfied with only one-sided observations. We always seek to gather new evidence to reassure ourselves that we have examined all sides of an issue.

I have already spoken in my last lectures about the importance of dreams and have mentioned that in ancient times, and among all peoples, dreams played a significant role. We can find importance attributed to

---

[5] A large department store in Vienna.

dreams in *The Bible* and among the ancient Romans and Egyptians who regarded dreams as a hint from the gods and as a decisive indicator for the future.

We have instinctively recognized that only those people dream who are not quite sure of themselves. When we look at our dreams, we can see that if someone feels secure, if he knows what to do, he does not dream. This fact tells us that when someone has a problem that he feels cannot be solved while he is awake, then he will dream because he needs something else to deal with his difficulties. Individual Psychology has demonstrated that dreaming establishes an emotion, an affect, an inner direction that points along a particular path the dreamer wishes to follow. A dream really means to create a mood, to give ourselves a feeling that our problem-solving capacities cannot deal with a given problem without the mood generated in our dream. When a person is immersed in a problem, a dream will evoke a mood and establish a guideline for him to follow in order to arrive at ways to deal with that problem which cannot be resolved with only logic and within the parameters of that person's lifestyle. There is actually no basic difference between our dream world and our awakened stare. When we want to convince ourselves of something, we employ moods and feelings. Take for example Chekhov's novel, "The Siren," in which the author shows that by creating a certain mood, hunger can be generated in a character in the novel simply by describing various fine dishes. The yearning for food becomes so strong that this otherwise dutiful official rushes out of his office in order to satisfy his sudden need for it. In this instance, officials were torn away from their work by creating a mood that led them to forget their duties.

The human psyche tends to be governed not only by logic, but also by feelings and can create moods that contradict logical considerations. All of us try to forego logical solutions to our problems and arrive at less logical solutions by drawing on our feelings and moods. Many actions cannot be understood logically. We can also create moods while awake such as when we think of sad occasions, or when we anticipate an impending disaster that might befall a person close to us. In such circumstances, our moods will be in harmony with those thoughts. When we imagine that we are in pleasant company and among happy people, our mood will be formed accordingly. Coue, for example, using this method, wants to help people become happy and wise by convincing them through autosuggestion that things will always get better. We can understand that a child will give in to moods and feelings that are not in harmony with logic. But we also recognize the limits of creating moods. We do not recommend generating feelings and moods with selective fantasies and giving psychological emotions concrete form in order to attain a personal superiority, such as by losing oneself in heroic and god-like ideals. We can draw conclusions from various clues, for example, when a child, who has no self-confidence and a lifestyle that causes him to shirk from solving problems, manifests moods and feelings that agree with that lifestyle.

Then some children want to solve problems by overcoming difficulties in useful ways. They create appropriate moods and feelings, and choose fantasies which are not exaggerated, of fantasies will not be exaggerated.

In our dream world where we have free reign, reality exerts little control. I can create fantasies and moods appropriate for my goals, which will help me find the path I would have followed even without devising these feelings. This mood justifies my actions. It means a great deal when someone can say that he acted in accordance with his feelings. Feelings are only part of the general lifestyle because the individual has worked to create them and has called them forth because they suit him. They are his. If someone goes to bed feeling embroiled in a particular problem and unable to resolve it, that problem will pursue him in his sleep and will begin to have an effect undeterred by logic or common sense. That person will evoke pictures, find comparable situations, and look for solutions that he feels necessary in order to create those feelings. He will seek to justify following a path dictated by his lifestyle. The means the dreamer calls on to serve him are the same that he would employ when awake to allow him to act in conformity with those feelings, further confirming our point of view.

I would like to demonstrate with an example how we can arouse our feeling in dreams. During the war, I was head of a large military hospital for soldiers suffering from neuroses caused by the war. I can say without exaggerating that I liked that place because I did not enjoy sending neurotics to the front lines. The patients were quite happy, did not fear unjust treatment, and I experienced good results. Once a young man came to me complaining about weak nerves and asked me to relieve him from military duty. His complaint turned out to be invalid, even though he walked around bent over as if he were deformed. I had to present my reports on patents to the chief of the local garrison hospital, who had the final authority to decide each case. When the day came that this young man was to leave my hospital, I told him that his condition did not warrant deferment from military duty. He suddenly straightened out and begged me to free him because he was a poor student and had to support his elderly parents. Not relieving him of duty would mean the end of his entire family. Consoling him, promised that I would do everything in my power, and that I would try to get him assigned to guard duty, which would allow him to find half-day employment. He was not satisfied. He begged me, crying, to find further relief for him. I had to expect, however, that given wartime conditions the chief of the garrison hospital would oppose any unjustified relief and would send him immediately to the front lines. I went home that night, and giving his case further thought, saw no other choice but to assign him to guard duty.

That night I dreamed that I was a murderer. I did not know whom I had killed. I walked around in dark alleys and felt like the murderer, Raskolnikov, who vacillated between feeling guilty and not guilty. I awakened trembling, feeling that I had committed a murder. I soon realized that the dream related to this particular young man and in an exaggerated manner represented what I would have been guilty of doing if I did not comply with his plea.

Logically, I could not have acted in any other way than I did without endangering him. I would only have harmed him. However, I still had the feeling that I should do more for him. In my dream I wanted to cancel my logic; I wanted to obtain for him an even lighter assignment so that he could save his parents. When I uncovered this self-delusion, I re-affirmed sustained my logically conceived recommendation.

Since I made that discovery, I have not allowed myself to be captured again by exaggerated feelings. In this case, common sense could hardly have suggested that I was a murderer. That conclusion would have been too far a reach. I was sufficiently sympathetic, however, that the dream was able to expand my sympathy and paint a picture of me as a murderer, thus creating a metaphor. Our aesthetic development enables us to think in terms of metaphors. Although we are fond of metaphors, we must not forget that any metaphor is a cunning deception. In light of actual circumstances, of logic, it is a forgery. This view also applies to the use of metaphors by poets. We use metaphors when we wish to explain or describe something and are unable to apply the naked truth. A comparison lets us see where a particular individual wants to go. A teacher will also reach for metaphors to augment what he is describing. They are an artful trick.

Chapter VIII

On the Theory of Dreams

On the subject of dreams we have thus far noted the following: (1) The dream has the task of creating a mood meant to lead the dreamer, against his own logic regarding a given situation in his life, to where his lifestyle actually takes him. (2) The dreamer employs certain means, which also relate to his lifestyle, in that in his dreams he reaches back to images in his memory that will ease his task and seem desirable to him for solving his problem. (3) The dreamer likes to find metaphors and similes in order to reinforce the mood he needs in order to attain his goal. On one point our observations converge. The dreamer requires a particular mood in order to follow the path that he fears losing if he were to use logic or his intellect. For that reason, he must not be able to understand his dream. We might say that he is intoxicated by his dream in which reality does not influence him and has no control over him at every step.

In order to integrate our observations, we have established a selective guideline, a direction that takes effect in the dream. The selection process is purposeful in that events and actions surface from the dreamer's memory that, like childhood memories, fit his lifestyle. The individual's lifestyle rationalizes his interests, which will further his personal striving for superiority. We also want to establish with dreams the type of child or adult we have before us, which is not to say that we believe a dream can tell us everything. However, a dream can be quite beneficial in establishing the uniform lifestyle, given that we also have information from a different perspective. Another means the dreamer employs to create emotions and establish a mood, in effect to deceive or intoxicate himself, is to foreshorten his problem so that he fails to grasp its full extent by selecting only one point as if that were the entire problem.

We don't act differently when awake. We can see this principle in thousands of daily occurrences, such as when a boy who does not want to learn to swim refuses to go into the water. At that point we try to get around his problem by saying: "Listen, you'll just get a little wet. Why not try it?" We then make it seem as if that is all that keeps the boy from going into the water. The dreamer also often selects just one aspect of his problem as if everything else does not matter. The other side of foreshortening a problem is exaggerating it. I have already mentioned an example of this exaggeration when I spoke of the dream I had during the war in which I tried to find a solution to a problem I faced. Thus, we can come to some resolution through dreams which often provide information we can also gather from daydreams, fantasies, and childhood memories and which provide us with an understanding of a child's attitude when confronting his tasks.

Some typical dreams often recur. Even if these dreams do not have the same meaning, they always evoke the same mood, and in some ways are similar. These recurring dreams provide us with starting points. Frequently we encounter "falling dreams" in which the dreamer falls somewhere. In some individuals, this dream is reduced to merely a feeling of falling. In some cases, such a dream can be so intensive that the person actually falls out of bed. That dream naturally represents the most extreme consequence of what the dreamer imagines might happen to him if he is not careful. It creates a mood that warns him to be on guard: "Be careful, don't cross the Halys River. You are in danger and could face defeat."

Because of the frequency of this dream, we are forced to conclude that most people lack courage and that caution and fear play a big role in their lives. We may well say that people are deeply fearful and that the history of individuals, as well as that of humankind as a whole, would have been quite different if people had more courage.

Another frequently occurring dream involves flying, which represents a simile for striving to attain superiority. The flying dream expresses a way to achieve something that in reality is unattainable, to create something that is beyond human ability, and that requires super-human strength. Children who have such dreams exhibit characteristic traits that point to a desire for superiority. The flying dream is occasionally linked with a dream about falling. The point of connecting the two can be expressed with the proverb: "He who climbs high falls far," or in a Vienna dialect: "Had you not climbed up, you would not have fallen down."

In a third frequently occurring dream, someone is being chased by a person or an animal. This dream clearly shows us an individual who by nature sees himself as weak and another person as strong. Such dreams reflect an intense feeling of inferiority. Dreams of robbers fall in the same category. They dream, for example, that they are in great danger and have no way of escaping, or that they are being pursued and attempting to shut behind them a door that does not close. These dreams

Individual Psychology in the Schools

also remind us of nightmares in which the dreamer experiences irresistible pressure and a feeling of being awake.

We have also found dreams in which the dreamer just missed a train or streetcar. The people who have such dreams often feel that they live under an unlucky star and believe that bad luck happens only to them and not to anyone else. A person who faces a difficult situation and who wishes not to become involved could also experience such dreams. He wants to withdraw unnoticed from having to resolve that situation. We also have seen dreams about having to take tests. For some time now, we have interpreted dreaming about taking a test as a disturbing sign associated with a feeling of terror, serving to create a fearful mood. Many different people experience these typical, frequently recurring dreams.

Sometimes dreams recur repeatedly for an individual. These periodic recurring dreams, if properly understood, clearly demonstrate a person's character. In such dreams, a person under the most varied circumstances will look for the same bridge in order to reach his goal of superiority. These dreams evoke the appropriate mood for his lifestyle so as to advance in that direction.

Interestingly, some people dream a lot, while others dream little or not at all. The reason for the lack of dreaming seems to be that people who dream little or not at all do not like to lie or deceive themselves. They are not subservient to their moods, and are not driven by their emotions. People who do not dream also find themselves in situations in which they feel content or at least have no desire to escape, or feel no impulse to solve a problem in which they are entangled. People dream more who are often guided by strong emotions, rather than by logic, in their daily lives. Some people have short dreams, which tell us they have found a shortcut to solving their problems and are determined to create an appropriate mood. Longer and complex dreams tell us that the dreamer was unable to create a consistent mood. Often, we cannot clarify the meaning of a dream, which usually happens when the dreamer is undecided how to fool himself and how to create an appropriate mood.

At this point, I would like to present the following children's dreams:

The dream of a boy in the third grade of public school: "I never dream at night. During the day I dream very rarely."

We can assume that this resolute child knows his way and does not try to fool himself.

"Only sometimes do I imagine that when I grow up I shall marry our maid."

This child stands for no nonsense, but is decisive and already knows what he will do when he grows up.

"I like her because she is good to me. When she is at the altar with her bridegroom, I shall jump up and push the man aside."

We can see that he takes this matter seriously and is ready to intercede forcefully, and if necessary, might even get physical.

The dream of a girl in the fourth grade of public school: "I slept in my bed and dreamed. This time it was a terrible dream. I stood in a bleak, scary hall. It had two large windows, but was still very sinister. I saw death dressed in a long white cloak, wandering around the room. He had neither eyes nor hair, but seemed to want to look at me. I wanted to scream, but my voice failed me. Then I saw my father. He looked quite different. He had a brown pointed beard, four feet, and looked very young. Suddenly I saw nothing more."

Although this dream seems complicated, we can analyze it clearly. This child recalls the death of a relative and contemplates how the death of someone close to her would affect her. Her father appears in her dream as very young and she wants to mollify herself with the thought that his death is far off. She seems concerned about what she will do when her father dies. She seems to feel closer to her father than to her mother. At this point, I would like to point out that some psychologists assume this concern about her father's death reflects the wish of all children for their parents to die. I have never encountered such a death wish. The sad mood in this case was created by the dream. The child thinks of the future, imagining how terrible it will be after her father dies and what she will do then. At the same time, she reassures herself with the thought that while her father could die, he is still very young. That she sees her father in her dream with four feet may be regarded in the context of a curse when someone says, for example: "You donkey, you cow, etc." I don't dare go any further on that point.

The dream of a girl in the fourth grade of public school:

"I once had a beautiful dream about an angel. I was in my garden when a man tried to throw me into the water. Suddenly, an angel appeared before me and held me in his arms. He said: 'If you throw this child into the water, you will die.' Then the angel flew with me into heaven. He also took my parents along. It was very nice there. Afterwards I was very happy."

This child is obviously looking for support. A relationship with a man appears to her as a dangerous situation. He wants to throw her into the water, meaning that a man is dangerous and we need an angel on our side for protection. Further proof of her pampering is her desire to take her parents into heaven with her.

"I once dreamed that the Christ Child was there. The day before, I had written Him a letter and that is why I had this dream. I dreamed that I was given a Christmas tree that reached into heaven. I was very happy..."

Nothing can occur in a dream other than the continuation of a psychological episode from the previous day. She comes to this psychological conclusion on her own.

"...because so many sweets were hanging from its branches."

She clearly has a strong interest in food.

"I then opened my eyes wide and saw a big teddy bear in a carriage."

We can assume that she is a visual child.

"When I was about to take a candy from the tree, the door suddenly opened and St. Nicholas entered and then ran out again."

That is forbidden: to sneak candy.

"When I awoke, I looked for the tall Christmas tree and the big teddy bear in the carriage. Everything had disappeared. Mother had kissed me in my dream."

Undoubtedly, this child is closely tied to her mother and has big wishes, represented by the tall Christmas tree. A spoiled, greedy child, as we can see in the last sentence, describes her dream. She still did not get enough and at least had to have a kiss from her mother.

The dream of a girl in a fourth grade class for slow learners:

"My father and I went for a walk. We walked for one hour and then another, but never reached our destination. Finally, we came to a house that we entered."

This child feels insecure somehow and not equal to the task.

"We entered and saw silver everywhere. We were so engrossed in looking at the silver that we fell asleep."

They fall asleep in the dream.

"We dreamed that the devil grabbed us and carried us to a mountain. We both slid down; one landed in one place and the other in another. Then I woke up and had to get out of bed since it was already 7 o'clock."

There is always trouble. Finally, after an outing, the devil suddenly appears, carries them up a mountain, and they slide down. They face difficulties and they cannot stay at the top. The child's handwriting shows an upward slant, which may be merely accidental, but she routinely slackens and believes that things will not work out.

Thinking she will only slide down, she asks herself why she should make the effort, which probably relates to her being in a slow learner class.[6]

The dream of an eleven-year-old boy in the second grade of middle school:

"I once dreamed about a brook. I walked along the brook until I arrived at an arid spot and saw a young shark. I pulled out my cap pistol and shot the fish dead."

This young hero takes it easy. He has a revolver; the fish does not.

"When I lifted him up, he had more than three bullet wounds."

This seems like a particularly heroic act.

"I carried him home and sliced open his stomach and pulled out his innards. Then I awoke because it was so gruesome."

This has to be explained. This boy may be interested in what is inside things, but is not too enthusiastic about it.

The development of a dream also reflects something of the dreamer's intelligence. The dream shows us not only that individual's uniqueness, but also reveals more about him.

The dream of another student in the same class:

"Recently I had a very peculiar dream. I was a locksmith and had no parents."

He was probably thinking ahead of what will occur in the future.

"I lived in a small room in the home of a very nice lady who looked very much like my mother...."

This could also be an orphan reflecting on the past and thinking about his mother.

"...and who did not ask me to pay any rent."

(A teacher told me that this child actually had no parents.) Here we see a child who is now twelve years old and cannot forget that he has no mother. He cannot forget it and contemplates what it might be like if he had a mother.

"One day when she brought me breakfast, I suddenly shouted for joy because I recognized my mother in that woman. I awoke immediately thereafter."

This boy believes that if he had a mother, life would be pleasant for him. He would get breakfast, would have to pay no rent, and would always be happy.

---

[6] Unfortunately, we have no dream material from mentally retarded children. Based on my cases, I seem justified in concluding that such children do not dream often, if at all. If this conclusion can be confirmed, it would be valuable to use in a diagnosis.

Orphans often overrate the meaning of the sad fact that they have no mother. Such children relate all the problems and troubles in their life to having no mother, frequently causing a bitter mood and a feeling of being shortchanged.

I recall an orphaned apprentice boy. In that situation, he was maltreated and committed suicide. He left behind a letter in which he wrote: "I would rather be with my parents." In his case, there was too great a contrast between fantasy and reality, which he could no longer face.

The dreams that we discussed so far tell us that these children are not particularly courageous, except for the boy who wanted to win over the stronger challengers and marry the girl. In the other cases, we are dealing with children who lack courage. In dreams, we constantly discover that we all have too little courage. We can establish from dreams and recollections that basically these children are weak. Tortured by all sorts of fears, they are preoccupied with dangers and defeats. They will never draw on enough strength in order to gain their goal. Instead of approaching a problem with courage, through their dreams they create a mood allowing them to evade solving their problems, or to approach them with great care. The behavior of these children reflects a peculiar philosophy of life, manifested in the way they view all problems, how they confront them, and what conclusions they draw. For example, if a person acts as if he were constantly in a race, always in great haste, is dissatisfied, fearful, and afraid that someone might overtake him, how else can he be helped, but by demonstrating that his philosophy of life is wrong? The "struggle against all" is also a philosophy of life, but has no social validity. The falseness of this view must be exposed and people must be brought to recognize the validity of a philosophy of life that adheres to common sense, is useful, and beneficial to all.

Chapter IX

Overview: Social Feeling

In this lecture I would like to review what has been discussed so far, and also interpret the history of a problem child. During the course of this discussion, we will see that the best method for understanding a child is to empathize and identify with him. When we pass a house and see a maid cleaning windows on the third floor, moving as if she were standing on a narrow windowsill, we sense tension that can only be explained by the feeling that we are standing in her place. We have the same sensation when watching a tightrope walker. Also, when a speaker is suddenly at a loss for words, we feel his embarrassment as if we were in his place.

Understanding is really an act of empathizing, which plays an important role beginning in early life and remains with us at every moment of our existence. For example, in a theater we empathize with the role played by the actor; when we read a book we identify with the hero. Thousands of examples show how understanding relates to empathizing with a person. However, empathy must be practiced. We often do that when reading a novel and come upon scenes that seem familiar to us when, in fact, we had actually empathized with the person being described.

Thus, if we truly understand a problem child, we will have the following feeling: If I were in that child's situation, I would act the same way, and given the same environment, would make the same mistakes and set the same goal. When we can feel as one with such a child, then we can understand him. If we cannot do that, then all efforts are in vain and useless. At that point, nothing can be done for that child because the mistake that was made in the creation of his lifestyle will not become known. We have available to us the best weapons and with the aid of the network of Individual Psychology, we can uncover the point where that mistake occurred.

We all know the most important question to ask in order to recognize the mistake: Since when did these complaints begin? Such mistakes develop mostly at a time when the child was ill prepared to move from his past into the present in which he lives. We have learned of several new situations that we can use as proof tests and from responses, or from a lack of responses, we can determine if that child has been correctly or incorrectly prepared. The questions we must ask are always of a social nature. These questions concern how a child relates to life, to other people, and to his tasks. Life consists of social questions, the responses to which demand a certain degree of social feeling. We have matured to where we recognize that a child who cannot perform what is expected of him has never learned, has never been prepared, to do so. This places the matter of punishment in another light. We are saddled with the task of finding out why that child is not properly prepared to correct mistakes and of providing him with the right preparation.

We have reviewed the various situations that play a role in the development of a child's lifestyle. This forming of a lifestyle begins with the relationship to the mother. We shall be able to establish from the child's later behavior whether that relationship has been correctly developed. All the child's organs will function according to the quality of that development. He will observe, listen, and act to the extent that the mother succeeded in expanding his devotion to her to others. The birth of a sibling presents another new situation, measuring whether a child has enough social feeling, or he is interested only in himself. Then come other situations such as beginning kindergarten; a lengthy illness of one of the parents to whom he was particularly close and who is now unable to attend to him; or the child, having recovered from an illness, is shocked to move from a warm and caring environment into one where he is no longer given excessive care. Other difficult situations occur when a pampered child faces a stepmother or stepfather, or is orphaned; or when a child in his early years grows up in a well-to-do home, but his parents then fall on hard times and are unable to provide for him as previously. Reversals a child encounters in life are also important. For example, a child may first live with generous caregivers or kind grandparents, then be moved to live with hostile stepparents, and finally come home to parents who mistreat him. We can establish whether a child had good preparation when he faces a difficult situation. The school and changes in teachers are also significant forces, as when one teacher is friendly and another strict. The extent of a child's social feeling can be gauged from problems he has with friends, and from his general interest in people.

Later in life, problems that arise from work, love, and marriage reveal the extent of a person's social feeling. Every case presents a unique situation. We are intrigued by the question: Why has this child no interest in others, no social feeling? Someone needs to know this network of guidelines exists, and how to understand it.

We have also come to know the three types of children who are inadequately prepared, and who have little or no social feeling: 1) Children with inferior organs, 2) pampered children, and 3) neglected children.

These children are far more interested in their own person than in others because they grew up under burdensome circumstances. In order to recognize a lifestyle, which has already become automatic during the fourth or fifth year of life, we have various hints that can reveal the line the child follows. We can draw conclusions from the child's expressions, his physical posture, and from all his movements. We can gather a child's reaction to life even from his sleeping posture. For example, if someone sleeps all balled up like a hedgehog, we can assume that he probably lacks in energy and courage. Another child whose sleeping position is as if standing at attention may always want to seem big. When lying on his stomach with his back turned toward another, a child usually manifests defiance. These sleep postures are also components of a lifestyle, like fear, that point to children who feel weak, which usually means pampered children. We also have been able to establish the extent to which a person holds on to early childhood memories. When we understand these hieroglyphics, we shall be able to uncover much from a child's original lifeform. The standing of a child within the family causes him to develop in certain ways, almost typically. The choice of occupation, fantasies, daydreams, and dreams provides us with clues to empathize with an individual's lifestyle and allow us to understand him better.

"Know thyself" has been our primary guide for bringing up children. This principle requires us to help a child fully understand his mistakes and help him eliminate them. When a child understands the connection between his behavior and his mistaken thinking, then he has one more way to determine the course of his life. He is no longer the same person as before. He can begin exerting control over himself and take steps to eliminate his mistakes. This is the true success achieved only by "knowing thyself," never with criticism, punishment, or bribery.

Where does the entire process of social feeling begin? The soul of every child contains the potential for the development of social feeling. It develops first with the mother because she is the first person with whom the child bonds. The first intimate person with whom the child has a social relationship, the mother must be the model of a trustworthy fellow human being. That is her first important function. Her second function, as I mentioned earlier, is to prepare the child for the tasks of life, to expand his interest toward others and all life on earth.

She must also understand how to awaken that interest toward the father and siblings. We can recognize in children as young as four or five whether they will become proper fellow human beings. With that knowledge, we can also prevent many mistakes, problems in upbringing, neuroses, the conditions that lead to criminality, the development that leads to suicide, prostitution, sexual crimes, etc. These mistaken directions reflect impairments in people who have little or no social feeling and who do not relate correctly to others. Only by recognizing this connection between social feeling and behavior can we see how little humankind has done to prevent mistakes and how much still remains to be done.

Bringing someone who has made mistakes to recognize them is not a simple task. The entire lifestyle of a problem child fights against being changed. Pestalozzi noted: "If you ever seek to improve a neglected child, he will oppose you in every respect, and will always want to make it difficult for you." That is the defense of an unconscious lifestyle. It resists changes, and like a machine, wants to continue along its familiar path. If we want to treat a problem child, we need a great deal of patience, friendship, and empathy. A child needs a fellow human being who is interested in others. The child feels our interest even if he does not understand it, just as he may be unsympathetic toward the characteristic traits of an egotist, someone interested only in himself. If we want to kindle social feeling in someone, we must perform the two functions of a mother: We have to win his interest and steer his interest toward others. We must not repeat the mother's mistakes by allowing the child to be interested only in us, or being unable to kindle social interest at all. We have no other choice since our primary task is to awaken social feeling.

Social feeling is closely tied to the development of a human being. A child who has social feeing hears and sees better, has a better memory, can achieve more, has the ability to win friends, plays well and probably has better sense than others. His social feeing allows his eyes to see better, his ears to hear better, and his heart to feel better. Those who have enough social sense are better achievers, can overcome problems, and have had more training. Also, those in prominent positions in school, in social circles, and at work, as well as those who can solve their problems, have a stronger social feeling. What, however, happens to the others? Certainly, they do not stand out in useful endeavors. Even if favorable circumstances put them in prominent positions, they will not hold those positions long. They will not be popular; they will fail in dealing with the three crucial tasks (friendship, work, and love) because they have insufficient interest in others. Only sufficient social feeing leads to the successful achievement of those tasks.

Later, I shall describe several cases of problem children and show how, with Individual Psychology and the help of our network, we can understand their characteristics and lifestyle.

Chapter X

Four Case Histories

Case #1

This case concerns an eleven-year-old girl in the second grade of middle school. The mother's complaint is that this usually well-behaved child can occasionally become very unpleasant.

We proceed on the assumption that no miracles occur in the psyche of a young child. Therefore, we are justified in asking: What situations cause this child to behave badly?

She behaves badly when her sixteen-months-older sister wants to borrow her younger sister's bathrobe and takes it out of he drawer. She then begins to yell and scream that her sister will dirty the robe.

Such cases are frequently found in family situations. We must ask what is happening when this otherwise well-behaved girl goes into a rage and starts to scream? Our answer is that she naturally wants to appear and act in front of her sister as the stronger of the two. We see a tendency to want to outdo her sister. We had earlier pointed out that generally two sisters grow up in a correlating frame of reference within which the younger strives to equal or outstrip the older. The older sister, on the other hand, strives to keep her position or strengthen it.

The older girl tends to make trouble for her younger sister and seeks to get her sister into situations where she will appear less deserving. She makes a test: She takes the coat and lets it fall to the ground.

This situation allows us to establish whether this girl is socially well prepared. It shows us that she has a great deal of interest in herself. We can assume that the younger sister really believes that she is the weaker of the two and that the only way she can assert herself is by screaming. She has a strong feeling of inferiority that does not give her any relief so that under certain circumstances, she lets herself go.

There is one other situation when the same scene plays out. It takes place when the older sister walks through the room while the younger one is dressing herself.

The younger sister seems to be more easily embarrassed than normal. The mother, also easily embarrassed, assumes this is the reason her younger daughter screams. We disagree and say that this child is embarrassed because of her feeling of inferiority. This raises the question how these two sisters physically compare to each other. The mother says that the older sister is remarkably beautiful, while the younger one is stocky and awkward to the point where it is difficult to avoid praising the older and making her appear the favorite whenever strangers come to the house. Seeing herself neglected, the younger sister believes she is disadvantaged by nature, and fears getting into situations where her disadvantaged position would become apparent.

I advised the mother that the younger child had to be taught that beauty does not play such a big role in life and that good health is much more valuable.

The child also demonstrates her dislike of school by being absent frequently. She does not think much of school. The mother told the following that occurred recently: One morning the younger sister did not want to get up at 7 o'clock in the morning to go to school and said so to her sister. The sister responded by saying: "Then don't bother to get up at all. Stay at home all day!" She actually did not go to school and stayed in bed until 10 o'clock. When she was asked to explain herself, she said that she stayed home because her sister had suggested it. As we can see, the fight continues unabated, as the younger sister uses every opportunity to put her older sister in a bad light. Her goal is to put her sister on an equal footing. But, how is that done? According to the parents, neither daughter is favored over the other. However, I believe that the older is regarded with more pride because she is more beautiful and as a result, the younger feels neglected. She also has the disadvantage of being unable to overtake her older sister. She can see no way of becoming superior to her sister. Her mistaken view should be pointed out to her and she should be made to understand that only a person who feels suppressed and weak screams in hopes of subduing another by screaming.

We can recognize this child's lifestyle and also see where mistakes were made. The mother failed in not being able to direct her child's interest toward the older sister. She was even unable to bond with the child herself. The mother said that her younger daughter favors her father because, "I am too abrupt with her." That is not a suitable method for winning over a child's affection. How is this child then to be regarded? If this child were a boy, beauty would not be a factor. However, since this is a girl growing up in a family that sees itself as well-to-do, achievement matters less than looking good. Where we overemphasize the traditional ideal of beauty, children naturally must suffer.

As the mother reported further, the younger daughter has no friends because she is clumsy, something that might have to do with her being chubby. She makes no friends because the children laugh at her and she, like someone in a race, is very sensitive on that point. In this regard, her social feeling has no chance of developing. She also cannot feel successful with her teacher because of the poor grades she gets for not making progress. This girl actually has very few prospects. However, I don't regard her chances in school as poor. School may yet provide some avenue for achievement, one that is also rewarding.

She cannot follow. When her mother purchases something for her, she declares: "If you do something for me, it means that I cannot do it myself."

She wants to distinguish herself by doing everything on her own and not following someone else.

We are not surprised to learn that she does not want to go to sleep at night. The parents had an arrangement by which the younger daughter goes to bed first. She finds that unfair and says she will not go to bed if her older sister is allowed to stay up late. The older sister, on the other hand, insists that her younger sister must go to bed first. When they finally agree to go to sleep, the race continues in bed. Both children read under a light over each bed. Then the mother comes into the room, tells the children that it is late and turns off the light over the younger daughter's bed. She remarks that the older girl can continue to read but "not you," to the younger. Here again, the younger child feels shortchanged.

The younger girl finds her mother's vulnerable point where she can stand up to her. At mealtime, she makes a big fuss. At least when they are eating, her mother has to pay more attention to her than to the other daughter.

I asked the mother whether the younger daughter has any determination. Parents usually do not understand that question correctly. The mother tells me that she is constantly being watched and is always together with her older sister. Besides, the maid is always present when the mother leaves the house. When asked whether the younger girl likes to be alone or is afraid, the mother answers that: "She always wants to have someone nearby."

This girl will constantly be tense. For example, she will have problems learning how to swim because she will not trust her swimming instructor, thinking that he is hostile toward her. If children with such an attitude could learn how to swim by themselves, they would not feel they are in a dangerous situation.

In regard to providing treatment for her, we would say the following: This child is in danger of becoming hostile to people. She is not a truly social person. She sees life as a struggle that turns on whether one is "on top;" one must be either the hammer or the anvil. If a person cannot be a hammer, then he is an anvil. She does not want to become an anvil. We should make clear to her that we gain much more in life with social feeling than by having people fight with one another. We must show her how her mistakes occurred in order to explain the delusion under which she lives when she assumes that she can never catch up with her sister, and, therefore, has to find ways to torment the sister whom she believes to be her superior in this race. We need to point out to her that because she is always tense, she cannot do well in school and make friends. Our task becomes to carry out the function of the mother: first, to win her over; then, to try to expand that affection toward others. We must help her win friends. We must try to help her stand out in school by becoming a better student who excels in schoolwork.

When asked what she wanted to become, she answered: "I want to work in my father's business." She wants to become like her father. We suspect from her answer that she has a tendency not to further her female side. Her father's business is in electro-technical articles. When I asked what the older daughter would like to become, the mother responded: "Oh, she doesn't bother with that!" She probably wants to get married and become a housewife. She believes that this will all take place by itself and she does not have to set goals for herself. Here again, we find stark differences. This is not a conscious thought process, but something that will occur by itself through the elimination of any problems. The younger daughter, on the other hand, feels that no one will like her, which is why she wants to go into her father's business.

The right path, to my mind, is giving this child the possibility of making progress in school. This direction would certainly be feasible if she were encouraged with optimism. She must be turned into a social person who does not always feel depressed and tense, who sees everything in its proper place, and who feels at home and not as if living in a hostile environment.

Case #2

I have two boys, ages 7 and 9. I have not yet been able to establish how well the younger is learning because he is only in the first grade at school.

We have here two boys, one older, the other younger. Children in families grow up in different situations. We cannot assume that they grow up under the same circumstances. The older boy was an only child for the first two years, obviously the center of attention and pampered. Suddenly, a second child appeared and his situation changed totally. He experienced a time when everything focused on him; he was like a ruler. Suddenly, his mother's attention is drawn to the second child. She no longer has as much time as before for her first child. Because preparing one child for the arrival of another is not easy, we shall see that in most cases the older child is ill prepared. He faces a difficult test period. Many cannot overcome strong jealously, beginning a mad struggle for the parents' favor and to regain their advantageous position, their former situation. The second child faces the situation of never being alone. He now has a leader in the race whom he can chase, someone he wants to reach. A child once said:" I am so sad that I can never be the same age as my older brother" (Esau and Jacob).

The older boy suffered a tragedy with the birth of his brother. If we hear that he now fears his younger brother will catch up to him and overtake him and that he is losing hope, we will understand that these negative feelings result from his mistaken lifestyle, an inscription in his soul that reads: "Suddenly, another has arrived and takes everything away from me." The behavior of these two children will be different, depending on (a) the extent to which the lifestyle of the older child is complete and whether it will be difficult or easy to change; (b) how the second child behaves; (c) how the parents conduct themselves; and (d) how they prepared the older child by extending his social feeling toward others. We must keep all these significant factors in mind.

We shall now hear how this boy developed:

As opposed to the older, in my opinion, the younger is a lazy learner.

He is procrastinating. We can deduce from this comment that the boy lacks the confidence to get ahead. He lost his courage. Thinking that the pursuit of useful endeavors will not succeed, he tries to gain esteem with useless activities. Laziness challenges the teacher; he must occupy himself with this student. This child attains what he strives for in an unusual way: He draws more attention to himself and makes others help him. Being a lazy learner is a way of distancing oneself from having to deal with problems. This is procrastinating. The unconscious lifestyle of a lazy child shows no confidence. Such children often say: "I am not any dumber than the others. I am just not interested." If this child could anticipate success, he would not be lazy. Laziness is a form of low self-evaluation. However, even laziness reveals a striving for esteem. Lazy children often become the center of attention. They make others work for them, which means devoting more time to them. We would not be surprised if such a boy were asked why he is lazy and replied: "You see, I am the laziest boy in class, but everyone busies himself with me and is always nice and pleasant toward me. The boy next to me is very diligent, but no one cares about him." The lazy boy enjoys the advantages of his laziness. He is like a wealthy person who also does not constantly think about his money; he just enjoys being rich.

When this boy achieves something, he is praised immediately. When he fails in something, he is told: "If you were not lazy, you could be at the head of the class." It is wonderful to see how such a lazy child can be satisfied feeling that he *could* be the best. He does not want to test himself. This again is a sign of being superior in a useless way.

All exhorting, whether kind or severe, has not succeeded thus far.

The boy is unaware of what goes on inside him because he acts in accordance with his lifestyle. He behaves as if he were in a trap. Allowing himself to be scolded means that he really wants to be at the center of attention. Some children even like to be spanked which makes them feel triumphant for having angered their father. Some children find pleasure and joy in being beaten, and sometimes even have a sexual experience. (Rousseau).

He always promises that he will be more diligent...

There we see it: "I will."

...however, he does nothing about it. When he does his homework, he allows himself to be distracted by everything.

He does not believe he can gain esteem by doing his homework. He has other ways.

Everything but his homework interests him. To make learning easier for him, I told him to report to me every evening what he had learned in school.

He has won attention again. Every night he speaks with the higher authority--his father.

When I come home at night, he does not report to me in keeping with his promise.

His father has to remind him of his commitment.

Only after I ask him directly does he respond. When I ask him: 'Why don't you want to learn?' He answers: 'I don't know.'

We know the answer: He believes that he cannot win esteem that way. We must encourage him and show him that by doing his homework, he can also get attention and tell him that he must find the right way.

Language, mathematics, and writing are most difficult for him and subjects he hates most.

Possibly left-handedness contributes to his serious feeling of inferiority; it would make writing difficult. This would be important to find out. Children who struggle with mathematics usually have been pampered and are looking for support. All subjects have easier ways of finding an answer, but not mathematics. It requires independent work and independent thinking. Pampered children for the most part show poor preparation for mathematics.

He proves with his reluctance to get to work on these subjects how much he really hates them. He seems more interested in science. He also would like to be able to draw. However, he can produce only terrible caricatures because he obviously lacks talent.

He is probably left-handed.

He can sit or lie for hours and stare into space.

The greatest enemy of children with low self-esteem is time. This boy has found a way to pass the time by staring into space.

In spite of the fact that he has to read many books, and has already started to read some, he has hardly finished any of them.

He has neither patience nor endurance. No one would pay attention to him if he read and he could expect nothing from others.

He looks for his toys and then abandons them shortly afterward, unsatisfied.

This social situation in which both children live is not the best, although neither boy has to be hungry.

Probably the saddest part in the lives of these children is that they spend their days in a child-care center.

This is a risky assumption. We would prefer that the correct viewpoint be adopted here, one that would encourage the boy.

The head of the center hates my 'big' boy because she is religious and we do not belong to any religion. She says that the boy lies, is deceitful and a coward, which is the result of his non-religious upbringing.

We have no doubt that these characteristics reflect his feeling of being without hope. I must confess that this non-religious boy attending a religious institution can be helped only with encouragement. When the head of the center says that he is this way because he was brought up in a non-religious home, she reveals her inability to reach him.

The father says:

To be honest, I have noted all these ugly characteristics in him. While the younger boy has none of them and while everyone speaks of him with love and admiration, everyone says bad things about the older boy.

The use of "while" shows me that the younger brother has pushed the boy into the background. Is it accidental that the older boy turns to bad things and the younger is good? Not at all. The older brother believes that he was crowded out of his pleasant situation by the younger boy, and the more he loses in friendship and love, the more he loses in resolve. The second child, who is now the victor, feels comfortable in his situation and has no need to gain attention with bad behavior.

Case #3

From my observations the following picture emerges about he student Bela K.: At first he was often in trouble during school breaks. Usually, he would walk around as if in a dream so that his fellow students were apt to make fun of him which, obviously, ended in quarrels and fights.

If these observations are correct and he walks around as if lost in a dream, it probably means that he is not involved and that school is something strange to him. His attitude shows that he is probably thinking of something else and that he does not feel comfortable in school. We must not forget that children usually are irritated by someone among them who does not have a sense of community, who does not play along. They pick him out to toy with, to tease, to push around, and molest. This type of behavior often goes too far, does not agree with our beliefs, and is wrong. It shows that these children want it to be known, without thinking about it, that within a social group there are certain rules of the game. The boy becomes noticeable because he does not play his social role. Pampered children are not liked by their fellow students. Constantly teased, they are considered childish, dependent, etc. Already in school something in children demands a social attitude, a feeling of associating. This absolute, present force that cannot be ignored integrates everyone, bringing social feeling to life. This force indicates that social feeling exists in every individual and in the masses as well, who tend to advance social feeling more strongly than the individual. In this mass-psychological phenomenon, if the masses are moved by something, if there is an urge to do or a desire for something, that force pulls everyone along. Often this movement happens against an individual's reason, which seems to have been suppressed, and he will act differently in a crowd than if he were alone.

In school, we often see what happens when a group asserts itself, which can lead to a situation in the classroom that does not always conform to what we demand of society. It can also lead to the class coming together to form a social order that carries out all sorts of transgressions. We can understand why anyone in a class who goes against social feeling is frowned upon. Someone who tells on another is equally frowned upon. Children never talk about a duty to be helpful toward the teacher and yet, everyone feels such a duty. Those who fail to see that as their duty are often scorned and excluded from the group. This dynamic helps us understand the attitude of this boy who failed to adapt and who walks around as if in a dream.

We can draw other conclusions as well: (1) Someone who cannot fit in at school, a necessary skill, probably lacks social feeling and has no interest in others. In order to confirm the assumption of a lack of social interest, we must verify whether the child was pampered and looks for a comfortable situation that will afford him relief, warmth, and love. (2) The boy's roughhousing proves he is not totally discouraged. Generally, fights are frowned upon, but for us they are a good sign and just as important to observe as his dream-like state. They show he has not lost resolve.

For several months now, there have been fewer such incidents.

That means he is beginning to fit in and allows us to conclude that he is capable of adapting, but it is difficult for him and will take time.

This student is quite isolated from his classmates.

That is not news to us. We would have arrived at the same conclusion.

In my class, I am particularly aware of his lack of concentration on my presentations.

Because we already believe we have recognized his uniform lifestyle, we are no longer surprised at his lack of concentration and expect that from him. Because he is not engaged, we cannot expect him to concentrate. He concentrates solely on how he can get away. If no one disturbs him in his reveries, he certainly will not concentrate on anything else.

Despite my efforts to stop him, he often bites his nails, at which he becomes deeply involved.

The nail-biting shows defiance. If we continue to be justified in believing he is defiant, it would indicate that he has not fully lost his courage and is still able to engage in fights and show defiance by biting his nails. I would like to note that nail-biting, picking one's nose, as well as devouring food, indicate defiance. This presumption may seem a little too daring for the novice. All children with this habit are nagged to stop such practices. If they continue to do so in spite of constantly being admonished, then drawing the conclusion that they are defiant is fully justified. They show a deficiency in the ability to cooperate. This boy does not play with others and has no interest in accepting the culture of his society. Although we can observe a great gap between him and the demands of life and society, we recognize nail-biting as a relatively good sign, showing that he is defiant and not totally discouraged.

Or else he plays with whatever he has at hand.

This also makes perfectly good sense to us because it shows the distance between him and his schoolwork. He does not occupy himself with what school requires of him, but toys with everything else.

On occasion he will chat with schoolmates whom he has known since elementary school, but not with the others.

Here again, we see the problem he has with adapting to new situations. If given enough time, he may have some success, but if he is expected to do something immediately, he is not prepared for it.

We regard his chatting in his favor. Clearly, we sometimes disagree with what is normally regarded as necessary school discipline. However, we feel justified in upholding our view. School discipline has no understanding of the individual, we do. We see his fighting and nail-biting as good signs, and consider his chatting favorably as well.

When he is asked to write something down, he sits there as if he does not understand the instruction.

This does not surprise us because he does not listen. Listening is a way of connection as much as watching. He does not want to get involved. He cannot become interested in what happens in school. He looks for a comfortable situation for which he is better prepared. He also distances himself from living a worthwhile life and from his future.

However, based on my observations, I cannot assume that he is resisting consciously.

We also do not assume that he resists consciously. But he is not encouraged to be a team player or team worker. We must change that situation and not merely punish the vestiges of his nature.

Because of the efforts of his parents, he rarely forgets his schoolbooks or assignments.
His objective responses are such that I can easily assume that he has enough mental capacity, understanding, and fantasy to fulfill the requirements at his grade level.

We also have recognized that he acts intelligently, in terms of his lifestyle. Faced with expectations of something for which he is not prepared, he cannot fulfill them. That is no reason to doubt his intelligence.

I am supported in my judgment by his German essays, spelling aside, which are always at an average level.

We can also find justification for that. When he is engaged in something by himself, he succeeds because he can delve into that subject. He will act no differently than he did at home as a pampered child in a household that deferred to him. There he was able to speak on various topics, could argue his point, was well received in a favorable environment, and became used to expressing himself effectively. Children not prepared early on to express their ideas at home and to argue, of course, are not well prepared to write essays without, at the same time, showing their limited ability. Such children have not prepared in the way that we can assume this boy did. He probably did not practice writing essays at home, but had prepared himself in his own way. He practiced at home by speaking, telling stories that hang together, etc. Such preparation for school activities is an extremely important element in Individual Psychology.

We must confess that we still do not really know what kind of practice ensures a child's success in school. It might have been expressed in something in which the child was interested and would not have been recognized as training for success in life. If we think how pampered children are trained, we find no easy explanation that in such training lies the eventual isolation of that person or his hostility toward others, and that, consequently, children are unable to make friends, socialize, and awaken social feeling. In this respect, we need a great deal of further research to establish how capable children and adults were brought up, as well as how those who failed in life were prepared. We use countless methods for training children and no one knows at a later stage what made a person successful. Here lies the starting point for prejudging talent. All children who are better trained will, of course, be seen as talented because of preconceived ideas. For the same reason, those who received little or poor training will, on the other hand, be regarded as untalented.

By the way, his spelling ability from when he took his entrance examination improved significantly by the beginning of the school year.

Spelling is an ability that still leaves us much in the dark. We don't know exactly why some children at times are bad at orthography and at other times do well. Individual Psychology, aside from other reasons, has correctly emphasized one aspect, which is that it depends greatly on circumstances whether a child is a visual or acoustic type. A visual child may possibly remember better and have a greater interest in what he has seen. The acoustic type spells as he hears words.

In Latin studies, he may one day give an answer that shows his full understanding, and the next day will fail on the same question.

This variation indicates that he is not involved. Perhaps on some days he is in a better mood in school than on others, or a question may once have been put to him in a friendly manner and at another time in an unfriendly way. He may also feel depressed on one occasion and not on another. Such differences would explain a great deal and should be investigated.

He often gives the impression that any intellectual interaction between him and me, and between him and his schoolmates, is impossible.

That impression is absolutely correct. It shows that he is not prepared for such interaction or for cooperation.

His recent failures seriously depress him and he cries hard when he becomes aware of them.

His crying can be understood from two vantage points: (1) it is the result of his feeling as if he were in a trap. As a boy who wants to be treated with kindness, warmth and understanding, he feels these failures and the subsequent punishment, as well as his poor grades, far more deeply than another boy would. (2) Apparently this boy has practiced crying because he comes from an environment in which crying is a good way to make an impression. It has become a weapon for him with which he can soften up others. Waterworks!

Very bothersome, of course, is his stuttering which in the course of a year has worsened.

We now learn that he not only uses his eyes and ears to avoid interacting, but also uses language. Stuttering means that he refuses to accept any approach made to him because he has a lifestyle unsuitable for making contact. We can look at all his symptoms as being a metaphor for stuttering. He stutters when he should interact, he stutters when he has to spell, and he stutters when doing his Latin assignment. All these manifestations come together in stuttering. We are concerned that his stuttering has grown significantly worse over the past year. It shows that he has not only failed to strengthen his connections in school, but has actually weakened them and he wants to distance himself even further from his tasks at school. It also proves that the method used in school, whether consciously or unconsciously applied, is wrong.

The extent to which the teacher has doubts about how all this began and how he can help the boy is shown in his final statement:

The boy grew a lot since September, but he also became very thin.

This comment indicates that the teacher may believe a physical explanation comes into play here, an idea that we must reject, of course. Let us be clear about this case. This boy should be enlightened about his faulty behavior toward his teachers, schoolmates, and schoolwork. As long as he fails to see his behavior as something wrong, he will always feel that, "Whatever you ask of me is too difficult." Thinking that he cannot do what others can damages his development immeasurably. He fails to be an achiever because he does not understand how to interact with others, fails to practice socializing, and simply is not involved. Such enlightenment would, in the first place, change his attitude. He should be shown that advancing in school is possible only if he connects with his teachers, his schoolmates and the school itself and if he stops acting as if all this were strange to him and none of his affair. He should be shown that winning friends would be to his advantage. Encouraging the teacher would greatly help the situation.

The question that arises which this report does not answer is: How did this boy get started on such a path? Based on my experience, we understand that he was a pampered child, and, as I established in speaking with his mother, an only child. We often find with only children that with pampering they become incompetent at establishing contact with others and regard all other situations as uncomfortable and difficult. They face every situation outside the framework of their experience as dangerous. Stepping out of their comforting atmosphere is like having the sword of Damocles hanging over their heads. We can easily understand that when they encounter a difficult situation, they cannot advance. Stuttering is a common occurrence in situations for which children are not prepared because they were too spoiled. I have never met a child who stutters who was not pampered, at least during the early years. These experiences have not been properly understood and have been underestimated for their importance. For example, we hear about a child who begins to stutter after a fall. The falling is made responsible for the stuttering, or we simply smile ironically because the stuttering is seen as the result of a faulty development of the nervous system. However, if we consider that this fall concerns a child not prepared for such an accident, for the problems in life, because he has always been pampered, then we can understand how he reacts to falling differently from other children. We also hear of children who, on seeing Santa Claus, are so scared that from that moment on they begin to stutter. Or we hear of cases where a child does not want to accept a new nursemaid, and possibly even gets spanked by her, which to some, but not to the child, may seem appropriate, and who from then on begins to stutter.

Stuttering is never caused organically. This can already be seen when a stutterer is alone and talks out loud to himself, and he does not stutter most of the time. He begins to stutter only when a second person appears on the scene. He lives as if surrounded by hostile people who represent problems and danger to him. As we know, these are significant character traits in pampered children.

Case #4

Lotte is 9 ¾ years old. She suffers from fatigue, headaches, and has heart problems.

A clinical examination found that she is organically sound and her symptoms stem only from "nervousness." This is the usual way to express it: "only" nervous. Patients become very upset about this "only." If we are to accept this report as genuine, we must assume that her condition results from great inner tension that Lotte has been unable to overcome, leading to a state of hopelessness. Such tension and fatigue will not occur as long as a person believes he can attain his goal.

The grandmother, who is bringing up the child, is counseled to pay little attention to the child's complaints.

In some cases such advice might work well, in others not. It is no panacea, as some physicians think. In any case, it does not change the child's situation. Another situation could be created toward which the child with her lifestyle will take another position, but it will bring about no changes in the child's personality.

The grandmother seems to follow that advice, but because of her fatigue, the child will often skip school for days.

In any case, the child is rewarded in one way. As a result of tension, she is relieved of one burden from which she suffers, going to school. We cannot assume that she does not like school, but rather that she associates school with something in particular. If we find out that Lotte is tense because of school, then she would want to find relief in that direction. We must assume that she does not feel hopeless in school, that she strives there, but is not sure of herself. She seems ambitious, but does not trust herself to attain the goal of her ambition. We already have confirmation of that in the following statement:

Lotte likes school and works a lot harder than she has to.

The fact that she works harder than she has to fully confirms our theory that she expresses some insecurity in her attitude. She wants to achieve something important which she can attain only if she excels.

She exerts herself to please one of her teachers.

We can now broaden our view. When this child is drawn to someone, when she achieves a friendly response, she is much more apt to excel and make a good impression on that person. That is not against human nature. Her insecurity about making a good impression cramps her efforts, causing her to feel exhausted. Her fatigue can lead to various physical symptoms, such as palpitations and fatigue in general. Her headaches can still not be explained. We know that in such cases headaches can occur. However, we not only want to emphasize the results of an exaggerated ambition, but also want to know how tension leads to headaches. We can possibly gain more insight when we remember that many people get headaches when angry.

We also know that anger affects blood circulation and the composition of the blood itself. This condition can be observed outwardly in many people, for example, when they turn pale or their veins stand out. We can assume from this connection that such disturbances in circulation also affect the brain where, as a result of circulatory problems, irritation ensues which understandably would cause headaches. Heart problems manifested in palpitations show how a person's mood and tension affect circulation. Perhaps when this child feels insecure, she suffers from symptoms similar to those caused by anger.

Recently, she has broken out in tears as a result of most insignificant incidents to tyrannize her parent, her 1 ½ year older brother, and her grandmother.

She believes that in her family tears are an excellent means for getting ahead. She strives to achieve her goal with tears and to gain esteem in useless ways. She tries to feel superior without doing anything worthwhile.

She does not want to be alone.

She obviously is a pampered child, which we can gather from learning that her grandmother has been taking care of her. When we also learn that she is staying with her grandmother, we can already come to some conclusion. Her tears mean even more because not wanting to be alone does not say it all. These tears must also relate to the tension of which we heard earlier. Her crying will manifest itself in fear, which gives further proof of her feeling insecure. She feels esteem only when someone is there for her.

When she read about a murder in the newspaper, she became so upset that her grandmother did not dare leave her alone at night.

This fear is not unusual in children and adults. People collect tragedies like busy bees in order to keep them for an excuse not to be left by themselves. If she had not found the story of a murder, she would have found another event. She can easily find such incidents.

She will no longer go swimming alone.

Pampered children usually have problems learning to swim. They do not like swimming because it requires independence, something children have not practiced if someone has always helped them.

The child always makes a scene when she is asked to go for a walk. She prefers to stay at home.

We see more evidence that she would like to keep her range of activities as narrow as possible. She wants to express with her behavior that, "I am too weak to carry out all the tasks placed before me." She wants to be better than anyone else which makes all her tasks too great. If someone takes everything lightly, not trying to outdo everyone else, life will not be problematic and the individual will not try to limit the range of his activities.

She would stand all alone at the market for three consecutive days and for two hours each time, in order to make observations for a class assignment from her favorite teacher.

This is part of her restricted activities by which she hopes to attain desperately sought-after superiority.

Her self-pity, lack of independence, and timidity are contrary to her behavior when she was younger.

We must assume that something obviously had happened to her, something that heightened her discouragement, which became part of her character as a pampered child. As we have learned, over the past few years she felt herself to be in a poorer situation and has much more difficulty with running her life than she had experienced earlier. We have no clue how this situation has come about.

Earlier she was different from her older brother in that she showed more fortitude, such as enduring pain more easily (she did not cry, as he did, when visiting the doctor), being independent and outgoing.

As we now know, she is the second child in her family. More eager to be first, such children are constantly racing. This must also have been the way she behaved earlier, striving to be ahead of her brother. Something must have happened that made the race more difficult for her. Today, she looks for superiority only within a narrow range of activities. We can already form some opinion as to what might have happened to her. Over the last few years, her brother may have appeared unsurpassable to her. He obviously feels quite strong, believing that he can win this race without any trouble. As a rule, in the relationship of an elder brother to a younger sister, the younger girl is heavily favored since girls develop mentally and physically quicker and, in this respect, win the race. When we now hear that the brother has gained superiority, then perhaps the boy had some kind of a head start. We still do not know how this situation came about.

The turnabout cannot be explained by any outward change in her life.

At this point, we don't know what caused this change. The turnabout could only have been that of a racer who became tired. She is a racer, but would like to have an easy race. She is no longer as confident of winning as she once was, perhaps because of the recognition paid her brother, or lack of recognition paid to her. We have to wait and see.

It is noteworthy that at the same time, there was a change in her brother.

This description touches on a point I had mentioned earlier; the brother's behavior must have changed.

He has become, like his grandmother reported, less insufferable, more sensible, independent, and more sociable.

Naturally, we want to know the reason that he changed. Possibly, in this race he became more sociable because he noticed that he was ahead and his sister lagged behind. He may have been promoted (possibly in school) and as a result, his sister saw her efforts as particularly difficult and decided to give up.

When he does something he likes, he is pleasant. Earlier, he rejected everything without any reason by bawling, being fresh, teasing his sister, etc.

The whole picture seems to have turned around in that he originally felt he could not win this race; now his sister feels she cannot win. Both siblings function as a unit and can only be understood that way. We want to gain some understanding of what could have happened which caused her to suddenly give up. Perhaps, he now succeeds in school and she does not. We are searching for possibilities that would cause a child suddenly to fail in getting ahead. Perhaps, he had some influence on his friends that allowed him to gain socially, or was physically advantaged being handsome while his sister was ungainly. We must establish what had made such a great impression on this girl.

We might find an explanation in her personal history:

Lotte required particular care during the first weeks of her life because of a problem with her navel. Subsequently, she developed a stomach problem that required constant care from her mother.

These inferiorities occurred during her earliest years, requiring extra care and particular efforts to draw close to her.

During the day, the child was pleasant and patient.

Obviously because someone was around her constantly.

At night, she realized that by wetting her bed, she was able to call on her mother to serve her. Finally, with much crying, she forced her mother to take her into her bed. This continued until she was three years old.

These are clear indications of a pampered child. If someone doubts that bed-wetting comes from pampering, I would recommend an old Individual Psychological rule which is to lay aside this symptom and look for other manifestations of pampering. These factors would relate to the child's being pampered and would then confirm bed-wetting as another symptom.

In her speech development, Lotte was noticeably slow.

This does not surprise us because we know that pampered children often are slow in learning how to speak.

She learned to speak very late and her language was childish.

Her activity in this regard supports her role as a younger child. These are consequences, not evidence that she energetically tries to overcome her problems.

When in her presence there was a discussion about young children who spoke much better than she, Lotte suddenly and unexpectedly said: 'Paul says 'uh-huh' instead of 'yes'.

She becomes critical when she hears that someone speaks better than she. We can see that she clearly tends not to regard herself as inferior.

Between the ages of 2 and 4, she tended to become increasingly obstinate.

This is a developmental tendency. In running this race with her brother, she wants to demonstrate that she is strong and a big girl.

She does not want to eat or go to sleep, particularly when she is staying with her mother.

Individual Psychology in the Schools

We frequently find these characteristics in pampered children.

Because of her work, the mother was no longer able to care for her constantly. The maid neglected the girl over the boy, who was more attractive and active.

Here again we see a view that comes close to what we had expressed earlier. Perhaps at this point, this ten-year old girl began to feel insecure for reasons that can probably be found in her school environment.

When he did not beat her, she allowed her brother to take care of her.

She liked being taken care of by her brother. Signs of a race surface periodically.

Prodded by him, she rebelled against their parents and then did not relent as quickly as he.

We are familiar with such behavior in second children. First-born children are more agreeable than second-born. They have a greater appreciation for the balance of power.

She shows more courage than he.

We have to get more details on this point from the person who wrote this report.

At age four, she was sent to a children's home where no one made any particular effort to get close to her.

This must have made a particularly strong impression on her. She had become used to having someone care for her all the time and we know that she favors those who are good to her. She can easily be guided with friendliness, goodness, and warmth. Under those conditions, she can control herself.

Her speech development did not improve.

She probably did not like the teaching methods in this home.

In general, she made no improvements. In this hostile climate, she got along well with her brother.

While in this home, they both felt they belonged together. We can see that in an integrated system, they can develop.

He liked the role of protector.

That is conspicuous. This boy was probably not easy to beat. If this had occurred at a later stage, we would not have been concerned.

She no longer wets her bed.

We have often observed that children cease to wet their bed when they come into another environment. On the other hand, many children do not stop bed-wetting, thinking they would be expelled from such a home and could then return to their own home. There is some sense in that. Sometimes they stop bed-wetting if the people in the new environment pay it no attention.

She was given a spanking for bed-wetting and nothing else. She also ate and went to sleep quickly. Then she came to her grandmother. She bonded with her as closely as she had with her mother.

We can see a strong need for kindness.

She again began to wet her bed.

Bed-wetting here again was worth something. It gained in value.

Only with extensive effort was it possible for her to give up bed-wetting. She first had to be awakened three to four times a night.

She seems to see some advantage over her brother with her bed-wetting. This confirms our earlier observation: At night she belongs to her mother and grandmother. With bed-wetting, she can draw her mother and grandmother away from her brother.

She continued her baby talk until she entered the Montessori kindergarten. Then she began, at first unsuccessfully, to make the effort to speak more adult-like.

If looked at closely, anything a person tries to do for the first time does not seem successful. It only seems like progress when some children starting out can do something better, when in fact they had some practice before, and for them learning a particular skill is not a new start. If it were new for them, they would not be successful. An example is learning how to swim, at which no one succeeds at first. It does not work the first time because the person does everything wrong. However, this must not keep a person from trying again.

At first she took speech lessons in order not to be laughed at.

This child always had difficulties in her life and we must assume that she knows about problems.

She adapted herself very well at this school. She soon read to the younger children.

We have often observed that children who start out speaking poorly later speak much better than others (for example, Demosthenes). The fact that she adapted herself speaks well for the school where children probably were treated kindly. It also explains why this girl adapted herself so successfully.

Today she speaks well and likes to give talks. She overcame her chubbiness and clumsiness with exercise. In that respect, she surpassed her brother.

As this indicates, for the time being she is the winner. We should recall, however, that her brother excelled in sports.

She does everything to please her brother and even lets him take advantage of her, such as giving him coins. Unlike her brother, who is stingy, she likes to give presents.

She seems to recognize her brother's strength and worth. This does not mean, however, that she forgoes her final victory. She merely does not want to fight and prefers to make a pact with him, similar to a political treaty. She has a strong accord with her brother which actually means that in this relationship, she feels the stronger of the two.

He treats her poorly.

He takes advantage of that situation. We can see that her insecurity grows out of her feeling of weakness. She feels how difficult overtaking her brother would be.

She found a substitute in friendships with younger boys.

This is again a sign that she does not feel strong. Seeking the friendship of younger boys is understandable. She already feels that men are superior and even accepts it, which must play a significant role in the behavior of such children. The change in this girl obviously came at a time when she began to sense sex differences and understood the consequences of these differences in our culture. In this case, we have to count on the girl having overestimated men and underestimated women. This pattern, her friendship with younger boys, and placing herself under her brother's protection, shows us her attitude toward men.

Her best friend is a boy who looks like a girl.

She seems to want to steer toward some form of parity. She does not want to be all girl and does not want boys to be too masculine. Her underestimation of women must already be a part of her.

She mothers him, which is something she likes to do in general.

This is again an indication of her feeling superior.

She is always afraid to hurt one of her friends, such as liking one more than another. She herself is easily hurt.

She seems to have courtiers and has to be careful not to insult them. She herself is easily hurt, like anyone who feels insecure and believes every minor incident could by upsetting.

In contrast to her brother, in school she is well liked by her teachers and by the children. In the first essay she wrote of a hero, a little girl who saves a big boy.

This clearly indicates striving: to make a little girl stronger than a bigger boy.

She wants to get married and become a mother.

She understands the role of women, and in some form of resignation, wants to take a bite out of the sour apple. She has the idea that marriage is related to becoming a mother and to being guided by the stronger man. We do not entirely believe that she is satisfied with her female role.

She worries, however, about obtaining furniture and diapers.

Here a new element emerges: The difficulties a girl faces in trying to get everything necessary for a marriage. She seems aware of what a dowry means and her problem with having no possessions gives her thought.

She has a very affectionate relationship with her father, whom she rarely sees, perhaps once very several years.

He obviously is tender toward her and shows his affection for her.

In a fantasy that she told and improvised on, her father appeared in all sorts of ludicrous situations.

She seems favorably disposed toward her father, but sees him in ludicrous situations as a man. This depreciation tendency occurs often in girls and women who regard men as laughable and incapable of dealing with minor matters. When boys pass a girls' school where girls are congregating outside, the girls can be seen giggling. To make men seem funny degrades them, even if they overestimate them in thinking they are superior.

The following conversation was overheard two years ago: 'Peter, when I am grown up, will you still be my brother?' 'Of course!'

She looks forward to becoming an adult. Although I don't want to exaggerate my powers of uncovering evidence, I cannot keep secret that this exchange fits my theory very well.

Individual Psychology in the Schools

> *'However, when I have a husband, what then?' 'Then he is your husband and I am your brother!'*

This needs no clarification. We can see how she tries to sort this out.

> *'But, what kind of a husband?' 'Well, someone whom you will like!' 'How is that possible?' 'Well, you just look him over.' 'But, how can I see that he has work?'*

She seems to understand quite clearly the differences in sexual roles. She perceives that the husband is there to work.

> *The boy laughs. She says to him, almost crying: 'I don't want to do everything myself. He should also cook and not be like Papa who is always reading a newspaper!'*

Here we see again her goal of attaining parity. We can help this girl by encouraging her. She lost her resolve for two reasons: 1. Her brother seemed too strong to her. 2. She fears that her role as a woman will not get her anywhere and she is convinced that she will never gain equality or be superior. We must understand how to speak with this child. She could be told that whatever her brother's successes are, they don't mean that much, and even if he is now ahead of her, she can reach the same level of success if she trains herself toward that end. If she believes she cannot achieve something, she should be shown that she can do it. She should be encouraged about her future and told that as a girl and eventually as a woman, she is not dependent on a man for help. She should understand that working, earning money, buying furniture, etc. are not only a man's privilege.

At the same time, she should recognize that housework is not to be disdained, but that such work as cooking does not pay for the man to engage in if he has a job at which he can earn more money. Housework should be seen as equal to what a man does in his job and meant to establish a foundation for the husband, so that the couple can be more effective by ensuring peace and harmony in their home. We should make clear to her that she can work alongside her husband and cooperate in a thousand different ways. We should encourage her to change her perception of her role as a woman and not look to a future fraught with hostility.

Part 2

The Education
of Children[7]

---

[7]Originally translated by Eleanore and Friedrich Jensen and published by George Allen & Unwin Limited, London, 1930. Edited for readability by Laurie J. Stein, 2006.

Chapter I

Introduction

From a psychological point of view, the problem of education reduces itself, in the case of adults, to the problem of self-knowledge and rational self-direction. In the case of children education may be approached in the same manner, but with this difference: because of the immaturity of children, the question of guidance—never wholly absent in the case of adults—takes on supreme importance. If we wished, we could allow children to develop of their own accord, and if they had twenty thousand years to grow and a favorable environment, they would eventually approach the standards of adult civilization. Of course, this method is out of the question, and the adult must necessarily take an interest in guiding the child in his development.

Here the great obstacle is ignorance. The adult has difficulty enough knowing himself, the cause of his emotions, his likes and hates—in short, understanding his own psychology. He has even more difficulty understanding children and guiding them on the basis of proper knowledge. Individual Psychology is especially concerned with the psychology of children, both for its own sake, and for the light it sheds on adult traits and behavior. And unlike other psychological approaches, it allows no gap to exist between theory and practice. It focuses on the unity of personality and studies its dynamic struggle for development and expression. From such a point of view, scientific knowledge is already practical wisdom, for the knowledge is a knowledge of mistakes, and whoever has this knowledge, whether the psychologist, the parent, the friend or the individual himself, immediately sees its practical application in the guidance of the personality concerned.

The doctrines and methods of Individual Psychology hang together as an organic whole. Because we see the behavior of individuals as motivated and directed by the unity of personality, whatever Individual Psychology has to say about human behavior reflects the same unity manifested in the activities of the psyche. In this opening chapter, therefore, I will attempt to present the viewpoint of Individual Psychology as a whole, and treat the various interrelated problems introduced here at fuller length in later chapters.

The fundamental fact in human development is the dynamic and purposive striving of the psyche. From earliest infancy, a child is engaged in a constant struggle to develop, and this struggle supports an unconsciously formed but ever-present goal—a vision of greatness, perfection and superiority. This struggle, this goal-performing activity, reflects, of course, the peculiarly human faculty of thinking and imagining, and it dominates all our specific acts throughout life. It dominates even our thoughts, for we do not think objectively but in accordance with the goal and style of life we have formed.

The unity of personality is implicit in each human being's existence. Every individual represents both a unity of personality and the individual's unique construction of that unity. The individual is thus both the picture and the artist. He is the artist of his own personality, but as an artist he is neither an infallible worker, nor a person with a complete understanding of soul and body; he is rather a weak, extremely fallible and imperfect human being.

In considering the construction of a personality, the chief defect to be noted is that its unity, its particular style and goal, is not built upon objective reality, but upon the subjective view the individual takes of the facts of life. A perception, a view of a fact, is never the fact itself, and for this reason human beings, all of whom live in the same world of facts, mold themselves differently. Each one organizes himself according to his personal view of things, and some views are more sound, while other views are less so. We must deal with these individual mistakes and failures in the development of a human being. We must especially deal with the misinterpretations made in early childhood, for these errors dominate the subsequent course of our existence.

The following case shows a concrete example of this process. A fifty-two-year-old woman habitually disparaged women older than herself. She related that when she was a tiny child, she felt humiliated and undervalued because of an older sister who received all the attention. Looking at this case with what we might call the "vertical" point of view of Individual Psychology, we can see the same mechanism, the same psychological dynamics both at the beginning of her life and at present—that is to say, near the close of her existence. She retains the fear of being undervalued and the anger at finding others favored or preferred. Even if we knew nothing else of this woman's life, or of her particular unity of personality, we could almost fill in the gaps in our knowledge on the basis of the two facts given. The psychologist acts here like a novelist, who has to construct a human being with a definite line of action, style of life, or pattern of behavior, constructing him in such a way that the impression of a unified personality is not disturbed. A good psychologist would be able to predict the conduct of this woman in certain situations, and to describe clearly the traits which accompany this particular "life line" in her personality.

The striving or goal-forming activity responsible for the construction of individual personalities presupposes another important psychological fact: the sense or feeling of inferiority. All children have an inherent feeling of inferiority which stimulates the imagination and incites attempts to dissipate the psychological sense of inferiority by improving the situation. An improvement of one's situation results in a lessening of the feeling of inferiority. From a psychological point of view, this striving for improvement may be regarded as a compensation.

Now the important thing about the sense of inferiority and the mechanism of psychological compensation is that it opens up a vast possibility of making mistakes. The sense of inferiority may stimulate objective accomplishment; it may also result in a purely psychological adjustment, widening the gulf between the individual and objective reality. Or, again, the sense of inferiority may appear so tragic that the only way it can be overcome is by the development of psychological compensatory traits, which in the end may not overcome the situation at all but which are nonetheless psychologically necessary and inevitable.

For example, three classes of children clearly manifest the development of compensatory traits. They are children who come into the world with weak or imperfect organs; children who are treated with severity and with no affection; and, finally, children who receive too much pampering.

We may take these three classes of children as exemplifying three basic situations in terms of which the development of the more normal types of children may be studied and understood. Not every child is born a cripple, but a surprising number of children manifest, to a greater or lesser degree, psychological traits based on some physical difficulty or weak organ—psychological traits of which the archetype may be studied in the extreme case of the crippled child. As for the classifications of pampered and hated children, practically all children fall to a greater or lesser degree into one, or even both groups.

All three of these primary situations produce a feeling of insufficiency and inferiority, and by way of reaction, an ambition beyond the realm of human possibility. The sense of inferiority and the striving for superiority are two aspects of the same fundamental fact in human life, and are thus inseparable. In pathological situations, we cannot easily say whether the exaggerated feeling of inferiority or the exacerbated striving for superiority is most harmful. They both go together in more or less rhythmical waves. In the case of children we find inordinate ambition, aroused by an exaggerated sense of inferiority, acting like a poison in the soul, forever making the child dissatisfied. Such a dissatisfaction does not lead to useful activity. It remains fruitless because it is fed by a disproportionate ambition. This ambition may be seen twisting itself into character traits and personal mannerisms. It acts like a perpetual irritant making the individual supersensitive and on guard lest he be hurt or trodden upon.

Types of this nature—and the annals of Individual Psychology are full of them—develop into people whose abilities remain dormant, who become, as we say, "nervous," or eccentric. Individuals of these types, when driven too far, wind up in the world of the irresponsible and the criminal because they think only of themselves and not of others. Their egotism, both moral and psychological, becomes absolute. We find some of them avoiding reality and objective facts and constructing a new world for themselves. By daydreaming, by embracing imaginative fantasies as if they represented reality, they finally succeed in creating psychological peace. They have reconciled reality and the mind by constructing reality in the image of the mind.

In all such developments, the tell-tale criterion which the psychologist and parent need to watch is the degree of social feeling which the child or individual manifests. Social feeling is the crucial and deciding factor in normal development. Every disturbance which results in a lessening of the social or communal feeling has a tremendously harmful effect on the mental growth of the child. Social feeling is the barometer of the child's normality.

Individual Psychology bases its pedagogical technique on the principle of social feeling. Parents or guardians must not permit a child to attach himself to one person only. If this unhealthy attachment is permitted, the child will find himself badly or insufficiently prepared for later life.

A good way of evaluating a child's degree of social feeling is to observe him when he enters school. At that time, he meets one of his earliest and severest tests. Because school is a new situation for him, it will reveal how well he has been prepared to face new situations, and particularly how well he has been prepared to meet new people.

The general lack of knowledge about how to prepare a child for school explains why so many adults look back on their school years as a sort of nightmare. Of course the school, when properly administered, often makes up for deficiencies in the earlier rearing of the children. The ideal school should serve as a mediator between the home and the wide world of reality, and be a place not merely for book knowledge, but a

The Education of Children

place in which the knowledge and art of living is taught. But while we are waiting for the ideal school to develop so that it may overcome the deficiencies in the parental education of children, we can also put our finger on the faults of the parents.

The school may serve as an early warning system, indicating the faults of family upbring, precisely because it is not yet an ideal environment. Children who have not been taught how to make contact with others feel alone when they enter school. As a result, they are regarded as peculiar, and thus the initial tendency grows stronger and stronger with time. Their proper development is thwarted, and they become behavior problem children. People blame the school in such cases, although the school has here merely brought out the latent defects in the home education.

Individual Psychology has always questioned whether behavior problem children can make any progress in school at all. While we have proved that a child's failure in school is a danger sign, it is not so much a sign of failure in studies, as it is a psychological failure. It means that the child has begun to lose faith in himself. Because he is discouraged, he begins to avoid useful roads and normal tasks, searching all the time for another outlet, a road to freedom and easy success. Instead of the road which society has mapped out, he chooses a private road where he can erect a compensation for his inferiority by attaining a sense of superiority. He chooses the path that always attracts discouraged individuals, the path of quickest psychological success. Someone can more easily distinguish himself and give himself the feeling of being a conqueror by throwing off social and moral responsibilities and by breaking the law, than by following the established social paths. But this easy road to superiority indicates underlying cowardice and weakness, no matter what apparent daring and bravery are manifested in the outward acts. Such a person tries to do only those things which guarantee him success, thus showing off his superiority.

Just as we observe that criminals, despite their surface recklessness and bravery, are cowardly underneath, so we can see how children in less dangerous situations betray their sense of weakness by various small signs. Thus, we commonly see children (and for that matter adults, too) who are unable to stand upright, but must always lean against something. Under the old methods of training children and understanding such signs, the symptom was treated but not the underlying situation. We used to say to such a child, "Don't lean on something all the time." Actually what matters here is not that the child leans, but that he constantly feels the need of support. We can readily persuade the child, either by punishment or reward, to give up this sign of weakness, but his great need for support is not thereby relieved. The disease continues. With sympathy and understanding, a good educator can read the signs and eradicate the underlying disease.

We can often draw conclusions about many qualities or traits from a single sign. In the case of a child obsessed with the need to lean on something, we can immediately see such traits as anxiety and dependence. By comparing him with similar individuals whose cases we know thoroughly, we can reconstruct his personality, seeing, in short, that we have to deal with a pampered child.

We turn now to the character traits of another group of children, those who have gone without love. The traits of this group, in their most developed form, can be observed by studying the biographies of all the great enemies of humanity. In all the life stories of these men, the one fact that stands out is that as children they were badly treated. Consequently, they developed a hardness of character, envy and hatred. They could not bear to see others happy. Envious people of this type are found not merely among obvious villains, but also among supposedly normal individuals. When such individuals are in charge of children, they think that the children should not be any happier than they themselves were as children. We find such a view applied by parents to their children, as well as by guardians to the children of others who are put in their charge.

These views do not spring from bad intentions. They simply reflect the mentality of those who have been harshly brought up. Such people can produce any number of good reasons and maxims, as for example, "Spare the rod and spoil the child!" And they give us endless proofs and examples, which do not convince us inasmuch as the futility of a rigid, authoritative education is proved by the clear result that it estranges the child from his educator.

By exploring various symptoms and interrelating them, the psychologist can, after some practice, organize a system to help him uncover the hidden psychological processes of an individual. While every point we examine in this system reflects something of the complete personality of the individual under investigation, we can feel satisfied only when we get the same indications at every point of our examination. Individual Psychology is thus an art as well as a science, and I cannot emphasize too strongly that we cannot apply our speculative scheme, our network of concepts, in a rigid and mechanical fashion to any individual. In all investigations, we must focus on studying the individual; we must never draw far-reaching conclusions from one or two modes of expression, but look for all possible supporting details. Only when we are successful in confirming our tentative hypothesis, only when we have been able, for example, to find the same stubbornness and discouragement in other aspects of his behavior, can we say with certainty that this stubbornness or discouragement permeates the entire personality.

However, we must remember that the subject under examination has no understanding of his own forms of expression and is thus unable to conceal his true self. We see his personality in action, and it is revealed not by what he says or thinks about himself, but by his acts interpreted in their context. The patient does not deliberately want to lie to us, but we have learned to recognize a vast gulf between a man's conscious thoughts and his unconscious motivations, a gulf which can best be bridged by a disinterested but sympathetic outsider. The outsider —a psychologist, parent, or teacher—should learn to interpret a personality on the basis of objective facts seen as the expression of the purposive, but more or less unconscious, strivings of the individual.

Thus, the attitude of the individual toward the three fundamental tasks of life reveals his true self, as nothing else can. The first task concerns social relationships, which we have already discussed in the context of the contrast between the private and objective views of reality. How does the individual solve the problem of making friends and getting along with people? What is his answer? When a human being believes he can evade the question by saying that the matter of friends is of complete indifference to him, then indifference is his answer. From this indifference we can, of course, draw conclusions as to the direction and organization of his personality. Moreover, we should note that social relationships are not confined merely to the physical making of friends and meeting of people; all the abstract qualities like friendship, comradeship, truthfulness and loyalty cluster around this relationship, and the answer to the question of social relationships indicates the individual's answer on all these points.

The second great task concerns how the individual wants to make use of his life—what part he wants to take in the general division of labor. If the social question may be said to be determined by the existence of more than one ego, by the relationship I-you, then we may say that this question is determined by the fundamental relationship Man-Earth. If we could reduce all mankind into one person, this person would have mutuality with the earth. What does he want from the earth? Just as in the case of the first question, the solution of the problem of occupation is not a one-sided or private matter, but a matter between man and earth. It is a two-sided relationship in which man hasn't got it all his own way. Success is determined not by our private will, but in relation to objective realities. For this reason the answer an individual gives, and the manner in which he gives it, to the question of occupation throws a revealing light on his personality and attitude toward life.

The third fundamental task arises from mankind's division into two sexes. The solution of this problem is again not a private, subjective matter, but must be solved according to the inherent, objective logic of the relationship. What is an individual's position toward the other sex? The typical private conception is again a mistaken conception. A correct solution can be arrived at only through a careful consideration of all the questions which cluster around the sex relationship. And it stands to reason that every departure from a correct solution of the problem of love and marriage indicates a mistake, an error in the personality. Also, we can interpret many of the harmful consequences following a wrong solution of this problem in light of the underlying error in the personality.

We can see, therefore, that we are in a position to discover the general style of life and particular goal of an individual from the way in which he answers these three questions. The goal is omnipotent. It decides a person's style of life and will be reflected in every one of his acts. Thus, if the goal is a striving toward being a fellow man, on the useful side of life, the stamp of that goal will be apparent in the individual's solutions of all his problems. All the solutions will reflect constructive usefulness, giving the individual the sense of happiness, worth, and power that go with constructive, useful activity. If the goal is directed otherwise, to the private and useless side of life, the individual will find himself unable to solve fundamental problems, and he will also lack the joy that comes from their proper solution.

The interconnection between these fundamental problems is strengthened by the specific tasks of life, which can be accomplished properly only in a social or communal setting, or, in other words, on the basis of social feeling. These tasks begin in the earliest years of childhood, when our sense-organs are developing in accordance with the stimulus of social life, in looking, speaking, hearing—in our relationships to our brothers, sisters, parents, relatives, acquaintances, comrades, friends and teachers. They continue through life in the same manner, so that he who gets out of social touch with his fellows is lost.

And so Individual Psychology stands on firm ground when it regards as "right" that which is useful for the community. We realize that every departure from social usefulness is an offense against right and brings with it a conflict with objective laws and necessities of reality. This clash with objectivity makes itself felt first of all in the feeling of worthlessness on the part of the offending individual, and also emerges—with even stronger force—in the retaliations of others who feel themselves aggrieved. Finally, the departure from social usefulness violates an inherent social ideal which every one of us, consciously or unconsciously, carries in himself.

With our rigorous emphasis on social-mindedness as a test of development, we can easily use Individual Psychology to understand and evaluate the style of life of any child. For as soon as the child faces a life problem, he will reveal, as if he were under examination, whether or not he has been "rightly" prepared. In other words, he will show whether he has social feeling, courage, understanding, and a generally useful goal. We then try to uncover the form and rhythm of his upward striving, the degree of his feeling of inferiority, and the intensity of his social consciousness. All these factors are closely interconnected and influence one another, forming an organic and unbreakable unity—a unity that cannot be broken until we discover the fault in construction and accomplish a reconstruction.

Chapter II

The Unity of the Personality

The psychic life of a child is a wonderful thing, fascinating at every point. Perhaps the most remarkable fact is the way we must unroll the whole scroll of a child's life in order to understand a single event. While every act seems to express the whole of his life and personality, it is unintelligible without a knowledge of this invisible background. To this phenomenon we give the name, unity of personality.

The development of this unity—the co-ordination of actions and expressions into a single pattern—begins at a very early age. The demands of life compel the child to respond in a unified manner, which not only constitutes his character, but also individualizes each of his acts, making them distinct from the similar acts of other children.

Most schools of psychology overlook the unity of the personality; or, if they do not entirely overlook it, they do not give it the attention it deserves. As a result, we often find both in psychological theory and practice, a particular gesture or expression is singled out for consideration as if it were an independent entity. Sometimes such a manifestation is called a complex, with the assumption that it can be separated from the rest of an individual's activity. But such a procedure resembles singling out one note from an entire melody, attempting to understand the significance of this one note apart from the string of notes which make up the melody. This process is futile, but unfortunately widespread.

In Individual Psychology, we take a stand against this widespread error, which is especially harmful when applied to the education of children. Our response to the theory of punishment clearly shows our contrasting point of view. What happens generally when a child does something that invites punishment? In a sense the total impression made by a child's personality is usually taken into account, but is usually a disadvantage because in the case of an oft-repeated mistake, the teacher or parent tends to be prejudiced in approaching the child, regarding him as incorrigible. Also, on the basis of a total impression, we are apt to deal less harshly with the mistakes of a child whose behavior is otherwise quite good. Nonetheless, in neither instance do we reach the real root of the problem as we should on the basis of the total comprehension of the child's unity of personality. We are in the position of trying to understand the significance of a few individual notes torn from the context of the whole melody.

When we ask a child why he is lazy, we cannot expect him to know what we must know, i.e. the fundamental connection between his mistaken thinking and his behavior. Neither can we expect him to tell us why he lies. For thousands of years, Socrates, who understood human nature so well, has spoken in our ears: "How difficult it is to know one's self!" By what right, then, can we demand that a child answer such complex questions, which even psychologists have difficulty answering? To be able to understand the significance of individual expression presupposes having a method for understanding the whole personality. Understanding means more than merely describing what a child does and how he acts; it means understanding his attitude toward the tasks which lie before him.

The following example illustrates the importance of our understanding the entire context of a child's life. A boy of thirteen was the older of two children. For five years, he was the only child of parents who had seen better days. Then a sister was born. Before her birth, every person in his environment was only too glad to fulfill every desire the boy had. The mother undoubtedly pampered him. The father was a good-natured, tranquil sort of person, who enjoyed his son's dependence on him. The son, naturally, was closer to his mother, since the father was an army officer and frequently away from home. A clever, well-meaning woman, the mother tried to satisfy every whim of her dependent but insistent son. Nonetheless, she was often annoyed at his display of ill-breeding or threatening gestures. A state of tension was created, expressed chiefly in the boy's constantly trying to tyrannize his mother—ordering her about, teasing her, and in short making himself disagreeably the focus of attention wherever and whenever he could.

Although the boy's conduct annoyed his mother, because he had no other particularly bad traits, she yielded to him, kept his clothes in order, and helped him with his school work. He was always confident that his mother would help him out of any difficulty he got into. Undoubtedly an intelligent child and just as well educated as the average, he went through elementary school with fair success until his eighth year. At that time, a great transformation took place which made his relationship with his parents unendurable. Not only did he drive his mother wild by his complete neglect of himself and personal carelessness in connection with all bodily functions, but he also pulled his mother's hair whenever she did not give him what he wanted; he never left her in peace, constantly pinching her ear or pulling her hand. He refused to

The Education of Children

abandon his tactics, and as his baby sister grew up, he clung all the more to the behavior pattern he had devised. His little sister soon became the target of his tricks. Although he did not go so far as to harm the child physically, his jealousy of her was clearly apparent. His great deterioration began when his sister was born and began to play a role in the family constellation.

When a child's behavior grows worse, or particular, new symptoms appear, we must consider not only the time when the condition started, but also the stimulating cause. We use the word, "cause," reluctantly because the birth of a sister is not automatically the reason for an older brother's becoming a problem child. Nevertheless, this negative response to the birth of a sibling happens frequently, and this relationship cannot be regarded other than as a mistaken attitude on the part of the child. It is not a matter of causality in the strict physical-scientific sense, for we cannot claim that because a younger child is born, the older one must deteriorate. When a stone fulls to the ground, it must fall in a certain direction and with a certain speed. But our investigations, using Individual Psychology, confirm that in a psychic "fall," strict causality does not play a role, only bigger or smaller mistakes which, after they are made, affect an individual's future development.

We can readily understand how mistakes appear in the development of the human psyche, and that these mistakes and their consequences lie side by side, revealing themselves in some failure or wrong orientation. The reason for these mistakes begins with the goal-setting activity of the psyche. Because this goal-setting involves judgment, it inevitably involves the possibility of making mistakes. This setting or determining of a goal commences in the earliest years. In his second or third year, as a rule, the child begins to fix for himself a goal of superiority which pulls him and toward which he strives in his own manner. Most often, the fixing of the goal involves some degree of incorrect judgment; nonetheless, it controls the child. The child concretizes his goal in his specific acts, and arranges his entire life so that it becomes a constant striving toward this goal.

We see, then, the crucial value of remembering that a child's development is determined by his personal, individual interpretation of things, and that he always behaves in the restricted circle of his personal mistakes whenever he approaches a new, difficult situation. The depth or character of the impression which the situation makes on a child does not depend on the objective fact or circumstance (as for example the birth of a second child), but rather on how the first child regards the fact.

This is sufficient ground for refuting the theory of causality; necessary connection exists between objective facts and their absolute meaning, but not between mistaken views of facts.

The remarkable aspect of our psychic life is that our point of view determines the direction we take, not the facts themselves. This principle is extraordinarily important, inasmuch as all our activities are regulated and our personality is organized on the basis of it. A classic example of the effect of subjective ideas in human action is furnished by Caesar's landing in Egypt. As he jumped ashore he stumbled and fell on the ground, which the Roman soldiers took as an unfavorable omen. Brave as they were, they would nonetheless have turned around and gone back, had not Caesar thrown out his arms and announced, "I have you, Africa!" We can see from this example how little the structure of reality is causal, and how its effects can be molded and determined by an organized, well-integrated personality. The same principle holds true with mob psychology and its relationship to reason; if a condition of mob psychology gives way to common sense, it is not because either the mob psychology or common sense were causally determined by the situation, but because both represent spontaneous points of view. Usually, common sense does not appear until after mistaken points of view have been tried out.

Coming back to the story of the boy, he soon found himself in a difficult situation. No one liked him any more, he made no progress at school, and yet he continued to behave in the same way. His behavior, which was continually disturbing to others, had become a complete expression of his personality. And so what happened? Whenever he disturbed some one, he was immediately punished. He received a bad report card, or a letter of complaint was sent to his parents. Things went on in this way until at length his parents were advised to remove him from school, as he did not seem suited for school life.

Probably nobody was happier than the boy about this solution. He did not want anything else. The logical consistency of his behavior pattern revealed itself again in his attitude. It was a mistaken attitude, but once assumed it expressed itself consistently. He had made his basic mistake when he set for himself the goal of always being the center of attention. And if he was to be punished, this mistake is the one for which he should have been punished. He tried constantly to make his mother wait on him. Also as a result of this mistake, he acted like a king who, after eight years of absolute power, is suddenly deprived of his throne. Up to the moment of his dethronement, he had been the only one who existed for his mother, and she for him. Then his sister arrived, and

The Education of Children

he struggled violently to recover his lost throne. That was again his mistake, but such a blunder does not involve any inherent badness or viciousness. Viciousness first develops when adults bring a child into a situation for which he is totally unprepared, and then allow him to struggle without any guidance. Take a child, for example, who has been prepared only for a situation in which some one devotes herself entirely to him; suddenly the contrary is true. The child is at school, where the teacher must divide his attention among many, and is rather annoyed when one child demands more than his proportionate share. Such a situation is full of danger for the pampered child, but at the outset the child is far from vicious or incorrigible.

In this boy's case, we can understand how a conflict arose between his personal scheme of existence and the scheme of existence demanded by the school. The conflict may be represented diagrammatically by picturing the direction and the goal of the child's personality, and the goal set by school life. The goals point in diverging directions. But his goal determines everything that happens in his life, so that no motion, so to speak, occurs in his whole system except in the direction of this goal. On the other hand, the school expects a normal scheme of existence from every child. The conflict is inevitable, but the school fails to appreciate the psychological facts in the situation and neither party makes any allowances for them, nor attempts to obviate the source of the conflict.

We know that the boy's life is motivated by the dominant desire to make his mother serve him and him alone. In his psychological scheme of existence, everything converges on this thought: I must dominate my mother; I must be the only one to possess her. But other things are expected of him. He is expected to work alone, to take care of his school books and papers, and to keep his possessions in order. It is as if a fiery race horse were hitched to a truck wagon.

Of course the boy's performance is not the highest, but when we know the real circumstances , we are much more inclined to be sympathetic. Punishing him in school would be useless because that would definitely convince him that school is no place for him. When he is expelled from school, or when the parents are asked to take him away, he is that much closer to his goal. His false scheme of apperception acts like a trap. He feels that he has gained, because now he really has his mother in his power. She must again devote herself exclusively to him. And that is just what he wants.

When we recognize the true state of affairs, we must admit the futility of picking one fault or another and punishing the child for it.

Suppose for example that he forgets a book—it would be a wonder if he didn't, for when he forgets, he gives his mother something to do. His forgetting is not an isolated, individual act; it is part of the whole scheme of personality. When we bear in mind that all the expressions of a personality are consistent parts of a whole, we can see that this boy simply acts in accordance with his style of life. Furthermore, his consistency, in accordance with the logic of his personality, at the same time disproves any presumption that his inability to perform his school tasks is due to feeble-mindedness. A feeble-minded person cannot construct and follow a style of life.

This highly complex case brings up still another point. We are all in a situation similar to that of this boy. Our own schemes, our own interpretations of life, are never in complete harmony with current social expectations. In the old days, social traditions were considered sacrosanct; however, we now realize that nothing about social institutions is sacred or fixed. They are all in the process of development, and the motive power in that process is the struggle of individuals to improve that society. Social institutions exist for the sake of the individual, and not the individual for the sake of social institutions. The salvation of the individual lies indeed in being social-minded, but social-mindedness does not imply forcing the individual into a Procrustean social mold.

These ideas about the relationship of the individual to society, which lie at the basis of Individual Psychology, apply with special force to the school system and its treatment of maladjusted children. The school must learn to regard the child as a unique personality, with valuable potential to be cultivated and developed, and at the same time it must learn to use psychological insight to evaluate specific acts. It must regard these specific acts, as we have said, not as single notes but in the context of the whole melody—the unity of personality.

Chapter III

The Striving for Superiority and Its Educational Significance

Next to the unity of personality, the most important psychological fact about human nature is the striving for superiority and success. This striving, of course, directly relates to the feeling of inferiority, for if we did not feel inferior, we would have no desire to improve the immediate situation. The two problems—the desire for superiority and the sense of inferiority—are really two aspects of the same psychological phenomenon, but for purposes of exposition, we will treat them separately. In this chapter, we will try to confine ourselves to the striving for superiority and its educational consequences.

The first question we may ask about the striving for superiority is whether it is innate, like our biological instincts. This is a highly improbable supposition. We cannot really speak of the superiority striving as being in any definite sense inborn. However, we must admit that a foundation must exist; there must be an embryonic core with the possibilities of development. Perhaps we may put it best this way: human nature includes the possibility of the development of the striving for superiority.

Obviously, we know that human activities are confined within certain bounds, that some abilities can never be developed. For example, we can never attain the smell faculty of a dog; nor is it possible to perceive with our eyes the ultraviolet rays of the spectrum. But other functional abilities can be developed further, and in this possibility of further development, we see the biological root of the striving for superiority and the whole source of the psychological unfolding of personality.

As far as we can see, this dynamic urge to assert ourselves under all circumstances is common both to children and adults. We cannot exterminate it. Human nature does not tolerate permanent submission; humanity has even overthrown its gods. The feeling of degradation and depreciation, the mood of uncertainty and inferiority, always lead to a desire for reaching a higher level in order to obtain compensation and completeness.

We can show that certain unique characteristics of children betray the pressure of environmental forces which develop in them feelings of inferiority, weakness and uncertainty, which in turn stimulate their whole mental life. They strive to free themselves from this condition, reach a higher level, and gain a feeling of equality. The more disturbing the inferiority feelings are, the higher the child sets his aims, looking for proofs of his strength—proofs which often transcend the limits of human powers. Because of the support he sometimes obtains from various quarters, a child can project a picture of the future bordering on God. In one way or another, the imagination of children often betrays that they are possessed with the idea of divine resemblance. This generally occurs in children who feel weakest.

One child of fourteen found himself in a very bad mental situation. When asked for childhood impressions, he remembered how painful it was for him to realize that he was unable to whistle at the age of six. One day, however, as he came out of his house, he succeeded in whistling. He was so surprised that he believed God whistled in him. This example shows clearly the intimate connection between the feeling of weakness on one hand, and the nearness of God on the other.

This aspiration for superiority relates to striking character traits. By observing this tendency, we witness the whole ambition of such a child. When this desire for self-assertion becomes extraordinarily intense, it will also involve an element of envy. Children of this type easily develop the habit of wishing their competitors all kinds of evil; and not only wishing—which often leads to neurosis—but also doing actual harm, causing trouble, and even sometimes manifesting serious criminal traits. Such a child can slander, betray domestic secrets, and degrade the other fellow in order to feel that his own value is enhanced, especially when he is being observed by others. No one is supposed to surpass him; therefore, whether he himself rises or the other fellow sinks in value does not matter to him. When the desire for power becomes very strong, it expresses itself in malevolence and vindictiveness. These children display a militant, defiant attitude, shown in their external appearance —in the flashing of their eyes, their sudden outbursts of anger, and their readiness to fight imaginary foes. For children aiming at superiority, to be submitted to a test is an extremely painful situation, for in this way their worthlessness might easily be exposed.

Consequently, we must adapt the tests to the uniqueness of the child. A test does not mean the same thing to every child. We can often find children for whom a test is a highly burdensome event, who blush and turn pale, begin to stutter and tremble, who are so paralyzed by shame and fear that their minds become blank. Some can answer only in unison with others, otherwise they cannot answer at all because they suspect that they are being watched. This desire for superiority will also

The Education of Children

manifest itself in play. An intense desire for superiority will not allow a child to play the part of a horse, while others play the part of drivers. He must be the driver himself, attempting to lead and direct. But when he is prevented by past experience from assuming such a role, he will content himself with disturbing the games of others. And if he is still further discouraged by numerous defeats, his ambition will be thwarted, and any new situation will drive him back instead of stimulating him to go forward.

Ambitious children who have not yet been discouraged display inclinations for competitive games of all kinds, and they equally manifest consternation in the event of defeat. The degree and direction of the desire for self-assertion can often be inferred from favorite games, tales, historical figures, and people. Adults often worship Napoleon, who serves well as a model for ambitious people. Megalomania in day-dreaming reveals a strong feeling of inferiority, which stimulates disappointed people to look for satisfaction and intoxication in feelings produced outside of reality. Something similar often takes place in dreams.

When we observe the different directions children take in their striving for superiority, we clearly see variations which we can divide into certain types. We cannot make this division into types a precise one because the variations are innumerable, and determined primarily by the amount of confidence the child has in himself. Children whose development has not been hindered direct this striving for superiority into the channels of useful accomplishment; they try to please their teachers, be orderly, and develop into normal school youngsters. We know from our experience, however, that these cases are not in the majority.

Some children want to excel others, manifesting a suspicious intensity in their struggle to surpass. Frequently, such striving reveals a note of exaggerated ambition, which is easily overlooked because we are accustomed to regard ambition as a virtue stimulating the child to further effort. This is usually a mistake because the development of a child suffers from too much ambition. A swollen ambition produces a state of tension which the child can bear for a while, but inevitably we will see signs that the tension grows too great. The child may spend too much time at home with his books and his other activities will suffer. Such children frequently avoid other problems only because of their eagerness to be ahead in school. We are not completely satisfied with such a development because a child cannot thrive mentally and physically under these circumstances.

The way such a child arranges his life in order to surpass all others is not best suited to a normal growth. At some point, he must be told not to spend so much time with his books, to go out into the air, to play with his friends and occupy himself with other things. Such children are not in the majority, but they occur frequently enough.

In another situation, two students in a class may be involved in a tacit rivalry. Observing closely, we will find that such competing children occasionally develop some disagreeable traits. They become envious and jealous, qualities which certainly do not belong to an independent, cooperative personality. They resent the success of other children; they begin to have nervous headaches, stomachaches, etc., when someone else forges ahead. They withdraw to one side when another child is praised, and of course, they will never be able to praise somebody else. This sign of envy does not throw a good light on exaggerated ambition.

Such children do not get along well with their comrades. They want the leading part in everything and are unwilling to subordinate themselves to the general organization of a game. Consequently, they do not like to play with others and act haughtily toward their schoolmates. The more insecure they believe their position to be, the more unpleasant they find every contact with their peers. Such children are never sure of their success and are easily rattled when they feel themselves in an insecure atmosphere. They are overburdened by the expectations of others, and by their own expectations of themselves.

These children also feel sharply the expectations their families have of them. With the vision of surpassing all others, of being a "shining light," they fulfill every task presented to them with excitement and nervousness. They feel the weight of the hopes resting on them, which they will carry only as long as circumstances are favorable.

If human beings were blessed with absolute truth and able to find a perfect method to spare children such difficulties, we would probably have no behavior problem children. Because we do not have a perfect method and the conditions under which children must learn cannot be ideally arranged, the anxious expectations of such children create a dangerous situation. They will face difficulties with quite different feelings from those of other children who are not burdened with unhealthy ambition. By difficulties, we mean those which are unavoidable. We cannot prevent a child from encountering difficulties, partly because our methods need further improvement and do not suit

The Education of Children

every child. Also, exaggerated ambition undermines the confidence children have in themselves. They do not face difficulties with the courage necessary to overcome them.

Gaining no satisfaction from accomplishing the task itself, over-ambitious children care only about the end result, which is the recognition of their success. Success does not satisfy them without recognition. Often, a child needs to maintain his mental balance when difficulties present themselves more than he needs to conquer these difficulties at once. A child forced into an overly-ambitious direction does not know this, and feels he cannot possibly live without the admiration of others. We see the result everywhere in the number of people dependent on the opinion of others.

We can see the importance of maintaining a sense of balance in relation to over-valuing immediate success when we consider, for example, children who come into the world with organ inferiorities. Such cases are, of course, quite common. Many children are better developed on the left than on the right side, a fact which is generally unknown. A left-handed child has many difficulties in our right-handed civilization. We can use certain methods to discover whether a child is right or left-handed. Almost without exception, left-handed children are generally awkward with their hands, and have exceptional difficulty in writing, reading, and drawing. One simple, but not entirely conclusive method for finding out whether a child is congenitally right-or left-handed, is to ask him to cross his hands. Left-handed children usually cross their hands so that the left thumb lies over the right. An astounding number of people are born left-handed and have never known it.

Investigating the history of many left-handed children, we find the following facts: first, they were usually regarded as clumsy or awkward (which is no wonder in our right-handed arrangement of things). To understand the situation, we need only think how perplexing it is, for those of us accustomed to right-handed traffic, to attempt to cross the street in a town where traffic moves to the left (England, for example, or Argentina) . A left-handed child finds himself in an even worse situation in a family where all the others are right-handed. His left-handedness disturbs both the family and himself. When he learns to write in school, he finds himself below the average. Because the reason for his poor performance is not understood, he is scolded, receives bad grades, and is often punished. The obvious interpretation of his situation is for him to believe that he is in some way less capable than others. A feeling will grow in him of having been shortchanged, of being in some way inferior, or of not being able to compete with others. Because he is also scolded at home for his clumsiness, he sees there only a confirmation of his inferiority.

Naturally, he does not have to accept this judgment as a final defeat, but many children give up the struggle under these disheartening conditions. Because they do not understand the real situation and no one explains to them how to overcome their difficulties, they struggle to keep on fighting. For this reason, many people have illegible handwriting because they have never trained their right hands sufficiently. However, we know this obstacle can be overcome because so many left-handed people become outstanding artists and painters, and also script engravers. These individuals have developed the ability to use their right hands simply by force of training despite their congenital left-handedness.

We are aware of the superstition that all left-handed people trained to use their right hand become stutterers. The explanation for this superstition is that the difficulties these children face are sometimes so great that they may lose their courage to speak. This reason also explains why we find so many left-handed people among those who manifest other forms of discouragement (neurotics, criminals, sexual deviants, suicides, etc.). On the other hand, we often find that those people who have overcome their left-handedness have also achieved a high position in life, frequently in an artistic atmosphere.

No matter how insignificant the single characteristic of left-handedness may appear, it still teaches us something of great importance: namely, that we can determine nothing of a child's ability until we have brought his courage and perseverance up to a certain point. When we frighten children and take away their hope for a better future, they may still seem capable of carrying on. But if we increased their courage, they would be capable of accomplishing much more.

Children with inordinate ambition are in a bad situation because we usually judge them by their success, not according to their preparedness to face and conquer difficulties. In our current civilization, we also tend to be much more concerned with visible success than with thorough education. Because we know the impermanence of success that comes to us with little effort, we can see no advantage in training a child to be ambitious. We serve his needs far better by training him to be courageous, persevering and self-confident, to recognize that failure should never discourage, but should be tackled as a new problem. His development would also be much easier if the teacher were able to recognize at what point a child's efforts seem futile and whether he makes sufficient effort in the first place.

The Education of Children

We see, therefore, that a striving for superiority can express itself in a character trait like ambition. Some children whose striving for superiority originally took the form of ambition relinquished this ambition as unattainable because another child had already gotten so much further ahead. Many teachers follow the practice of treating children who do not manifest sufficient ambition severely, or giving them bad grades in order to arouse their dormant ambition. Occasionally, this method succeeds if the child still has some courage left. However, we do not recommend this method for general use. Children already close to the danger line in their studies become completely confused and are driven into a state of apparent stupidity by such treatment.

On the other hand, we are often astounded at the unsuspected intelligence and capability which children manifest after being treated with gentleness, care, and understanding. Admittedly, some children who change in this fashion frequently exhibit a greater ambition. This is simply because they fear falling back to the old state. Their old way of living and former lack of accomplishment remain before their eyes like warning signals, continually urging them forward. In later life many of them behave as if possessed by a demon; they occupy themselves day and night, suffer constantly from the effects of overwork, and believe that they are never doing enough.

All this becomes much clearer when we keep in mind the dominant idea of Individual Psychology that every individual's personality (child as well as adult) is a unified whole, and that it always expresses itself in accordance with the behavior pattern which he has gradually built up. To judge an act detached from the personality of the actor is wrong because a specific and single act can be interpreted in many ways. The uncertainty in judging vanishes at once when we comprehend the particular act or gesture—for example, tardiness—as the inevitable answer of the child to the tasks he faces at school. His tardiness means simply that he would rather have nothing to do with the school; consequently, he does not bother to fulfill the school's requirements. In fact he does what he can not to comply with them.

From this standpoint, we can see the whole picture of the "bad" school child. We see the tragedy that takes place when the striving for superiority expresses itself not in the acceptance of school, but in the rejection of it. A series of typical behavior symptoms appear, gradually approaching closer and closer to incorrigibility and retreat. The child may turn into the court jester type, playing pranks to make others laugh and doing little else. Or he may annoy his comrades. Or else he plays truant and falls in with evil companions.

We see, then, how not only does the fate of the school child lie in our hands, but the later development of the individual as well. The education and training furnished by the school determine in a crucial fashion the future life of the individual. The school is placed in between the family and life in society. It has the opportunity of correcting the mistaken styles of life formed under family upbringing. It also has the responsibility of preparing the child's adjustment to social life and of ensuring that he plays his individual role harmoniously in the orchestral pattern of society.

When we view the role of the school historically, we see that it has tried to turn out individuals according to the social ideal of the time. It was successively an aristocratic, religious, bourgeois, and democratic institution, educating children according to what the times and rulers demanded. Today, in accordance with the changing social ideal, the school must also change. Thus, if today's ideal man or woman is independent, self-disciplined, and courageous, the school must aim to turn out individuals approaching that ideal.

In other words, instead of regarding itself as an end in itself, the school needs to keep in mind that the individual must be trained for society and not for the school. Thus, it must not neglect those who have given up the ideal of being model children at school. These children do not necessarily have less of a striving for superiority. They may turn their attention to other things where they do not have to strain themselves, and where they believe, either rightly or wrongly, that success is easier to achieve. They may have this belief because in their earlier years they have unconsciously trained themselves for other activities. Although they may not become brilliant mathematicians, they may distinguish themselves in athletics. The educator should never dismiss any salient accomplishment, but should use it as a point of departure to encourage the child to improve in other spheres of activity. The educator's task is much easier when he starts with a single encouraging accomplishment, using it to make the child believe he can be just as successful in other things. He is enticing the child, as it were, from one fruitful pasture to another. Because all children, except the feeble-minded, are quite capable of coping successfully with their school work, what needs to be overcome is simply an artificially constructed barrier. This barrier arises from taking abstract school performance, instead of the ultimate educational and social goal, as the basis for judgment. On the child's side, the barrier is reflected in a lack of self-confidence, with the result that his striving for superiority may detour from useful activity because it does not find its proper expression.

What does the child do in this situation? He thinks of a way to escape. He may find some unusual characteristic which does not draw praise from the teacher, but attracts his attention, or may only arouse the admiration of the other children at such a display of impertinence or stubbornness. Such a child, by virtue of the disturbance he creates, often regards himself as a hero, and as a little giant.

Such psychological manifestations and deviations from proper conduct arise in the course of the school experience. Their origin cannot be traced altogether to the school, although that is where they come to the surface. The school, taken in a passive sense, that is to say, apart from its active educational mission, is an experiment station where the defects in early family upbringing are brought to light.

A good, observant teacher can see many things in a child on the first day of school. Many children immediately show all the signs of a pampered child to whom the new situation (school) is most painful and disagreeable. Such a child has had no practice in making contacts with others, and his ability to make friends is essential. A child who comes to school with some knowledge of how to establish contact with others is better prepared. Also, he must not be dependent on one person to the exclusion of all others. The faults of family upbringing must be corrected at school, but of course we hope that a child comes to school more of less free of such faults.

We cannot expect a child who has been pampered at home to suddenly be able to concentrate on his work at school. He will not pay attention. He will manifest a desire to remain at home rather than go to school; in fact, he will have no "school sense." We can easily detect the signs of this aversion to school. For instance, the parents need to coax the child to get up in the morning; they must constantly urge him to do this or that; they find him dawdling over breakfast, and so on. Such a child seems to have constructed an impassable barrier to prevent his making progress.

The cure for the situation is the same as for left-handed individuals; we must give such children time to learn, and we must not punish them when they come late to school because that only increases their sense of unhappiness there. Punishment at school confirms the child's feeling that he does not belong there. When parents spank a child to force him to attend school, he will not only not want to attend school, but will look for means to make his position more bearable. These means will, of course, be means of escape, not means of actually meeting

The Education of Children

the difficulty. The child's aversion to school, his inability to cope with the school problem will be apparent in every gesture and movement. He will never have his books together, and he will constantly forget or lose them. When a child makes a habit of forgetting and losing books, we can be certain that he is not on good terms with his school.

In examining these children, we usually find that they have no hope of achieving any success at school. This self-undervaluation is not entirely their own fault. The environment has helped them along in this mistaken direction. At home, someone in anger has prophesied a dark future, or has called them stupid or worthless. When these children find at school what appears to be a confirmation of such accusations, they lack the judgment, the power of analysis (which their elders often also lack) to correct their misinterpretation. They thus give up the battle before they even make an attempt at combat, considering the defeat which they themselves bring about an insurmountable obstacle and confirmation of their inability or inferiority.

Because circumstances are usually such that, once a mistake is made, it will probably not be corrected, and because these children usually lag behind in spite of their apparent efforts to forge ahead, they soon give up the effort and turn their attention to inventing excuses for staying away from school. Absence from school, or truancy, is one of the most dangerous symptoms. Regarded as one of the worst sins, it usually leads to drastic punishment. Thereafter, children believe themselves compelled to take refuge in cunning and misrepresentation. A few paths lead them into still further misdeeds. They may forge notes from home and falsify report cards. They may spin a net of lies at home about all they are supposed to be doing at school, which place they have not attended for some time. They also have to find a place to hide during school hours. Obviously, they frequently find in such hiding places other children who have already trodden this path. And so the children's striving for superiority remains unsatisfied after merely playing truant; it urges them to further acts, that is to say, to lawbreaking. They go further and further, ending up with full-fledged criminality. They form gangs, begin to steal, learn sexual perversions, and feel quite grown up.

The great step having been taken, they now search for more food for their ambition. Because they have remained undetected in their acts, they feel they can commit the most clever of crimes, which is why so many children will not give up their life of crime. They want to go further along this road because they believe they can never achieve success in any other direction. They have excluded everything which might stimulate them to useful activity. Their ambition, continually

The Education of Children

stimulated by the deeds of their comrades, drives them to new a-social or anti-social acts. A child with criminal tendencies is always extremely conceited. This conceit has the same source as ambition, and it forces the child to continually distinguish himself in some way or other. When he cannot make a place for himself on the useful side of life, he turns to the useless side.

In one case, a boy killed his teacher. If we examine the case, we find all the characteristic traits in this boy. He had a careful but too nervous upbringing under the guidance of a governess who believed that she knew everything there was to know about the expression and function of mental life. The boy lost faith in himself because his ambition passed from exaggerated heights to nothing—that is to say, to sheer discouragement. Life and school did not fulfill his expectations, so he turned to law-breaking. In breaking the law, he passed out of the control of the educator and the child guidance expert, for society has not yet devised the apparatus for treating criminals, especially juvenile criminals, as educational problems whose psychological mistakes need correction.

A curious fact familiar to anyone involved in pedagogy is the number of wayward children in the families of teachers, ministers, doctors and lawyers. These children belong not merely to educators without much professional standing, but also to those whose opinions we regard as important. Despite their professional authority, they seem unable to achieve peace and order in their own families. The explanation is that in all such families certain important viewpoints have either been entirely overlooked or not comprehended. Part of the difficulty comes, for instance, from the strict rules and regulations which the educator-parent, by means of his assumed authority, tries to force on his family. He disciplines his children too severely. He threatens their independence and often actually robs them of it. He seems to arouse in them a mood which compels them to take revenge for his severity, rooted in their memory of the rod with which they have been beaten. Also, we must remember that professional pedagogy leads to an extraordinarily sharpened observation. For the most part this is a great advantage, but in the case of one's own family, it often results in the children wanting to be constantly in the center of attention. They regard themselves as a display experiment, viewing their parents as the responsible, determining parties. They expect their parents to remove all difficulties, while they feel free of any responsibility.

Chapter IV

Directing the Superiority Striving

Every child has a striving for superiority. A parent or educator must direct this striving into a fruitful and useful channel. He must ensure that the striving produces mental health and happiness instead of neurosis and disorder.

How is this task accomplished? On what basis do we differentiate between useful and useless manifestations of the striving for superiority? The answer is interest in the community. We cannot think of any achievement, anything worthwhile that anyone has ever done, that has no connection with the community. If we recall the great deeds which seem noble, lofty and valuable, we see that these deeds have been valuable not only to the doer, but to the community at large. Hence, the education of a child must be so organized that he will develop social feeling or a sense of solidarity with the community.

Children who do not understand the notion of social feeling become problem children. They are simply children whose striving for superiority has not been guided in a useful direction.

Although opinions differ widely as to what is useful to the community, one thing is certain: we can judge a tree by its fruit. The results of any act show whether it has been useful or useless to the community. This means that we must consider the place and time of an action, as well as its results. Eventually, the action must coincide with the logic of living, and this intersection with the logic of living will show whether the action has any relevance to the needs of the community. Universal values are the standards of communal life, and sooner or later the contradictions or agreements with these standards are bound to emerge. Fortunately, in daily life, we do not often find ourselves in situations that require complicated judgments. Social movements and political trends, whose effects we cannot clearly foresee, are controversial. However, in the lives of individuals as well as groups, the results ultimately determine the usefulness of certain acts. From a scientific point of view, we cannot call anything good or useful for everyone unless it is a correct solution of the problem of life, which is inextricably related to the earth, the cosmos, and the logic of human interrelationships. We can decide on the correctness of an action only when we test it in the light of the solution of the problem. Unfortunately, sometimes the opportunity to test the value of a solution comes so late that we have no time to correct mistakes.

Individuals who do not regard their life's structure from a logical and objective point of view are for the most part unable to see the coherence and consistency of their behavior pattern. When a problem occurs, they are appalled, and instead of tackling it, they think they have erred in taking a road on which they encounter problems. In the case of children, we must also remember that when they leave the road of usefulness, they are not in a position to learn positive lessons from negative experiences simply because they do not understand the significance of problems. Therefore, we need to teach a child to view his life not as a series of unconnected events, but as a continuous thread connecting all his experiences. No one event can be removed from the context of his whole life; it can be explained only in relation to everything that has gone before. When a child understands this connection, he will be able to comprehend why he blundered onto the wrong path.

Before discussing further the difference between the right and wrong direction for the striving for superiority, we should consider the kind of behavior which seems to contradict our general theory. This behavior is laziness, which on its surface, seems to contradict the view that all children have an innate striving for superiority. In fact, a lazy child is ordinarily scolded because he appears to have no striving for superiority, no ambition. But if we examine his situation more closely, we see how the ordinary view is mistaken. The lazy child possesses certain advantages. Not burdened with other people's expectations of himself, he is to some extent excused for not accomplishing much. He does not struggle, therefore assuming a negligent, indolent attitude. However, because of his laziness, he often succeeds in pushing himself into the limelight, where his parents feel obligated to occupy themselves with him. When we consider how many children want a position in the foreground at any price, we can see why some of them discover the idea of making themselves noticeable by being lazy.

This, however, is not a complete psychological explanation of laziness. Many children adopt a lazy attitude as a means of easing their situation. Their apparent incapacity and lack of accomplishment are attributed to laziness. We rarely hear them being accused of incapability; on the contrary, their families usually say : "What couldn't he do if he were not lazy ?" The children content themselves with the recognition that they could accomplish anything, if only they were not lazy. This assumption is balm for the ego of the child who has too little confidence in himself. It is a substitute for success, not only in the case of children, but for adults as well. This fallacious if-sentence, "If I were not lazy, what couldn't I do ?" quiets their feeling of having failed. When such children really do something, their small deed assumes extra significance in their eyes. The one unimportant accomplishment contrasts sharply with their uniform lack of accomplishment before, so they receive praise for it, while other children who have been consistently productive receive less recognition for greater accomplishments.

Thus, we can see the hidden and misunderstood diplomacy in laziness. Lazy children are like tight-rope walkers with a net underneath the rope; when they fall, they fall softly. Criticism of lazy children is milder than of other children, and it insults their ego less. Being told that one is lazy is less painful than being told that one is incapable. In short, laziness serves as a screen to hide the child's lack of faith in himself, protecting him from trying to cope with the problems confronting him.

Current educational methods fulfill precisely the wishes of the lazy child. For the more we scold a lazy child, the closer he is to his goal. We constantly occupy ourselves with him, and the scolding diverts attention from the question of his ability, thus fulfilling his desire. Punishment works much the same way. Teachers who think they can cure a child of laziness by punishing him are always disappointed. The severest punishment cannot make an industrious child out of a lazy one.

If a transformation takes place, it occurs because of a change in the situation, as for instance, when such a child attains an unexpected success. Or again it may happen when he passes from a strict teacher to a more gentle one, who understands the child, talks with him encouragingly, and gives him new courage instead of weakening the little courage that he has. In such a situation, the change from laziness to activity is sometimes surprisingly sudden. Thus, some children who were backward in the first years of school, on coming to a new school, become unusually industrious because of the change of environment.

Some children who do not seek escape by means of laziness avoid useful activity by playing sick. Other children are unusually excited at examination time because they think they will be shown some preference because of their nervous tension. The same psychological tendency is manifested by children who cry: the crying and the excitement are pleas for privilege.

In the same group with these children are those who demand special consideration for having some defect -- stutterers, for example. Adults who work closely with tiny children will have noticed that almost all of them show a faint tendency to stutter when they begin to speak.

The Education of Children

The development of speech is, as we know, quickened and hindered by many factors, principally by the degree of social feeling. Children who are socially-minded, who want to make contact with their fellow human beings, will learn to speak much more quickly and easily than those who avoid others. There are even situations in which speech is a superfluous activity; for example, in the case of a child so protected and pampered that his every wish is divined and fulfilled before he has time to make his desires known (as is necessarily done with children who are deaf mutes).

When children do not learn to speak before the age of four or five, the parents begin to fear deaf-mutism. But they soon notice that the children can hear quite well, which of course excludes the hypothesis of deaf-mutism. However, these children live in an environment in which speech is superfluous. When everything is handed to a child "on a silver platter," so that he has no urge to speak, then he will learn to speak late in life. Speech indicates the child's striving for superiority and the direction of its development. He must speak in order to express his superiority striving, whether this expression takes the form of bringing joy to his family by his utterances, or helping him attain his ordinary needs. When a child feels no possibility for this type of expression in either form, then we can naturally expect difficulties in his speech development.

There are other speech defects, such as difficulty in the pronunciation of r, k, and 8. They are all curable, so the large number of adults who stutter, lisp, or speak unintelligibly is rather remarkable.

Most children grow out of stuttering. A small percentage must be treated. The case of a thirteen-year-old boy will illustrate what the process of treatment involves. A doctor started the treatment when the boy was six years old. The treatment lasted a year and was unsuccessful. A year followed without professional assistance, then another year with another doctor; the treatment was still unsuccessful. The fourth year nothing was done, and during the first two months of the fifth year, the boy was entrusted to a speech doctor who made his condition worse. Some time later he was sent to an institute specializing in speech defects. The treatment, which lasted two months, was successful, but after a period of six months he had a relapse.

He then spent eight months with yet another speech doctor. This time, instead of any improvement being achieved, a gradual deterioration set in. One more doctor was tried, but again without success. During the next summer he improved, but at the end of the vacation period he sank back into his old manner of speaking.

Most of the treatment consisted of having the boy read aloud, in slow speaking, exercises, etc. Some forms of excitement produced temporary improvement, only to be followed by relapse. The boy had no organic defects, although as a tiny child he had suffered a fall from the second story of a building, which resulted in concussion of the brain.

The boy's teacher, who had known him for a year, described him as "a well-bred, industrious lad who blushes easily and is somewhat irritable." French and geography were the boy's hardest subjects, he said. At examination time, he was especially excited. Of his special interests, the teacher noted a taste for gymnastics, sports, and technical work. The boy did not manifest in any way the nature of a leader; he got along well with his schoolmates, but quarreled occasionally with his younger brother. He was left-handed, and the year before he had had a stroke of paralysis on the right side of his face.

In his family environment, his father, a businessman, is very nervous and often scolds the older son severely when he stutters. Nevertheless, the boy fears his mother more. He has a tutor at home, so he seldom leaves the house. He misses his freedom. He also thinks his mother is unfair because she favors the younger boy.

On the basis of these facts, we can offer the following explanation. The boy's ready blushing indicates the increased tension which comes as soon as he must make a social contact. It is, as it were, a relative of his stuttering habit. Even a teacher whom he likes does not succeed in curing him of his stuttering because this stuttering has become automatic and expresses his general dislike for others.

We know that the motive for stuttering does not lie in the external environment, but in the way the stutterer apperceives that environment. His irritability is psychologically very significant. He is not a passive child. His striving for recognition and superiority expresses itself in irritability, as it does with most weak natures. He reveals further proof of his discouragement in quarreling only with a younger boy. His excitement before an examination shows his increased tension due to the fear that he will not be successful and the feeling that he is not as capable as others. He has a strong feeling of inferiority, which diverts his striving for superiority in a useless direction.

Because the situation at home is not as agreeable as at school, the boy gladly goes to school. At home, the younger brother occupies the center of the stage. Although an organic wound or fright could not possibly have caused his stuttering, one or the other may have helped rob him of his courage. His younger brother, who has pushed him to one side in the family constellation, has had a greater effect on him.

Significantly, the boy suffered from enuresis (bed-wetting) until he was eight years old, a symptom found for the most part only in those children who were first spoiled and pampered and later "dethroned." The bed-wetting is a sure indication that he fought for his mother's attention even at night. It is a sign in this case that the child could not reconcile himself to being left alone.

The boy can be cured through encouragement and being taught how to be independent. He must have tasks put in his way which he can accomplish, and from which he can gain faith in himself. He admits that the arrival of his younger brother was disagreeable to him; he must now be made to understand how his jealousy has driven him into a useless direction.

We can say a great deal about the symptoms which accompany stuttering. Thus, we want to know what happens in a state of excitement. When many stutterers become angry, they can scold without a trace of stuttering showing in their speech. Also, older stutterers frequently speak flawlessly when reciting, or when they are in love. These facts indicate that the crucial factor lies in their relationship to others. The decisive moment is the confrontation, the tension aroused in the child when he must establish a connection between himself and another, or when he must achieve expression by means of speech.

When a child learns to speak without undue difficulty, no one pays much attention to the progress of his speech; however, when he shows difficulties, nothing else is mentioned in the house and the stutterer occupies the center of attention. The family occupies itself exclusively with him, resulting, of course, in the child paying too much attention to his speech. He begins consciously to control his expression, something that children who speak normally do not do. We know that the conscious control of functions which should operate automatically results in a restriction of the function. A pretty example of this is given by Meyrink in his fairy tale, "The Flight of the Toad." The toad meets an animal with a thousand feet and immediately begins praising the powers of this remarkable animal. "Can you tell me," asks the toad, "which one of your thousand legs you move first, and in what order you move the other nine hundred and ninety-nine legs?" The millipede begins to think, starts observing the movements of his legs, and in his attempts to control them, becomes confused and cannot move a single one.

Although exercising conscious control over our lives is important, trying to control each individual movement is harmful. We are able to produce works of art only when we can permit the physical movements necessary to produce these works to flow unconsciously.

The Education of Children

Despite the disastrous effect stuttering has on a child's potential, and despite the obvious disadvantages that accompany stuttering during the child's upbringing (the sympathy and special attention given him by his family), many people still take refuge in excuses rather than seeking to improve the condition. These excuses apply both to parents and children, both of whom may have no faith in the future. The child is especially content to lean on others, maintaining an advantage by a seeming disadvantage.

How frequently apparent disadvantages may be turned to advantage is illustrated in one of Balzac's stories. He tells of two tradesmen who tried to get the best of each other in a bargain. While they were thus bargaining, one of them began to stutter. The other one noticed, quite surprised, that the stutterer won enough time with his stuttering to think before making his point. Searching quickly for a counter-weapon, he suddenly made himself unable to hear any more. The stutterer was then at a disadvantage, because he had to strain himself in order to make the other one hear. Equality was thereby re-established.

Stutterers should not be treated like criminals, even though they sometimes use this habit to win time for themselves or make others wait. Children who stutter should be encouraged and treated gently. Only through friendly enlightenment and increasing a child's courage can successful cures be accomplished.

Chapter V

The Inferiority Complex

The striving for superiority and the sense of inferiority coexist in every human being. We strive because we feel inferior, and we overcome our feeling of inferiority by successful striving. The sense of inferiority does not become psychologically significant, however, unless either the striving for success is obstructed, or it is exaggerated by the psychological reaction to organ inferiority. Then we have an inferiority complex—an abnormal feeling of inferiority which necessarily seeks easy compensations and specious satisfactions, while at the same time obstructing the road to successful accomplishment by magnifying the obstacles and decreasing the supply of courage.

Let us consider again in this connection the case of the thirteen-year-old boy who stuttered. As we have seen, his discouragement is partly responsible for his continued stuttering, and his stuttering increases his discouragement. We thus have here the usual vicious circle of a neurotic inferiority complex. The boy wants to hide himself. He has given up hope; he may even have had thoughts of suicide. His stuttering has become an expression and a continuation of his life's pattern. It makes an impression on his environment, puts him in the center of attention, and thus eases his psychological malaise.

The boy has set for himself a somewhat overvalued and mistaken goal of counting in the world and amounting to something. Always striving for prestige, he must appear to be good-natured, able to get along with others, and have his work in order. On top of that, he thinks he must have an alibi in case he experiences a defeat, and this alibi is his stuttering. This boy's case is all the more significant because for the most part his life is usefully oriented; his judgment and courage have deteriorated in only one arena.

Of course, stuttering is merely one of innumerable weapons which discouraged children use when they do not believe they will be able to succeed on the strength of their own ability. These weapons of discouragement may be compared to the weapons which nature has given animals for their protection—claws and horns. We can easily see how these weapons have their origin in the child's weakness, and his despair of being able to cope with life without such extraneous equipment. A remarkable number of things may serve for such weapons. Some children have no other weapon than their lack of control of stools and urine. This lack of control indicates that they do not want to leave their infancy, the state in which we can live without work and pain. Such children seldom have any organic weakness of the intestines or the bladder. They merely resort to these things as tricks to awaken the sympathy of the parent or educator, even though these same tricks may sometimes evoke ridicule from their comrades. These manifestations should therefore not be treated as sicknesses, but as expressions of an inferiority complex, or of an endangered striving for superiority.

We can visualize how the stuttering developed, most likely from a small physiological core. The boy was an only child for a long time, and his mother was constantly occupied with him. As he grew up, he probably felt he was not receiving enough attention, that his self-expression was being curtailed, so he discovered a new trick with which to draw attention to himself. Stuttering assumed a greater significance; he noticed how the person to whom he spoke watched his mouth. By stuttering, he was thus able to secure for himself some of the time and attention that would otherwise have been devoted to his younger brother.

In school, he found the same situation. His teacher devoted a great deal of time to him. Thus, as a result of his stuttering, he was able to assume a role of superiority both at home and at school. He missed none of the popularity of the good students and for which he yearned. He clearly was a good student, but things were made easier for him.

On the other hand, though his stuttering had the effect of inducing his teacher to be lenient with him, it is scarcely a method to be recommended. The boy is hurt much more than other children when he fails to receive what he considers his quota of attention. This securing of attention became in fact a sore subject with the appearance of the younger brother in the family constellation. Unlike normal children, he never developed the ability to extend his interest to others. He made his mother the most important person in his family environment, to the exclusion of everybody else.

We must begin the treatment of such children by increasing their courage and getting them to believe in their own strength and ability. Although establishing a friendly relationship with a sympathetic attitude and not frightening these children with stern measures is valuable, this is still not enough. We must use the friendly relationship to encourage them to make continued improvement. This can be done only by making children more independent, by bringing them, through various devices, to the point where they necessarily acquire faith in their own mental and physical powers. They simply must be convinced that what they have not

The Education of Children

yet achieved can be readily attained by diligence, perseverance, practice, and courage.

The worst mistake in the education of children is for the parent or educator to prophesy a bad ending for a child who has strayed on the wrong path. Such a stupid prophecy makes the situation infinitely worse because it increases the child's cowardice. We should do just the opposite: inspire the child with optimism. As Virgil said, "They can because they think they can."

We must never believe that we can influence a child to really improve his conduct by humiliating or shaming him, even though we sometimes see that children who are afraid of being laughed at seem to change their behavior. The following case illustrates the unsoundness of this stimulation by ridicule. One boy was constantly teased by his friends because he could not swim. Finally, he could stand the ridicule no longer, so he jumped from the diving board into deep water. He was saved from drowning only with great difficulty. Perhaps a coward in danger of losing his prestige may do something to counteract his cowardice, but it is seldom the proper act. It is often a cowardly, useless way of meeting his original cowardice, as we see from the case just cited. The real cowardice lay in the boy's fear of admitting that he could not swim because he would thereby lose standing among his friends. Desperately jumping into the water did not cure that cowardice, but rather reinforced his cowardly propensity not to face facts.

Cowardice destroys relationships. A child so worried about his own person that he can no longer consider others is willing to achieve prestige at the cost of his fellow human beings. Cowardice thus brings in its wake a self-centered, combative attitude which abolishes social feeling, without abolishing the fear of others' opinions. A coward fears being ridiculed by people, being overlooked, or degraded. He is thus always at the mercy of the opinions of others. Like someone living in an enemy country, he develops the character traits of suspicion, envy and selfishness.

Children of this cowardly type frequently become critical and nagging, reluctant to praise others and resentful if others are praised. Thus, wanting to surpass others not through one's own accomplishments, but through degrading others, is a sign of weakness. To rid children of inimical feelings toward others is a pedagogical task which cannot be avoided by those who have recognized the symptoms. He who does not see them is, of course, excused, but he will never know how to correct the resulting unfavorable character traits. But when we know that the problem is to reconcile the child to the world and to life, to show him his mistake and explain to him that what he wanted was to have the prize of prestige without having worked to achieve it, then we also know in what direction to work with the child. We know that we have to strengthen the friendly feelings that children should have for one another. We know that we also have to teach children not to look down on someone because he has received a bad grade or because he has done something wrong. Otherwise, these poor grades and mistakes build up an inferiority complex and rob the child of his courage.

When a child is robbed of his faith in the future, he withdraws from reality and builds up a compensatory striving on the useless side of life. An educator's most important task, we might almost say his holy duty, is to ensure that no child is discouraged at school, and that a child who enters school already discouraged regains his confidence in himself through his school and his teacher. This goes hand in hand with the vocation of the educator, for education is possible only with children who look hopefully and joyfully to the future.

One type of discouragement is merely temporary, and occurs particularly in the case of ambitious children who, despite the progress they are making, sometimes lose hope because they have passed their last examination and must now turn to the choice of an occupation. Also, some ambitious children often give up the fight for a while, when they do not achieve first rank in their examinations. The conflict which has unconsciously been long in preparation suddenly breaks out. It may express itself in complete confusion, or in anxiety neurosis. Such children—if their discouragement is not checked in time—will always be starting something without finishing it. When they are older, they will change jobs frequently, never believing that anything can end well for them and constantly fearing defeat.

The self-evaluation of a child is then of the greatest importance. It is impossible, however, to discover what a child really thinks of himself by asking him. No matter how diplomatically we go about it, we receive uncertain or indefinite answers. Some children will say they think rather well of themselves; others will say they are worth nothing. Investigation in the latter cases may often disclose that the adults in their environment have said to them hundreds of times, "You aren't worth anything!" or "You are stupid!"

Few children can hear so scathing a reproach without being wounded by it. Others protect and shield their ego by undervaluing their ability.

If questioning a child does not inform us as to his judgment of himself, we can, however, observe the manner in which he approaches

The Education of Children

his problem—whether, for example, he goes forward in a confident, decisive manner, or he exhibits the sign found most frequently among discouraged children, a hesitating manner. Schematically, this movement may be illustrated by the example of a child who starts to go bravely forward, but then slows down and falters the nearer he approaches his tasks, and finally stops altogether at some distance before actual contact with them. Sometimes such children are described as lazy, or absentminded. The descriptions may be different; the result is always the same. The children do not tackle their work as we expect a normal human being to do, but are preoccupied with obstacles. Sometimes a child succeeds so well in fooling his elders that they fall into the mistake of thinking him lacking in ability. When we keep the whole picture in mind and illuminate it with the principles of Individual Psychology, we find that the whole trouble has been the lack of confidence--undervaluation.

When we consider a misdirected striving for superiority, we must remember that a completely self-centered individual is an anomaly in society. We often see children who, because of an inordinate superiority striving, have no consideration for anyone else. They are hostile, lawbreaking, greedy, and selfish. When they discover a secret, they will use it to hurt someone else.

But in those children whose conduct is most reprehensible, we find an unmistakably human trait; somewhere they have a feeling of belonging to mankind. The relationship of their ego to the world around them is implied or expressed in some way, although the further their life scheme is from the conception of cooperation, the more difficult it is to discover any social feeling. We must look for forms of expression which betray the hidden feeling of inferiority. These expressions are innumerable. They begin with the glance of a child. The eye is not only an organ which takes up rays and conducts them further, but also an organ for social communication. The way a person looks at someone shows the degree of his inclination to connect himself with others. That is why all psychologists and writers have emphasized an individual's glance so much. We all judge another person's opinion of us by the way he looks at us, and we try to discover part of his soul in his glance. Even though we may make mistakes or misinterpret, we can more easily conclude from the glance of a child whether he is friendly.

Obviously, those children who cannot look adults directly in the face open themselves to suspicion. These are not always children with a bad conscience. This glancing away may simply indicate an attempt to avoid tying himself, however momentarily, to another human being. It indicates the child's attempt to withdraw from the society of his comrades. How near a child approaches us when we call him is also an indication. Many children remain at some distance; they want to find out first what it is all about and will approach only when necessary. They regard close contact with suspicion because they have had some bad experiences, thus generalizing their one-sided knowledge and misusing it. Interestingly, some children have the tendency to lean, either on their mother or their teacher. The one to whom a child goes more willingly is much more important than the one whom he says he loves most.

Some children reveal a distinct feeling of confidence and courage in the way they walk, in their erect carriage and well-carried head, in their firm voice and lack of timidity. Other children shrink when they are spoken to and immediately betray their feeling of inferiority, their fear of not being able to cope with the situation.

In investigating this inferiority complex, we find many who believe that it is innate. The objection to this opinion is that any child, no matter how courageous, can be made afraid. A child whose father and mother are timid will probably be timid as well, not because he has inherited the timidity, but because he has grown up in an atmosphere permeated with fear. The atmosphere of the family, and the character traits of the parents are most important in the development of a child. Children who keep to themselves in school come more often than not from families having little or no relationships with others. Although we may be tempted to think of inherited characteristics in such cases, this is not a valid theory. No physical changes in the organs or the brain are able to produce an inability to make contact with others. However, while they do not necessarily compel such an attitude, certain facts make this peculiarity understandable.

The simplest case which will illustrate the matter theoretically is the example of a child born with weak organs, who has been sickly for some time, and oppressed by life because of pain and weakness. Such children are preoccupied with themselves, viewing the outer world as hard and hostile. A second harmful factor plays a role in such cases. A weak child must find a person who makes life easier for him, who devotes himself to the child, and who by this very devotion and protective attitude develops in the child a strong feeling of inferiority. All children, because of the disparity in size and strength between them and adults, have a relative feeling of inferiority. This feeling of being "less" is easily intensified when a child is told, as so frequently happens, "Children should be seen and not heard."

The Education of Children

All these impressions sharpen the child's perception of the fact that he is in a disadvantageous position. He cannot reconcile himself with the realization that he is smaller and less powerful than others. The more the idea that he is smaller and weaker stings him, the greater the efforts that he will make to become more. His striving for recognition has received an added impetus. Instead of trying to arrange his life so that it harmonizes with the lives of those in his immediate surroundings, he creates a new formula, "Think only of yourself." This type of child keeps to himself.

We may safely state that the majority of weak, crippled, and ugly children have a strong feeling of inferiority, which expresses itself in two extremes. Either they timidly shrink and withdraw when spoken to, or they are aggressive. These two forms of behavior may seem totally different, but in fact they have the same cause. In their striving for recognition, such children betray themselves by saying too little one time and too much another. Their social feeling is ineffectual either because they expect nothing from life and believe they are able to give nothing, or because they subvert the feeling to personal use. They want to be leaders and heroes, always in the center.

When a child has been training himself in a wrong direction for years, we cannot expect that a single conversation will change his pattern. The educator must have patience. In such cases where a child makes attempts to improve and has an occasional relapse, it is sometimes advisable to explain to him that improvement does not come quickly. This quiets the child and does not permit him to be discouraged. When a child has been deficient in mathematics for two years, he cannot possibly make up the deficiency in two weeks, but he certainly can make it up. A normal child, a courageous one, can make up anything. We see again and again that an inability is due to mistaken development, a peculiar, heavy, graceless formation of the whole personality. We can always help behavior-problem children who are not feeble-minded.

Inability or seeming stupidity, clumsiness, and apathy are not sufficient proof of feeble-mindedness. Feeble-minded children have physical indications of faulty brain development. This physical defect may be caused by those glands which affect the development of the brain. Sometimes such physical defects vanish in time, and only the psychic traces of the original physical deficiency remain. In other words, a child who was originally weak because of a physical deficiency may continue to act as if he were weak even after his body has grown strong.

We must go even further. Not only may psychological inferiority and an egocentric attitude be the result of a past history of organic inferiority and physical weakness, but they may also be brought about by entirely different circumstances that have nothing to do with organic inferiority. They may be brought about through the wrong kind of nourishment, or through a loveless and harsh upbringing. In such cases, life for the child becomes only a misery, and he assumes a hostile attitude toward his environment. The effects are similar, if not identical, with the disturbance in psychological life resulting from organic inferiority.

We have to expect great difficulties in treating children who have been brought up in an atmosphere devoid of love. They will view us as they view all others who hurt them; every encouragement to go to school will be felt as oppression. They will constantly feel restrained and will tend to revolt as much as they can. They will not be able to assume a correct attitude toward their peers because they envy those children who have had a happier childhood.

Such embittered children often develop into characters who like to poison the life of others. Not sufficiently courageous to overcome their environment, they try to compensate for their own feeling of lack of power by oppressing those who are weaker, or by being superior to others through apparent friendliness. This false friendliness, however, lasts merely as long as the others permit themselves to be dominated. Many children come to the point where they make friends only with those who are in worse circumstances, just as some adults feel particularly drawn to sufferers. Or they prefer younger, poorer children. Boys, too, sometimes prefer a particularly passive, submissive type of boy or girl, without gender entering into their preference.

Chapter VI

The Development of the Child: Preventing the Inferiority Complex

When a child takes an unusually long time to learn to walk, but can walk normally once he has learned, it does not mean that he must develop an inferiority complex for the rest of his life. We know, however, that a child whose mental development is otherwise normal is strongly impressed by any restriction in his freedom of movement. He feels that his situation is an unhappy one and he is likely to draw pessimistic conclusions from it, which may tend to govern his future course of action, even though the original physical, functional incapacity disappears later. Many children had rickets at one time and, though cured, still bear the marks of the disease: crooked legs, clumsiness, lung catarrh, a certain malformation of the head (caput quadratum), curved spine, enlarged ankles, feeble joints, bad posture, etc.

What remains psychically is the feeling of defeat which they acquired during their illness, and their consequent inclination to pessimism. Such children see the ease with which their comrades carry on and are oppressed by a feeling of inferiority. They undervalue themselves, and take one of two courses. Either they completely lose confidence and make little if any attempt at progress, or they are spurred on by the seeming desperation of their plight to catch up with their more fortunate playmates in spite of their physical handicap. Obviously, children do not have sufficient intelligence to judge their situations correctly. What determines the development of the child is neither his own intrinsic ability nor the objective environment, but the interpretation that he happens to make of the external reality and his relationship to it. The potential a child brings into the world is not of primary importance, nor is our adult judgment of his situation of any importance. We must see the child's situation with the eyes of the child himself, and interpret it with his own mistaken judgment. We must not suppose that he behaves logically, according to adult commonsense, but we must be ready to recognize that children make mistakes in interpreting their own positions. Indeed, we must remember that the education of children would be impossible if they did not make mistakes. We could not possibly educate or improve a child if the mistakes he made were innate. Consequently, he who believes in innate character traits cannot and should not educate children.

We do not always find a healthy mind in a healthy body. Sometimes we find a healthy mind in a sick body when a child faces life with courage in spite of physical defects. On the other hand, if a child is physically healthy, but through unfortunate circumstances has been led to make a fallacious interpretation of his abilities, he will not be mentally healthy. A failure in any given task often makes a child believe in his own incapacity. This is because such children are extraordinarily sensitive to difficulties and regard each obstacle as a confirmation of their lack of power.

Some children in addition to having difficulties in motor activities find it hard to learn to speak. Learning to speak should usually accompany learning to walk. The two are of course not actually connected, but depend on the rearing of the child and the circumstances of the family. Some children who would otherwise have no difficulty fail to speak because the family neglects to help them. Clearly, however, any child who is not deaf and whose speech organs are otherwise perfect should learn to speak at a reasonably early age. Under certain circumstances, especially in extremely visual types, speech is delayed. In other cases, parents spoil the child by saying everything for him instead of letting him make the attempt to express himself. Such a child takes so long to learn to speak that we sometimes think he is deaf. When he finally does learn to speak, his interest in speaking has become so intensified that he frequently becomes an orator in later life. Klara Schumann, the wife of the composer, could not speak until she was four and could speak only a little even when she was eight. She was an unusual child, very reserved, and she preferred to spend her time idling in the kitchen. We can deduce from this that no one bothered her. "Peculiar," said her father, "that this striking mental discord was the beginning of a life so full of wonderful harmony." Hers is an example of over-compensation.

We must be careful to see that deaf and dumb children receive special schooling, because more and more complete deafness seems to happen infrequently. No matter how defective a child's hearing is, his little ability to hear should be nursed to the utmost. Professor Katz, in Rostock, has demonstrated that he has been able to train children who were considered unmusical to a full appreciation of music and the beauty of sound.

Sometimes children who are successful in most of their school subjects fail terribly in one, frequently in mathematics, thereby arousing the suspicion of a light form of imbecility. Perhaps children who are not successful in arithmetic may have at one time been frightened by the

The Education of Children

subject and became discouraged in their attempts to cope with it. Some families, occasionally among artists, boast that they cannot calculate. In addition, the general idea that mathematics is harder for girls than for boys is wrong. Many women are excellent mathematicians and expert statisticians. Schoolgirls often hear "boys can count better than girls" and are discouraged by the remark.

Whether a child can use figures or not is an important indication. Mathematics is one of the few fields of knowledge which gives a human being security. It is a thought-operation which leads to the stabilization of surrounding chaos by numbers. People with a strong feeling of insecurity are usually bad calculators.

Other subjects also connect to feelings of security. Writing, the affixing to paper of the sounds known only to inner consciousness, gives security to the individual. Drawing permits making permanent a fleeting optical impression. Gymnastics and dancing express the attainment of physical security and, more especially, by virtue of the sure control of our bodies, a modicum of mental security. Probably this is why so many educators are such firm believers in sports.

A striking manifestation of a feeling of inferiority in children is the difficulty in learning to swim. When a child learns to swim easily, it is a good sign that he will also be able to overcome other difficulties. A child who has difficulty learning to swim shows lack of faith in himself and in his swimming instructor. Significantly, many children who have difficulty at first, become excellent swimmers later on. These are the children who, sensitive to the original difficulty, have been spurred on by eventual success to a goal of perfection and who frequently become champion swimmers.

We need to know whether a child is particularly attached to one person or is interested in several. Usually, a child is attached most deeply to his mother, or to another member of the family. Every child has this ability to attach himself unless he is feeble-minded. When a child has been reared by his mother and attaches himself to another person in the family, it is important to discover why. Obviously, no child should concentrate all his affection and attention on his mother, for a mother's most important function is to spread the interest and confidence of the child to his fellowmen. Grandparents also play an important role in the development of a child—usually a pampering role. They tend to pamper because aging people fear they are no longer necessary. They develop exaggerated inferiority feelings and as a result assume the role of nagging critics or of soft-hearted, good-natured elders who, in order to make themselves important to the children, deny them nothing. When visiting grandparents, children are often so spoiled that they refuse to return to their more disciplined homes. On their return, they complain that it is not as nice at home as it is at their grandparents'. We mention here the role that grandparents sometimes play in the lives of children so that educators will not overlook this important fact in investigating the style of life of any particular child.

Clumsiness in movement (Question Two of the Psychological Questionnaire in The Appendix) resulting from rickets and remaining unimproved over a long period, usually indicates that the child received too much special attention and was therefore pampered. Mothers should have enough intelligence not to kill a child's independence, even when the child is ill and needs special care.

An important question is whether the child has given much trouble (Question Three). When we hear that this has been the case, we can be sure that the mother has been too closely attached to the child. She has not been successful in establishing independence in him. This trouble-making usually manifests itself when going to sleep or getting up, in eating and washing, also in nightmares, or enuresis (bed-wetting). All these symptoms point to an attempt to get the attention of a certain person. One symptom after another appears; the child seems to discover one weapon after another to use in his fight to dominate the older person. When a child expresses such symptoms, his environment is not helping him develop. Punishment does not work, and such children usually provoke their parents into punishing them in order to show them that this punishment is futile.

An especially important question concerns the development of the child's intelligence. This question is sometimes difficult to answer correctly and we must occasionally resort to Binet tests, which, however, do not always give reliable results. No intelligence test is completely reliable and the results should never be accepted as constant for the entire life of the child. In general, the development of intelligence depends a great deal upon family circumstances. Families in better circumstances are able to help their children, and children with good physical development usually show comparatively good mental development. Unfortunately, our culture is arranged so that those children who progress more smoothly in their mental growth are predetermined to the "quality work," or better jobs, while those who grow more slowly are assigned to menial work. As far as we have been able to observe, the system newly introduced in many countries of having special classes for academically weaker children works out so that most of these children come from poor families. We can thus

The Education of Children

conclude that these poorer children, had they been surrounded by a more favorable environment, would undoubtedly have been able to compete successfully with children lucky enough to be born into families of better material circumstances.

We must also investigate whether a child has ever been the butt of ridicule or discouraged by teasing. Some children can bear such discouragement; others lose courage, avoid the difficult roads of useful work, and turn their attention to outward appearances, revealing little faith in themselves. An indication of a hostile environment is when a child constantly quarrels with others, fearing that if he is not the aggressor, others will attack first. Such children are disobedient, believing obedience to be a sign of subordination. They think that the courteous return of a greeting is a degradation, so they answer impertinently; they never complain because they regard the sympathy of others as a personal humiliation. They never cry in front of others, and sometimes laugh when they should cry, which looks like a lack of feeling, but only indicates a fear of showing weakness. No act of cruelty has ever been done which has not been based on a secret weakness. The really strong person has no impulse for cruelty. Such disobedient children often bite their nails, pick their noses, and are very dirty and stubborn. They need to be encouraged and we must make clear to them that their actions only indicate their fear of appearing as weaklings.

Question Four, whether the child makes friends easily or is unfriendly, whether he is a leader or a follower, has to do with his ability to make social contacts, with his degree of social feeling or discouragement. It also has to do with his desire to obey or to rule. When a child isolates himself, he indicates that he lacks sufficient confidence in himself to compete with others, and that his striving for superiority is so strong that he fears the subordination of his personality in the crowd. Children with an obsessive tendency to collect things may want to enrich themselves and surpass others. This tendency to collect is dangerous because it can easily go too far and develop into inordinate ambition or greed, the expression of a general feeling of weakness which seeks a point of support. Such children are easily led to steal when they believe that they have been neglected or overlooked, because they feel this lack of attention more than others.

Question Five concerns the child's attitude toward school. We must notice whether he is tardy or anxious about going to school (such anxiety frequently indicating reluctance). Children express their fears in the face of particular situations in various ways. When they have homework to do, they become irritable; they have what seems like a heart palpitation caused by the tense state into which they work themselves. One type may have certain organic changes, such as sexual excitement. The system of giving children grades is not always a commendable one. Children would be relieved of a great burden if they were not classified in such a way. School becomes a sort of constant examination or test in which a good grade is necessary to strive for, while a bad grade is like a permanent judgment.

Does the child do his homework willingly, or must he be forced to do it? Forgetting to do homework shows the tendency to avoid responsibility. Unsatisfactory school work and impatience with it are sometimes means used for escaping school, because the child wants to do something else.

Is the child lazy? When a child fails in schoolwork, he prefers to have laziness as the reason rather than inability. When a lazy child performs one task well, he is praised, and then he hears, "He could accomplish so much if he were not lazy." The child is satisfied with this opinion because he is convinced that he no longer has to prove his ability. To this type also belong the indolent children who lack courage, who cannot concentrate, who are constantly dependent. These pampered children disturb classroom work because they want to draw attention to themselves.

We cannot easily discover a child's attitude toward his teacher. Children usually mask their real feelings toward their teachers. When a child constantly criticizes, and tries to humiliate his school friends, we may assume that this tendency to degrade is an indication of his own lack of faith in himself. Such children are arrogant, nagging, and know everything better than the others. This attitude masks their own weakness.

The indifferent, apathetic, passive children are more difficult to handle. They also wear a mask because they are not really so indifferent. When such children are driven beyond control, their reaction generally takes the form of a fit of furious passion or an attempt at suicide. They never do anything until they are ordered to do so. They are afraid of setbacks and overvalue other people. They must be encouraged.

Children who show excessive ambition in sport or gymnastics may betray that they have been ambitious in other directions, but have been afraid of defeat. Children who read far more than usual, excluding most other activities, may lack courage and indicate that they hope to win power through reading. Such children have a rich imaginative life, but are timid in facing reality. It is also important to note what kind of stories children prefer: novels, fairy tales, biographies, travel, or

The Education of Children

objective, scientific works. During puberty, children are easily attracted to pornographic books. Unfortunately, every large city has bookstores that sell such printed matter. The increased sexual drive and the longing for experience turn their thoughts in this direction. Preparing children for their role as fellow men, clarifying sexuality at an early age, and fostering friendly relationships with their parents and peers will help combat such harmful influences.

Question Six concerns family conditions: sickness in the family, such as alcoholism, neuroses, tuberculosis, syphilis, or epilepsy. A comprehensive physical history of the child is also important. A child who breathes through his mouth frequently has a stupid facial expression, resulting from adenoids and tonsils which prevent correct breathing. An operation to remove such obstructions is important, and sometimes believing that the operation will help him gives a child more courage to tackle school when he returns.

Sickness in the family frequently harms the progress of a child. Chronically ill parents burden their children heavily. Nervous and psychic disorders oppress the whole family. Whenever possible, children should not be permitted to know that a member of the family has become mentally ill. A mental disorder casts a shadow over the whole family, apart from the superstition that it can be inherited. This is also true of the innumerable cases of tuberculosis and cancer. All these diseases make a horrible impression on the mind of a child and sometimes he should be removed from such a home atmosphere. Chronic alcoholism or criminal inclinations within a family act like a poison which a child frequently cannot resist. However, the proper placement of children taken from such homes does involve difficulties. Epileptics are usually irritable and disturb the harmony of family life. But syphilis is the worst of all. Children of syphilitic parents are usually very weak, inherit the disease, and find life tragically hard to cope with.

We cannot overlook that the economic condition of the family colors a child's outlook on life. Poverty in comparison with the better circumstances of other children arouses a feeling of insufficiency. Children who are moderately well-off have difficulty going without their customary comforts if the family's finances decline. The tension is still greater when grandparents are better off than the parents, as in the case of Peter Ghent, who could not rid himself of the thought that his grandfather was extremely powerful while his father failed in everything. A child often becomes industrious as a protest against an indolent father.

The first contact with death when it comes suddenly is frequently a shock great enough to influence a child's whole life. When a child is

The Education of Children

unprepared for death, than suddenly faces it, he realizes for the first time that life has an end. This may discourage him completely, or at least make him timid. In the biographies of doctors, we often find that their choice of a profession was caused by a brusque meeting with death, proof that a child is deeply affected by his realization of death. Children should not be burdened with this problem because they are not able to comprehend it entirely. Orphans or step-children often blame their unhappiness on the death of their parents. Knowing who has the deciding voice in the family is important. Usually, the father has it. When a mother or a step-mother dominates, the results are abnormal, and the father frequently loses the respect of his children. Sons of dominating mothers usually carry with them a certain fear of women of which they rarely can rid themselves. Such men either avoid women or make life unpleasant for the women in their families.

We need to know whether a child's upbringing has been strict or indulgent. Individual Psychologists do not believe that either strict or indulgent methods should be used in raising children. Parents needs to avoid major mistakes, while they give children understanding, and constant encouragement to face and solve problems, so that the children develop social feeling. Parents who nag their children harm them, for they completely discourage the children. A pampering environment develops a dependent attitude and a tendency to cling to one person. Parents should avoid both the painting of rosy pictures and the describing of the world in pessimistic terms. Their job is to give the child as good a preparation for life as possible, so that he will be able to take care of himself. Children who have not been taught how to face difficulties will seek to avoid every hardship, which leads to an ever-narrowing circle of activity.

Who has charge of the children? A mother does not need to be constantly with her children, but she should know the person in whose care she places them. The best way to teach a child is to let him learn from experience, within reason, so that his conduct is guided not by the restrictions placed on him by others, but by the logic of consequences.

Question Seven concerns the position of the child in the family constellation, which has a major influence on his character. An only child is in an unusual situation; a youngest child, and an only boy among girls or an only girl among boys are also in unusual positions.

Question Eight involves the choice of an occupation. This question is important because it reveals the influence of the environment, the amount of the child's courage and social feeling, and his life style. Day-dreams (question nine) are also significant, as well as early

The Education of Children

childhood recollections (question ten). People who have learned to interpret childhood recollections can frequently discover from them the entire style of life. Dreams may also indicate the direction in which a child is going, whether he is attempting to solve or evade his problem. Knowing whether a child has speech defects is important; further, whether he is ugly or good-looking, well-formed or badly-formed (question thirteen).

Question Fourteen. Will the child discuss his situation openly or not? Some children boast as a compensation for their feeling of inferiority. Others refuse to talk, fearing they will be taken advantage of, or fearing a new hurt if they betray their weakness.

Question Fifteen. A child who is successful in one subject, say in drawing or music, must be encouraged on the basis of this achievement to improve in his other subjects.

Children who at the age of fifteen do not know what they want to become may be discouraged and should be treated accordingly. The occupations, and social and professional accomplishments of parents, as well as older siblings, must be considered. The whole development of a child can be harmed by the unhappy marriage of the parents. A teacher's duty is to proceed carefully, to form an accurate picture of the child and his environment, to arrange his treatment, and to attempt to improve the child based on the knowledge gained from the questionnaire.

Chapter VII

Social Feeling and the Obstacles to Its Development

In contrast to the cases of superiority striving we have discussed in the previous chapters, many children and adults unite with others to accomplish tasks cooperatively and make themselves generally useful from a social point of view. Such manifestations may best be described by the term social feeling. What is the root of this feeling? The answer is a matter of some controversy. But as far as I have been able to discover, this phenomenon is at the core of what it means to be human.

We might perhaps ask in what sense such a psychological sensibility is more innate than the psychological striving for superiority. The answer would be that at bottom both have the same core—that the desire for supremacy and the feeling of social-mindedness rest on the same basis in human nature. They both express a root desire for affirmation; they differ in their form, and their different forms involve different implicit judgments about human nature. Thus, the unique striving for supremacy involves a judgment that the individual can do without the group, while the feeling of social-mindedness involves a belief in a certain dependence on the group. Of the two views of human nature, social feeling is clearly superior to the egotistical striving. The former represents a useful, socially logical outlook, while the latter, although common, represents a useless, selfish outlook.

If we want to see in what sense social feeling has truth and logic on its side, we have only to observe man historically and we shall notice that he has always lived in groups. This fact is not surprising when we reflect further that those creatures who are not able to protect themselves individually have always been compelled to live together for self-preservation. We have only to compare a human being with a lion to realize that man, regarded as a species of animal, is quite insecure, and that most other animals comparable in size to man are stronger and better armed by nature for physical offense and defense. Darwin observed that all animals whose defense equipment has been somewhat neglected by nature travel in packs. The orangutan, for example, with his extraordinary physical strength, lives alone with his mate, while the smaller and weaker members of the ape family live in groups. The formation of groups serves, as Darwin has pointed out, as a substitute or compensation for that which nature has denied to the animals individually—claws, fangs, wings, etc.

The Education of Children

The formation of groups not only balances what particular animals lack as individuals, but it also leads them to discover new methods of protection which improve their situation. For instance, some groups of monkeys know how to send out advance scouts to discover the presence of enemies. In this way, they are able to use their massed strength, thereby more than making up for the weakness of each member of the group. Buffalo herds also join together, successfully defending the group against individual enemies of far greater power.

Animal sociologists who have studied this problem report that in these groups we often find arrangements similar to laws. Thus, the scouts that are sent ahead must live according to certain rules, and every blunder or infraction is punished by the whole herd.

In an interesting connection, many historians assert that the oldest laws of mankind were those affecting the watchmen of the tribe. If this is so, we have a picture of the invention of the group idea out of the inability of weaker forms of animal life to protect themselves. And in a certain sense, the feeling of social-mindedness reflects physical weakness and fundamentally connects with it. Thus, with human beings perhaps the most important situation that fosters social feeling is the helplessness and slow development of infants and children.

In the whole realm of animal life, no creatures except man come into the world with such complete helplessness. Also, as we know, the human child requires the longest time to reach maturity. This long "pre-adult" period is not because of the infinite number of things way he develops. Children need the protection of their parents much longer because their physical limitations demand it, and the human race would die out if children were not given such protection. The physical weakness of the child links together education and social-mindedness. Education is a necessity because of the child's physical immaturity, and the goal of education is provided by the child's need to rely on the group in order to overcome his immaturity. Education must necessarily be social in purpose.

The idea of community life and social adjustment to it must provide the foundation of all our rules and methods for the education of children. Whether we know it or not, we are always impressed more favorably by what is good from the standpoint of the community, and less favorably by what is generally disadvantageous or harmful to society.

All educational mistakes which we observe are mistakes only because we judge that they will produce harmful effects on the community. All great accomplishments, and in fact all development of a human being's abilities occur under the pressure of social life and in the direction of social feeling.

Let us consider speech, for example. A person living alone needs no knowledge of speech. That human beings have developed speech indicates indisputably the necessity for communal life. Speech is a distinct bond between people and at the same time a product of their living together. The psychology of speech is conceivable only when we use the idea of the community as a point of departure. Individuals living alone have no interest in speech. Whenever a child lacks this broad base of participation in the community and grows up isolated, his ability to speak will be restricted. What we call a talent for speaking can be acquired and improved only when an individual relates to others.

People tend to assume that those children who can express themselves better than others are simply more talented. This is not true. Children who have difficulty speaking or making contact through speech usually do not have strong social feeling. Children who do not learn to speak well are frequently spoiled children, for whom their mothers do everything before the children have time to ask for anything. In this way they lose contact and the ability for social adjustment because they do not need speech.

Some children are reluctant to speak because their parents never permit them to finish a sentence or to answer for themselves; others have been laughed at or ridiculed, and thereby discouraged. This constant correcting and nagging seems to be a widely spread malpractice in the education of children. The dire result is that such children carry with them for years a feeling of degradation and inferiority. We can notice this feeling in adults who use the typical introduction before they begin a sentence: "But, please don't laugh at me." We often hear this plea and immediately recognize that such people were frequently laughed at as children.

In one case, a child could speak and hear, but his parents were both deaf and dumb. He cried without making any sound when he hurt himself. He needed to let his parents see his pain, but he knew that making his suffering audible was useless.

The development of other human capacities, such as the growth of understanding or of a logical sense, is unthinkable without social feeling. A man living absolutely alone has no need of logic, or at least has no more need than any other animal. On the other hand, a man in constant contact with others, who must use speech, logic, and common sense in dealing with them, must develop or acquire social feeling. This development of social feeling is the final goal of all logical thought.

The Education of Children

Occasionally the actions of people appear stupid to us, when in reality these actions are quite intelligent in light of their personal goals. This judgment frequently happens with those people who think that everybody else must think as they do, which shows us how significant the factor of social feeling or common sense is in judgment (not to mention that the development of common sense would not be necessary if communal life were not so complicated and did not present the individual with so many intricate problems). We can very well imagine that primitive people have remained at a primitive level because the relative simplicity of their existence did not stimulate them to deeper thought.

Social feeling plays a most important part in our ability to speak and think logically—two functions which we might almost regard as holy. If everyone attempted to solve his problems regardless of the community in which he lived, or to use a language of his own, chaos would result. Social feeling gives a security which each individual can feel and provides the main support in his life. It may not be completely identical with the confidence that we derive from logical thought and truth, but it is the most palpable component of that confidence. To use an illustration, why are calculating and counting so confidently accepted by everyone so that we tend to regard as precisely true only that which we can express in numbers? The reason is that numerical operations are more easily communicable to our fellow men, at the same time that they are easier for the mind to work with. We do not have much confidence in truths we cannot easily communicate to others and have others share with us. This train of thought was doubtless behind Plato's attempt to model all philosophy on numbers and mathematics. We see the connection with social feeling even more closely in his desire for the philosopher to go back to the "cave," to participate in the life of his fellow men. Even the philosopher, he felt, could not live properly without the security that comes from social feeling.

Children who have less of this feeling of security, reveal it when they come in contact with others or. when they have to perform certain tasks on their own initiative. They reveal it particularly in school in those subjects which require objective, logical thinking, as in mathematics.

The conceptions for which a human being is prepared in childhood (for example, moral feelings, ethics, etc.) are usually presented in a one-sided manner. A system of ethics for a human being condemned to live alone is inconceivable. Morals have value only when we think of the community and the rights of others. This view is a little more difficult to confirm when we think of aesthetic feelings, of our inclination to artistic creations. However, even in the realm of art, we can perceive a generally consistent impression which probably has its basic roots in an understanding of health, strength, correct social development, etc. So far as art is concerned, the boundaries are elastic, with perhaps more room for individual taste. On the whole, however, even aesthetics follows social lines.

If we are asked the practical question-- how can we tell the degree to which social feeling has been developed in a child ?--we must answer that certain conduct manifestations need to be considered. For example, when we see that children, in their striving for superiority, force themselves to the front with no consideration for others, we can conclude they have less social feeling than those children who avoid that particular behavior. We cannot imagine a child in our present civilization without some desire for personal supremacy. As a result, his degree of social feeling is usually not sufficiently developed. This deficiency is the condition which the critics of mankind, the old and modern moralists have always complained of —that man is by nature egotistical and thinks more of himself than he does of others. This criticism has always been expressed in the form of a sermon which has no effect on children or adults, because nothing can be accomplished with this axiom alone, and people have eventually consoled themselves by thinking that everybody else is no better.

When we deal with children whose ideas have become so confused that they have developed harmful or criminal tendencies, we must recognize that no amount of moral preaching has ever had any beneficial effect. In such a situation, we would do better to probe a little deeper in order to abolish the evil by pulling up the roots. In other words, we must relinquish our role of judge and assume that of comrade or doctor.

If we constantly tell a child that he is bad or stupid, he will become convinced in a short time that we are right and he will not have sufficient courage thereafter to tackle any task presented to him. What happens then is that the child fails in whatever he tries to do. The belief that he is stupid takes firmer root. He does not understand that the environment originally destroyed his self-confidence and that he is subconsciously arranging his life to prove this fallacious judgment correct. He feels less able than his comrades; he feels restricted in abilities and possibilities. His attitude shows unmistakably his depressed frame of mind, which is in direct proportion to the amount of pressure exerted upon him by an unfavorable environment.

The Education of Children

Individual Psychology has tried to show that the influence of the environment is evident in every mistake a child makes; for example, a disorderly child is in the shadow of a person who puts his things in order; a child who lies is under the influence of a domineering adult who wants to cure the child of lying by harsh means. We can even detect traces of the environment in a child's boasting. Such a child usually feels that praise is a necessity, not the successful accomplishment of a given task; and in his striving for superiority, he constantly seeks to evoke laudatory comments from the members of his family.

Parents usually overlook or misunderstand certain circumstances in the life of every child. Thus, each child in a family of siblings is in a different situation. The first child has the unique position of having been the only child for a while. This experience is unknown to a second-born. The youngest child experiences a set of circumstances which not every child goes through, because he remains for a while the smallest and weakest in the environment. We see many variations of these situations. When two brothers or two sisters grow up together, the one who is naturally older and more competent has overcome particular difficulties which the younger has yet to conquer. The younger of two such children is in a relatively unfavorable position and feels it. To compensate for this feeling of inferiority, the child may increase his striving in order to overtake the older brother or sister.

Individual Psychologists who have worked for a long time with children are usually able to detect the position that children have in the family constellation. When the older child is one that has made normal progress, the younger one has been stimulated to greater effort to keep up with the older. As a result, the younger is usually more active and more aggressive. If the older child has been weak and has developed slowly, the younger is not forced to make quite so strong an effort to compete.

Therefore, we need to know a child's position in the family in order to completely understand him. The youngest children in families bear unmistakable signs of being the youngest. Of course there are exceptions, but the most common type of youngest child wants to surpass all the others, is never quiet, and is constantly compelled to further action by the feeling and belief that he must eventually amount to more than all the others. These observations are significant because they require adopting certain educational methods for children. We cannot possibly follow the same rules in handling all children. Each child is unique, and while we classify children according to general types, we must be careful to treat each one as an individual. While this principle is

The Education of Children

almost impossible to implement in the school, it is definitely achievable at home.

The youngest child wants to be in the foreground of any picture and in many cases he succeeds. This important consideration weakens considerably the notion of the inheritance of mental characteristics. When youngest children of different families bear so much resemblance to each other, we have little reason to believe in inheritance.

Another type of youngest child, directly opposite to the active one described above, is the completely discouraged adolescent. Such a child is as indolent as possible. We can understand that the seemingly great difference between these two types is explainable psychologically. No one is so easily hurt by difficulties as he who has the inordinate ambition to excel all others. His ambition makes him unhappy, and when the obstacles seem almost insurmountable, he flees more quickly than one whose striving does not have such an important goal. We see in these two types of youngest child the personification of the Latin saying: "Aut Caesar, aut nullus" or, "all or nothing."

In the Bible, we find excellent descriptions of youngest children which coincide exactly with our experience—for example, the stories of Joseph, David, Saul, etc. The objection that Joseph had a younger brother, Benjamin, may be refuted by considering that Benjamin was born when Joseph was seventeen years old, so that Joseph as a child was the youngest. In life, we often see families supported by the youngest child. We find confirmation for our assertion concerning the youngest not only in the Bible, but also in fairy tales. In all fairy tales, the youngest surpasses all his siblings; in German, Russian, Scandinavian or Chinese fairy tales, the youngest conquers all. His victories cannot be mere coincidence. In former times the figure of the youngest child was much more prominent than it is today, and was probably better observed because it was easier to notice under primitive conditions.

Much more could be written about the characteristics which children develop in accordance with their position in the family constellation. Oldest children also have many characteristics in common and may be divided into two or three main types.

I had been studying the matter for a long time and was not quite clear about it when I accidentally stumbled on a passage in Fontane's autobiography. Fontane describes there how his father, a French emigrant, took part in a war between Poland and Russia. His father was always happy when he read, for example, that ten thousand Poles had beaten fifty thousand Russians and put them to flight. Fontane could not understand his father's joy. On the contrary, he objected very much on

The Education of Children

the ground that fifty thousand Russians simply had to be stronger than ten thousand Poles, and "if that isn't so, it doesn't please me at all because the stronger should always remain the stronger." In reading this paragraph, we immediately jump to the conclusion, "Fontane is an oldest child!" Only an oldest child could make such a sttement. He remembers his possession of power in the family when he was the only child and feels that being dethroned by a weaker person is an injustice. As a matter of fact, oldest children usually have a conservative trait. They are believers in power, in rule, and in unbreakable laws. They tend to accept despotism quite frankly and without apology. They have the right attitude for positions of power because they once occupied such positions themselves.

There are exceptions, as we have said, in the types of oldest children. One exception which has previously been neglected is the tragic position of an older boy with a younger sister. Descriptions of confused, completely discouraged boys have often indicated, without the fact itself being mentioned, that the trouble was a younger, clever sister. The frequency of this occurrence is no accident because it has a natural explanation. We know that in our present civilization men are considered more important than women. A first-born son is frequently pampered. His parents expect a great deal of him. His situation is a favorable one until a sister suddenly appears. The girl enters an environment which contains a spoiled older brother who regards her as an annoying intruder and who fights against her. This situation spurs the girl on to make extraordinary efforts, and if she does not break down, this stimulation affects her whole life. The girl develops rapidly and frightens the older boy, who suddenly sees the fiction of masculine superiority destroyed. He becomes uncertain, and since nature has so arranged matters that girls between the ages of fourteen and sixteen develop mentally and physically more rapidly than boys, his uncertainty is likely to end in a complete defeat. He easily loses his belief in himself and gives up the fight, arranges plausible excuses, or puts difficulties in his own way which he can then use as alibis for ceasing to struggle.

Many such first-born boys are confused, hopeless, inexplicably lazy, or suffering from nervousness for no other reason than that they did not feel strong enough to compete with a younger sister. Such boys sometimes maintain an unbelievable hatred of the female sex. Their fate is usually a sad one because few people understand their condition and can explain it to them. Sometimes it goes so far that parents and other members of the family complain, "Why isn't it the other way around? Why isn't the boy a girl, and the girl a boy?"

The Education of Children

Boys who are alone among several sisters also have characteristics in common. It is difficult to prevent a primarily feminine atmosphere in a house with several girls and only one boy. Either he is badly spoiled by all the members of the family, or all the women exclude him. While such boys develop differently, they have particular traits in common. We know that many people believe boys should not be educated by women exclusively. We cannot take this idea literally, because all boys are first reared by women. What the idea really means is that boys should not be brought up in an environment of women. This is not an argument against femininity, but against the misunderstandings arising from such a situation. The same idea applies to a girl who grows up with boys. The boys usually look down upon the girl and she tries, as a result, to imitate the boys in order to be their equal, which is an unfortunate preparation for her later life.

No matter how tolerant we are, we cannot join in the chorus of those who believe that girls should be brought up like boys. We can do it for a while, but certain unavoidable differences quickly become apparent. Men have different roles to play in life determined by their difference in physical structure. This difference plays a part in the choice of a profession, and girls who are not satisfied with their feminine role sometimes have great difficulty in adjusting themselves to the occupations open to them. When we come to the issue of preparation for marriage, clearly the education for the role of a woman must be different from that for the part of a man. Girls who are dissatisfied with their gender will object to marriage as a personal degradation, or if they do marry, they will try to dominate. Boys who have been brought up like girls will also experience great difficulty in adjusting themselves to our present form of civilization.

In considering all this, we must remember that a child's style of life is usually determined by the time he is four or five years old. Those are the years during which he must develop social feeling and the flexibility necessary for adjustment. By the time a child is five years old, his attitude to his environment is usually so fixed and automatic that it proceeds in more or less the same direction for the rest of his life. His apperception of the outer world remains the same; he is caught in the trap of his private perspectives and repeats unceasingly his original mental patterns and the resulting actions. Social feeling is limited by the boundaries of the individual's mental horizon.

Chapter VIII

The Child's Position in the Family:
The Psychology of the Situation and the Remedy

We have seen that children develop in accordance with their unconscious interpretation of the position they occupy in relation to their environment. We have also seen that first, second, and third children develop differently, each in accordance with his particular position in the family constellation. This early condition may be regarded as a test of the character developed by the child.

The education of a child cannot begin too soon. As a child grows, he develops a set of rules or formulas which regulate his conduct and determine his reactions to various situations. With a very young child, we have only slight indications of the particular pattern he is constructing to guide his future behavior. Later on, as the result of years of training, this behavior pattern becomes fixed and he no longer reacts objectively, but in accordance with his unconscious, subjective interpretation of the sum total of his past experiences. When a child has made a false interpretation of any particular situation or of his own ability to cope with a particular difficulty, this erroneous judgment will determine his conduct and no amount of logic or common sense can change the adult conduct until the original, childish misinterpretation is corrected.

The development of every child has some subjective quality, and this uniqueness should be the focus of investigation for educators. This individuality prevents the application of general rules in the education of groups of children. It is also the reason why the application of the same rule achieves different results with different children.

On the other hand, when we see children reacting to the same situation in almost the same way, we cannot say that this is because of a law of nature; human beings tend to make the same mistakes because of their common lack of understanding. Most people believe that a child always becomes jealous when another child appears in the family. The first objection to this generalization is that we do find exceptions; the second, is that a knowledge of how to prepare children for the arrival of a younger brother or sister would make jealousy impossible. A child who makes a mistake may be compared to a person who finds himself in the mountains in front of a footpath. He does not know where or how to proceed. When he has finally found the right path and has come to the

The Education of Children

next town, he hears people say in astonishment: "Almost everyone who wanders off that path gets lost." Mistakes made by children are often along such enticing paths. They look easy to tread, and thus attract the child.

Many other situations have immeasurable influence on the character of a child. How often do we see two children in a family, one who is good and one who is bad? If we investigate the circumstances a little more closely, we find that the bad child has an intense desire for superiority, wants to dominate others, and uses all his power to rule the environment. The house is noisy with his cries. The other child, by way of contrast, is quiet, modest, the family's favorite, and held forth as an example to the other. The parents do not know how to explain such opposites in the same family. Upon examination, we see that the good child has discovered that he gains much more recognition by his excellent behavior, thereby competing successfully with his sibling. In a rivalry of this nature between two children, we can understand how the first has no hope of surpassing the second by being better than the second, so he strives to excel him in the opposite direction, by being as naughty as possible. In our experience, such naughty children can be turned into even better children than their siblings. We also find that a strong desire for superiority may express itself in one extreme direction or the other. We see the same thing in school.

We cannot predict that two children will be exactly the same because they grow up under the same conditions. No two children grow up under exactly the same conditions. The character of a well-behaved child is greatly influenced by the presence of an ill-behaved one. As a matter of fact, many children who were originally well-behaved later turn into problem children.

In one case, a seventeen-year old girl was a model child until she was ten years old. She had a brother eleven years older who had been badly spoiled because he had been the only child for eleven years. The boy was not jealous of his sister when she arrived; he merely continued his usual behavior. When the little girl reached her tenth year, the brother began to be away from home for long periods. She assumed the position of an only child, which had the effect of making her want to have her own way at any price. She grew up in a rich home, so that when she was a child, her every desire was easily fulfilled. When she grew older, this was not always possible and she began to show her dissatisfaction. She began to incur debts at an early age on the strength of her family's financial reputation, and she soon owed a considerable sum of money. This situation means nothing more than that she chose

The Education of Children

another road to fulfill her wishes. Her good behavior vanished when her mother refused to accede to her demands. Quarrelsome and tearful, the girl developed into a most unpleasant character.

The general conclusion we can draw from this case and other cases resembling it, is that a child can satisfy his superiority striving by good behavior; therefore, we are never sure whether such good behavior will continue when the situation changes. The advantage of our psychological questionnaire is that it gives us a more comprehensive picture of the child and his activities, as well as his relationship to his environment and everyone in it. We will always have indications of his style of life, and when we have studied the child and the information gained from the questionnaire, we will find that his character traits, emotions, and style of life are all tools he uses to promote his striving for superiority, increase his feeling of importance, and obtain prestige in his world.

One type of child we frequently encounter in school seems to contradict this description. The indolent child is reserved, impervious to knowledge, discipline, or correction, living in a world of his own fantasy, and at no time displaying a striving for superiority. With enough experience, however, we can perceive how this behavior is also a form of striving, even though an absurd one. Such a child has no faith in his ability to achieve success by the usual means, so he avoids all means and opportunities for improvement. He isolates himself and gives the impression of a hardened character. This hardness, however, does not include his whole personality; behind it we can usually find an extraordinarily sensitive, trembling spirit which needs this outer callousness to protect itself from hurt. He encloses himself in an armor and nothing can come near him.

When we succeed in finding a way to induce this type to speak, we find that he is preoccupied with himself, daydreams constantly, and creates fantasies in which he appears great or superior. Reality is far from the daydreams of such children. They make believe that they are heroes, conquering all others; or tyrants who have robbed all others of power; or martyrs helping the suffering. We frequently find the tendency to play the savior among children, not only in their daydreaming, but in their actions. Some children can be depended on to spring to the rescue when another is in danger. Children who play the role of rescuer in their daydreams train themselves for the part in reality, and when not too discouraged, act the part when the opportunity offers.

Certain daydreams recur continually. In Austria during the time of the monarchy, many children had daydreams of saving the king or one of the princes from danger. The parents, of course, never know that their children have such ideas. Children who daydream a lot cannot adjust to reality and are unable to make themselves useful. For them, the gap between fantasy and reality is wide. Some choose the middle road: they retain their daydreaming while making a partial adjustment to reality. Others make no adjustment at all and withdraw more and more from the world into a private world of their own creation, while still others want to have nothing to do with products of the imagination and occupy themselves only with reality—stories of travel, or of hunting, history, etc.

Obviously, a child should have some imagination as well as a willingness to accept reality, but we must not forget that children do not regard these things as simply as we do and tend to divide the world sharply into two extremes. Most important, they tend to divide everything into opposites (above or below, all good or all bad, clever or stupid, superior or inferior, all or nothing). Adults also use this same antithetical scheme of apperception. Ridding ourselves of this type of thinking is difficult; for instance, thinking of hot and cold as opposites when we know scientifically that the only difference is in the degree of temperature. Not only do we frequently find this antithetical scheme of apperception among children, but we also find it in the beginnings of philosophical science. The early days of Greek philosophy are dominated by this idea of opposites. Even today, almost every amateur philosopher tries to measure values by means of opposites. Some of them have even established tables—life-death, above-below, and finally, man-woman. The present, childish division of everything into opposites and the old philosophical scheme of apperception are strikingly similar, and we may assume that adults accustomed to dividing the world into sharp contrasts have retained their childish way of thinking.

People who live according to such an antithetical device have a formula which can be expressed by the maxim "all or nothing." Of course, such an ideal is impossible to realize in this world, but nonetheless, they regulate their lives according to it. Human beings cannot have either all or nothing. A thousand and one gradations exist between these two extremes. We find this formula primarily among children who have a deep feeling of inferiority and become inordinately ambitious as a compensation. Several such characters are found in history, such as Caesar, for example, who was murdered by his friends when he sought the crown. Many of the peculiarities and character traits of children can be traced to this idea of all or nothing—for example, stubbornness. The lives of children provide so many proofs of this idea

The Education of Children

that we have been led to conclude that such children have developed a private philosophy, or a private intelligence contrary to common sense. As an illustration, consider the case of a four-year-old girl who was unusually stubborn and perverse. One day her mother brought her an orange and the child took it, threw it on the floor and said: "I don't want it when you bring it; I'll have it when I feel like having it!"

Indolent children who cannot have everything withdraw more and more into the emptiness of their daydreams, fantasies, and castles-in-the-air. We must not assume too quickly, however, that these children are lost. We know very well that hypersensitive natures easily withdraw from reality because their personally created fantasy world promises them protection from further wounding. But this withdrawal does not necessarily indicate complete maladjustment or unadaptability. A certain distance from reality is necessary not only for writers and artists, but also for scientists, who also need a good imagination. The fantasies evoked in daydreams are merely a detour which an individual attempts to take to avoid the unpleasantnesses and possible failures in life. We must not forget that precisely those people with rich imaginations who were later able to combine their fantasies with reality became the leaders of mankind. They became leaders not only because of better education and more perceptive observation, but also because of their courage and the positive attitude with which they approached the difficulties of life and successfully fought them. The biographies of great men often reveal that while they did not have much use for reality and were bad students as children, they did develop a remarkable ability to observe what went on around them; so that as soon as conditions became more favorable, their courage grew to the point where they once more approached reality and took up the fight. Naturally, there is no rule as to how to make great men out of children. However, we must remember never to approach children harshly, but to constantly encourage them, and always try to offer them an appealing, manageable picture of reality, so they do not create a gap between their fantasies and the world.

Chapter IX

The New Situation as a Test of Preparation

Psychic life is a unity, in the sense that all expressions of personality at any one time fit together on a continuum. The unfolding of personality in time takes place without sudden jumps. Present and future conduct is always consistent with past character. This is not to say that the events in an individual's life are automatically determined by the past and by heredity, but it does mean that the future and past fit together without a break. We cannot jump out of our skins overnight, although we never know what is in our skins—that is to say we never know our full capabilities, until the moment that we express them.

In this fact of continuity without automatic determinism, lies not merely the possibility of education and improvement, but also the possibility of detecting the state of character development at any given time. When an individual faces a new situation, his hidden character traits come out. If we could directly experiment with individuals, we could find out their state of development by putting them through new and unexpected situations. Their conduct in such situations must be consistent with their past character, and it reveals their character in a way that familiar situations do not.

We get perhaps the best insights into the character of children at those moments of transition, when they pass from home to school, or when their home conditions are suddenly changed. At that point, the limitations in the child's character come out as clearly as an image on a photographic plate put in a developing solution.

We once observed an adopted child. He was incorrigible, unpredictable, and prone to temper tantrums. When we spoke with him, he did not answer intelligently. He talked about things that had no connection with our questions. Considering the whole situation, we concluded that after he had been in the home of his foster parents for some months, he had developed a hostile attitude toward them. Consequently, he didn't like it there.

It was the only conclusion we could draw from the situation. His foster parents shook their heads at first and said that the child was well treated, in fact better than he had ever been treated before in his life. But that is not decisive. We often hear parents say: "We have tried everything with the child, gentleness and severity, and nothing has helped." Kindness by itself is not enough. Even though some children react favorably to kindness, we must not imagine that we have changed them. They believe that they are temporarily in a favorable position, but they have remained basically the same and the disappearance of the kindness would at once bring back the old condition.

We need to understand how a child feels and thinks—how he interprets his situation—and not what his parents think. We pointed out to the foster parents that this boy did not feel happy with them. We could not tell them whether or not he was justified in his attitude, but something must have happened to arouse such hate in him. We told them that if they did not feel capable of correcting his mistakes and winning his love, they would have to give him away to someone else, because he would continually rebel against what he considered an imprisonment. Later we heard that the boy had become a veritable fury, and was considered actually dangerous. He might have been slightly improved by gentle treatment, but that would not have been enough because he did not understand the whole scheme which became clear to us as we elicited further information. The real explanation of the case follows: He grew up with the children of his foster parents and believed that they did not care for him as much as they did for their own children. That is certainly no reason for such temper tantrums, but he wanted to get out of the house; consequently, every act which would further his desire seemed suitable to him. He acted intelligently in light of the goal he had set for himself, so we can disregard any consideration of possible feeble-mindedness. The family took some time to realize that they would have to give him away, if they felt incapable of changing his behavior.

When we punish such a child for his lapses, to him the punishment is a good reason for continuing his rebellion. It confirms his feeling that he is right in rebelling. We have a sound basis for our views, and from this perspective we can understand all of this boy's errors as the result of his fighting against his environment, the result of his facing a new situation for which he had not been prepared. Childish as these mistakes are, they need not surprise us, because we see the same childish manifestations in adult life.

The interpretation of gestures and subtle forms of expression is an almost unexplored field. The teacher is probably in the best position to arrange all these forms into a pattern and to examine their connection with each other and their origin. We must remember that one form of expression may have different meanings on different occasions and that two children can do the same thing without having it mean the same. Furthermore, the forms of expression in problem children vary even

The Education of Children

when they arise from the same psychological cause. In short, many roads exist to any specific goal.

We cannot speak here of right or wrong from the point of view of common sense. Children make a mistake because they have a mistaken goal. Consequently, what follows as the result of striving to achieve this goal is also mistaken. Although we have innumerable possibilities for making mistakes, only one correct path leads to productive, socially useful living.

Several significant forms of expression tend to be ignored, such as the position in sleep. An interesting case is that of a fifteen-year-old boy who suffered from the hallucination that the then Emperor Francis Joseph I had died and had appeared to him as a ghost, ordering him to organize an army and march against Russia. When we came to his room at night to see how he slept, we saw a striking picture. He was lying in bed in the position of Napoleon. When we saw him the next day, his posture was similar to the military pose expressed in his sleeping position. The connection between the hallucination and his waking attitude seemed rather clear. We inveigled him into a conversation in which we tried to convince him that the Emperor still lived. He did not want to believe it. He told us that he had always been teased about his small stature when he waited on the guests in the cafe. When we asked him if he knew someone who had the same posture in walking, he thought a little and then said, "My teacher, Mr. Meier." We seemed to be on the right track and were able to get over the difficulty by conjuring up the figure of Meier as another little Napoleon. What was still more important was this item: The boy told us that he would like to become a teacher. This teacher, Meier, was his favorite and he would like to imitate him in everything. In short, the whole life story of this boy was summed up in his posture.

A new situation tests a child's preparedness. If he has been well prepared, he meets new situations with confidence. If he lacks preparedness, a new situation brings a tension which leads to a feeling of incapacity. The feeling of incapacity distorts judgment, and his reaction is faulty—that is to say, it does not correspond to the demands of the situation—because it is not based on social feeling. In other words, a child's failure in school must be attributed not only to the inefficiency of the school system, but also to the primary deficiency in the child.

We must examine the new situation, not because we believe it causes the deterioration in a child, but because we know that it shows more clearly the primary inadequate preparedness. Every new situation may be regarded as a test of preparedness.

The Education of Children

In this connection we may again take up for discussion some points in the questionnaire (see Appendix I).

1. When did the cause for complaint begin? A new situation immediately catches our attention. When a mother remarks that her child was all right until he went to school, she tells us more than she really understands. The school has been too much for the child. It is not enough when the mother answers, "For the last three years." We must know what changes took place three years ago in the child's environment or in his own physical condition.

The first sign of a child's waning faith in himself is frequently found in his inability to adapt himself to school life. The initial failure is sometimes not taken seriously enough and may mean a catastrophe for the child. We must find out how often he has been spanked for receiving bad school grades, and what effect these grades or the spankings have had on his striving for superiority. The child may become convinced that he is incapable of accomplishment, especially if his parents are in the habit of saying, "You'll never amount to anything," or "You'll end up on the gallows."

Some children are spurred on by failure; others break down. Children who lose confidence in themselves and faith in the future must be encouraged. They must be treated gently, patiently, and tolerantly.

A brusque explanation of sex may shock a child into confusion. The brilliant success of a sister or brother may deter him from further effort.

2. Was it noticeable before? This means, was the child's lack of preparedness noticeable up to the time of change in his situation? We get all kinds of answers to this question. "The child was disorderly," which means that the mother used to do everything for him. "He was always timid," which means great attachment to the family. When a child is described as weak, we may assume that he was born with weak organs, was spoiled or pampered because of his weakness, or he may have been neglected because of ugliness. This question also refers to the possibility of feeble-mindedness. The child may have developed so slowly that he was suspected of being mentally deficient. Even though he later grew out of this condition, he would still retain the feeling of having been pampered or restricted, and these feelings would make much more difficult any attempt to cope with a new situation. If we are told that the child is cowardly and careless, we may be sure that he thereby secures someone's attention.

The first task of a teacher is to win the child, and thereafter to nourish his courage. When a child is clumsy, the teacher must find out

The Education of Children

whether he is left-handed. If he is clumsy to an exaggerated degree, the teacher should find out whether the child fully understands his sexual role. Boys who grow up in a feminine environment, avoid the company of other boys, or are teased, mocked, and often treated like girls accustom themselves to the part of girls, and later develop rather stormy internal conflicts. Ignorance of the organic sexual distinction between male and female leads children to believe that their sex can be changed. But they eventually discover that their physical constitution is unchangeable and try to compensate by developing either mental masculine or feminine traits, according to the sex to which they wish to belong. They express these tendencies in dress and deportment.

Some girls develop a loathing for feminine occupations. The chief reason is the supposed valuelessness of such work, which indeed expresses a basic failure of our civilization. The tradition still exists that men have privileges which are denied to women. Our civilization is distinctly to man's advantage and approves of certain rights which men assume for themselves. The birth of a son usually arouses more joy than the arrival of a daughter. This can only be a harmful influence on both son and daughter. The thorn of inferiority stings the girl very soon, while the boy feels burdened with expectations. Girls are restricted in their development. In some countries, such as America, this compulsive division is no longer so noticeable. But in social relationships, no balance has been achieved yet, even in this country.

We are concerned here with the whole mentality of mankind which is reflected in the children. The acceptance of the role of women involves some hardship which occasionally incites revolt. This revolt expresses itself frequently in unruliness, stubbornness, and indolence, all of which relate to a striving for superiority. When such symptoms appear, the teacher must find out whether the girl is dissatisfied with her sex.

This particular dissatisfaction may grow to include all other fields, so that life in general becomes a burden. Occasionally, we encounter the expression of a desire to live on another planet where mankind is not divided into two sexes. Such erroneous thought processes can lead to various absurdities, or to complete apathy, criminality, and even suicide. Punishment and lack of affection only strengthen the feeling of inadequacy.

Such unfortunate conditions can be avoided when the child learns in an unobtrusive fashion the difference between man and woman and is taught that each is worth as much as the others. Usually, the father seems to have a sort of superiority. He appears to be the possessor,

The Education of Children

makes the rules, directs, explains to his wife, and decides. Brothers try to be superior to their sisters, and make them dissatisfied with their sex by scorn and criticism. The psychologist understands that such conduct on the part of brothers springs from their own feeling of weakness. To be able to do something is quite different from merely seeming to be able. The argument that until now women have not been able to point to great accomplishments is quite worthless. Women have not previously been raised to do great things. Men have put stockings to mend in the hands of women, trying to convince them that this was their work. Although we have made some progress in this regard, the way we prepare girls today still does not indicate that we expect anything extraordinary of them.

To hinder preparation and then adversely criticize inferior accomplishment is short-sighted. Improving the present situation is not easy because not only fathers, but mothers as well look upon masculine privileges as justified and rear their children according to this idea. They teach their children that masculine authority is right, so their boys demand obedience and the girls resign themselves to it. Children should know as early as possible to which sex they belong, and also that their sex is unchangeable. Women, as we have said, have developed resentment against the masculine assumption of authority and superiority. When a woman's resentment is so great that she expresses it in refusing to accept her sex and strives to be as much like a man as possible, Individual Psychology calls her behavior, the "masculine protest." Secondary symptoms, such as deformity or incomplete development, often lead adults to doubt their sex in reference to anatomical norms (masculine physical characteristics in girls and feminine in boys). These beliefs are sometimes deeply embedded and related to constitutional weaknesses. A childish physical construction, more noticeable in the case of a man than a woman, leads to the remark that the man has feminine characteristics. This is untrue, for such a man more accurately resembles a child. A man whose body does not develop completely feels painfully inferior because the general ideal of our civilization is a fully grown man, whose achievements must surpass those of women. An incomplete development or lack of beauty in a girl also frequently leads to avoiding the problems of life because we overvalue beauty.

Disposition, temperament, and feelings are tertiary sexual indications. Sensitive boys are called feminine; poised, self-confident girls are described as masculine. Such traits are never innate; they are always acquired. These characteristics in early childhood are remembered later and adults refer to the fact that they were unusual as

The Education of Children

children, that they were withdrawn, or behaved like boys or girls, as the case may be. They developed according to the interpretation of their respective sexual roles. The further question, how far sexual development and experience has gone, means that a certain understanding is expected at a certain age. I have found that at least ninety per cent of the children, when parents or educators finally explain sexual matters to them, have already learned the facts long before. No hard and fast rules concerning sexual explanation can be made, because we cannot predict what a child will accept, or will believe in such an explanation, or in general what effect it will have on him. As soon as the child asks for an explanation, we should give it, after carefully considering the condition of the child at the time. Premature explanation is inadvisable, even though it does not always have a harmful effect.

The situation of an adopted child or a stepchild is a difficult one. Children belonging to either of these classes take good treatment as a matter of course and blame all severity on their special family position. Sometimes a child who has lost his mother attaches himself closely to his father. After a while, when the father re-marries, the child feels he has been shut out and refuses to make friends with the stepmother. Interestingly, a few children regard their real parents as stepparents, implying, of course, harsh criticism and complaint. Stepparents have acquired a bad reputation because of the many fairy tales in which they are the evil characters. Fairy tales, we may note in passing, are not ideal reading material for children. We cannot forbid them completely, because children learn a great deal about human nature from them. But we should have corrective comments written to accompany certain stories and to prevent children from reading tales containing cruelty or distorted fantasy. Fairy tales of strong men performing cruel deeds have been used occasionally to harden the child readers, to dwarf soft feelings —another mistaken idea springing from our hero worship. Boys think showing sympathy is unmanly. Scorning tender emotion is incomprehensible, because it is unquestionably valuable when it is not misused, although any emotion can of course be misused.

Illegitimate children, too, are in an extremely difficult situation. Obviously, having the woman and child bear the burden of illegitimacy while the man goes scot free is not right. The one who pays the greatest price is, of course, the child. No matter how we want to help such children, we cannot prevent their suffering, for their common sense soon tells them that all is not in order. They are scorned by their companions or else the laws of the country make living conditions hard, and illegitimacy is legally branded on them. Because of their sensitivity,

The Education of Children

they quarrel easily and develop a hostile attitude to the world, for every language has ugly, insulting, and painfully degrading words for such children. We can easily understand why so many orphans and illegitimate children become problem children and criminals. We cannot possibly attribute these asocial tendencies in illegitimate or orphaned children to innate or inherited dispositions.

Chapter X

The Child at School.

When a child enters school, he finds himself in an entirely new situation. Like all new situations, entrance into school can be regarded as a test of previous preparation. If the child has been properly trained, he will pass the test in a normal manner; if not, the defects in his preparation will become clearly apparent.

We do not often take records of a child's psychological preparedness at the time he enters nursery school and elementary school, but such records, if we had them, would shed great light on behavior in adult life. Such "new situation tests" would be infinitely more revealing than ordinary tests of scholastic performance.

What is demanded of a child when he enters school? Schoolwork demands cooperation with the teacher and with schoolmates, as well as an interest in the school subjects. By the child's responses to this new situation, we can measure his degree of cooperative ability and his sphere of interest. We can tell in what subjects he is interested; we can see whether he is interested in what another person says; we can tell whether he is interested in anything at all. We can ascertain all these facts by studying the attitude of the child, his posture and look, the way he listens, whether he approaches the teacher in a friendly manner, or whether he stays far away from him, etc.

How these details affect an individual's psychological development may be illustrated by the case of a certain man, who consulted a psychologist because he had difficulties in his profession. Looking back into the man's childhood, the psychologist discovered that he had grown up in a family in which all the other children were girls; also, the parents died soon after he was born. When the time came to enter school, he did not know whether he should register in the girls' or in the boys' school. Persuaded by his sisters to enter the girls' school, he was soon dismissed from there. We can imagine the impression this left on the child's mind.

Concentration on school subjects depends primarily on the child's interest in his teacher. Part of the teacher's art is to keep a child attentive and to find out when he is not attentive, or is unable to concentrate. Many children come to school without any ability to concentrate. Generally pampered, they are dazed by the presence of so many strange people. If the teacher happens to be a little strict, these children appear

The Education of Children

to have no memory. But this apparent lack of memory is not so simple as it is generally regarded. A child who is reproached by the teacher for having no memory has a memory for other things. He is even able to concentrate, but only for the situation in which he has been pampered at home. He is attentive to his desire to be pampered, but not for school work.

If such a child does not succeed in school, if he has bad grades and does not pass his examinations, criticizing or reproaching him is useless. Criticism and reproaches will not change his style of life. On the contrary, such things will convince him that he is not fit for school and will make him develop a pessimistic attitude.

Significantly, when pampered children are won over by the teacher, they are often very good students. They can work when they have a great advantage for themselves; unfortunately, we cannot guarantee that they will always be pampered at school. If the child changes schools or changes teachers, or even if he does not make progress in a particular subject (and arithmetic is always a dangerous subject for pampered children), he will suddenly come to a stop. He will not be able to proceed because he has been accustomed to having everything made easy for him. He has never been trained to struggle and does not know how to struggle. He has no patience for meeting difficulties and forging ahead by conscious effort.

We see, then, what sound preparation for school means. In bad preparation, we can always see the mother's influence. We can understand how she was the first to awaken the child's interest, and thus had the crucial responsibility of directing that interest into healthy channels. If she failed in her responsibility, as she often does, the result was evident in the child's behavior at school. In addition to the mother, every family member has an influence: the father, the rivalry of siblings, which we have analyzed in other chapters. Then, too, outside influences, bad circumstances and prejudices, all have an effect, about which we shall speak more in a succeeding chapter.

In short, with all these circumstances that explain the bad preparation of the child, we would be foolish to judge him on the basis of his scholastic record. Instead, we should take the school reports as indications of his present psychological condition. The grades themselves are not significant, but what they indicate as to his intelligence, interest, ability to concentrate, etc. Scholastic tests should not be interpreted differently from such scientific tests as intelligence tests, despite the difference in their construction. In both cases, the emphasis should be on what is revealed about the child's mind, and not the number of correct answers given to a test.

In recent years, so-called intelligence tests have been developed. They have a great weight with teachers, and sometimes they are worthwhile, because they reveal things not shown by the ordinary tests. Once in a while, they prove the salvation of a child. Thus, when a boy has had bad school reports and the teacher has wanted to put him in a lower class, the intelligence test may suddenly reveal a higher rating. Instead of being held back, the child is allowed to skip a grade. He feels successful, and thereafter acts differently.

We do not wish to undervalue the function of an intelligence test and of an I.Q., but we must say that when a test is used, neither the child nor the parents should know the I.Q. Neither the parents nor the child know the true value of an intelligence test. They imagine that it represents a final and complete point of view, that it indicates the fate of the child, who is henceforth limited by it. In reality, the findings revealed by intelligence tests are quite open to criticism, if they are taken as absolute findings. A good rating on an intelligence test is no guarantee for later life, and on the other hand, otherwise successful adults often make low scores.

Individual Psychologists have found that whenever intelligence tests reveal a great lack of intelligence, the scores can be improved, if we find the right methods. One of these methods is to let the child play with the particular intelligence test until he finds out the right trick, as well as the right preparation for taking such an examination. In this way, the child makes progress and increases his experience. He will make better scores on subsequent tests.

How much children are influenced by the school routine, and whether they are oppressed by the heavy school curriculum, are controversial issues. We do not undervalue the subjects in the school curriculum, and we do not believe that the number of subjects taught should be decreased. Clearly, subjects should be taught in a coherent manner so that children see their purpose and practical value, and do not regard them as purely abstract and theoretical. Many people now debate whether we should teach a child to learn subjects and facts, or educate the child's personality. We in Individual Psychology believe that the two can be combined.

As we have said, subjects of instruction should be made interesting and practical. Mathematics—arithmetic and geometry—should be taught in connection with the style and structure of a building, the number of people that can live there, etc. Some subjects can be

The Education of Children

taught together. In some of the more progressive schools, we have experts who know how to teach the interrelationships of subjects. They take a walk with the children and find out that they are more interested in certain subjects than in others. They learn to combine instruction; they learn to combine, for example, instruction about the plant with the history of the plant, the climate of the country, etc. In this way, they not only stimulate interest in subjects which would otherwise be uninteresting to the child, but they also give him a coordinated, interconnected approach to things, which is the final aim of all education.

Educators should not overlook that at school children feel they are in a personal competition, which affects their behavior. The ideal school class should be a cohesive unit, in which each of the children feels a part of the whole. The teacher should make sure that rivalries and personal ambitions are kept within bounds. Because children do not like to see others forge ahead, they either do not spare themselves in their efforts to overtake their competitors, or they fall back into disappointment and a subjective view of things. That is why the advice and direction of the teacher is so important; a proper word from him will transfer the energies of the child from competitive to cooperative channels.

In this connection, the institution of modified schemes of self-government in classes is helpful. We do not have to wait until children are completely ready for self-government to institute schemes of this kind. At first, we can allow children to merely watch what is going on, or to act in an advisory capacity. If children are allowed complete self-government without preparation, they are generally more severe and strict in their punishments than the teachers, or they may even use their political functions for personal advantage and superiority.

In terms of children's progress in school, we have to consider both the point of view of the teacher and the point of view of the children. Interestingly, children have very good judgment in this regard. They know who is the best in spelling, in drawing, in athletics. They can rate each other quite well. Sometimes they are not entirely just to others, but they realize this, and try to be fair. The great difficulty is that they minimize themselves: they believe, "Now, I can never catch up." This is not true; they can catch up. The mistake in their judgment must be pointed out to them; otherwise, it will become a fixed idea throughout life. A child who has such an idea will stay where he is and never progress.

The great majority of school children are usually at the same level; they are the best or the worst or the average, and they stay that way. This state of things does not reflect so much the development of the brain, as it does the inertia of psychological attitudes. It is a sign that children have limited themselves and cease to be optimistic after the first few mistakes. But, significantly, changes in relative position do take place once in a while, showing that no predetermination governs the intellectual status of a child. Children should be aware of this possibility for change, and be helped to understand its application in their own case.

Both the teacher and the children should also let go of the superstition that the results accomplished by children with normal intelligence can be attributed to special heredity. This belief in the inheritance of abilities is perhaps the greatest mistake ever made in regard to the education of children. When Individual Psychology first pointed out the error of this belief, people thought it was simply an optimistic conjecture on our part, not a generalization based on science. But now more and more psychologists and psychiatrists are coming to accept this point of view. Heredity is too easy a scapegoat for parents, teachers, and children. Whenever difficulties requiring effort arise, they can call upon heredity to relieve them of any responsibility for doing things. But we have no right to escape our responsibilities, and we should always be suspicious of any points of view that have the effect of releasing us from them.

No educator who believes in the value of his work, who believes in education as the training of character, can consistently accept the doctrine of heredity. We are not concerned with physical heredity. We know that organic defects, even differences in organic ability are inherited. But where is the bridge between the functioning of organs and the ability of the mind? In Individual Psychology, we have insisted that the mind experiences the degree of ability possessed by the organs and has to deal with it. Sometimes the mind overreacts, in that it gets frightened by some organic disability, and the fear lasts long after the organic cause is removed.

People like to trace things back to their origins, seeking the roots from which a phenomenon has developed. But this point of view, which we constantly use in evaluating individual achievements, is very misleading. The usual error in this process is to neglect most of the ancestors, forgetting that if we are to construct family trees, every generation has two parents. If we trace back five generations, there are 64 ancestors, and among 64 ancestors we can surely find a clever person to whom we can attribute the ability of his descendant. If we go back ten

The Education of Children

generations, we have 4,096 ancestors, and then undoubtedly we will find one very able person in the lot, if not more than one. We must also remember that the tradition established in a family by one extremely able person resembles the working of heredity. We can thus understand how some families produce more able people than other families, but not because of inheritance. Just consider how things used to work out in Europe when each child was forced to continue in the profession of the father. If we forget the social institutions, the statistics of heredity can be made to look quite formidable.

Next to the idea of heredity, the problem that causes the greatest difficulties for a child is punishment for bad school grades. If a child has bad grades, he is also not well liked by the teacher. He thus suffers in school, and then comes home and finds new scenes and new reproaches from his parents. His mother and father scold him, and often spank him as well.

Teachers should keep in mind the aftermath of bad report cards. Some teachers believe that a child will struggle harder if he has to show a bad report at home. But they forget the particular home circumstances. In some homes the child is brought up in a rather cruel manner, and a child of such a home will think twice before bringing back a bad report. As a result, he may not come at all, or sometimes he may be driven to the extremes of despair and commit suicide from fear of his parents.

Although teachers are not responsible for the school system, they can temper the impersonal severities of the system with a personal touch of sympathy and understanding. Thus, a teacher could be gentler with a particular student because of his home environment, and by being gentler could encourage him instead of driving him to despair. A child who consistently gets bad grades has a heavy weight on his mind, and when everyone tells him he is the worst student in the school, he eventually believes it himself. If we identify ourselves with such a child, we can readily understand why he does not like school. His response is only human. If anyone were in a place where he was constantly criticized, received bad grades, and lost hope of ever catching up, he would not like the place and would try to escape from it. And so we should not be surprised when we see such children staying away from school.

But while we should not be alarmed at such an occurrence, we should realize its significance. We should realize that it means a bad beginning, especially if it happens in the period of adolescence. Such children are clever enough to protect themselves by forging report cards, playing truant, etc. In this way, they meet others of their own kind, form gangs, and start out on the road that leads eventually to crime.

All this can be avoided if we accept the point of view of Individual Psychology that no child should be thought hopeless. We must feel that a method can always be found to help a child. Even in the worst of circumstances, we can still find some way to help him.

We almost do not need to mention the bad results of making children repeat classes. A teacher will agree that a child who repeats a class is a problem both for the school and for the family. This may not happen in every case, but the exceptions to the rule are few. Most of who repeat a class are chronic repeaters; they remain backward, presenting a problem which has been evaded, but not solved.

When to let a child repeat a class is a difficult question. Some teachers manage to avoid the problem successfully. They use the vacation periods to train the child, searching for the mistakes in his style of life and correcting them, so they are able to let him go on to the next class. This method could be practiced more widely, if we had the institution of special tutors at school. We have social workers and home teachers, but no tutors.

The institution of home teachers does not exist in Germany, and they do not seem entirely necessary. The classroom teacher in the public school has the best overall view of the child. He can know what is going on more than others, if he looks properly. Some say that overcrowding prevents the classroom teacher from knowing individual students. But if a teacher observes how a child enters school, he can soon see the student's style of life and avoid many difficulties. He can accomplish this task even with a great crowd. We can educate a large group of children better if we understand them than if we do not understand them. Overcrowded classes are far from a blessing and should be avoided, but they are not an insuperable obstacle.

From the psychological point of view, teachers should not change each year—or every six months as they do in some schools—but advance with the class. Keeping a teacher with the same children for two, three, or four years, would he a great advantage all around. Then the teacher would have an opportunity to know all the children intimately. He would be able to know the mistakes in each one's style of life and correct them.

Children often skip grades. Whether this practice has any advantage is debatable. Often, they fail to satisfy the high expectations that have been awakened in them by the skipping process. Skipping a grade should be considered in the case of a child who is too old for his grade. It should also be considered in the case of a child who was backward before and has since developed and improved. Skipping a

The Education of Children

grade should not be held out as a reward for better grades or because a child knows more than others. It is more to the advantage of a bright child, if he devotes time to extra-curricular studies, like painting, music, etc. What the bright child learns in this way benefits the whole class, because it stimulates the others. Depriving a class of the better students is not good. While some say we ought to separate the outstanding and bright children, we do not believe it. We believe rather than the bright children push the whole class forward , giving it a greater impetus for development.

Examining the two types of classes at school, the advanced and the remedial, is interesting. Amazingly, in the advanced classes a few are actually slow learners, while the remedial classes are not primarily composed of slow learners, as most people think, but of children from poor families. Children of poor families get the reputation for being slow because their preparation is not so good. And we can readily understand this situation. Because the parents have too much to do, they are not able to devote any time to the children, or perhaps they are not educated enough for this purpose. Such children who lack psychological preparation should not be put into the remedial classes. Being in a remedial class stigmatizes a child, who is then ridiculed by his peers.

A better way to take care of such children would be to apply the method of tutors, which we have already mentioned. Besides tutors, clubs should be available, where children could go for extra tutoring. There they could do their home work, play games, read books, etc. In this way, they would get training in courage instead of training in discouragement, which is what they get from classes for slow children. Such clubs, when combined with more playgrounds than we now have, would keep children completely off the streets and away from bad influences.

In all discussions of educational practice, co-education comes up. In principle, we should promote it. It is a good way for girls and boys to get to know each other better. However, co-education involves special problems that must be considered, or else the disadvantages will outweigh the advantages. For example, people tend to overlook that until their sixteenth year, girls develop more quickly than boys. If the boys do not realize this and see the girls get ahead faster than they do, they lose their balance and enter into a senseless race with the girls. Facts like these must be taken into consideration, either by the administration or by the classroom teacher.

A teacher who likes co-education and understands the problems involved can make it work successfully. But a teacher who does not like co-education will feel burdened by the system, and in his class co-education will fail.

If the co-educational system is not properly administered and if the children are not properly led and supervised, of course, problems involving sexuality will occur. For instance, sex education in school presents a complicated problem. In fact, school is not the right place for sex instruction, because the teacher cannot know how the children will take his words when he speaks before a whole class. If the children ask for information privately from the teacher, that is a different matter. If a girl asks the teacher for facts, he should answer correctly. In a later chapter, we will discuss sexual issues further.

Returning now to the main heart of the problem, after our digression on the more or less administrative phases of education, we find out how to educate children by identifying their interests and the subjects in which they can be successful. Nothing succeeds like success. This is as true of education as it is of other phases of life. And it means that if a child has an interest in one subject and succeeds in it, then he will be stimulated to go on to other things. The teacher's task is to utilize the students' successes as stepping-stones to greater knowledge. The student alone does not know how to do this—to lift himself by his bootstraps, so to speak, as all of us must do to ascend from ignorance to knowledge. But the teacher can arrange this building of confidence from success, and if he does, the student will see the point and cooperate.

What we have said about subjects of interest applies also to the sense organs of children. We must find out which sense organ is the most used and what type of sensations fascinate the child most. Many children are better trained in seeing and looking, others in listening, still others in moving, etc. In recent years, vocational schools have come into favor, and they utilize the sound principle of combining subjects of instruction with training of the eyes, ears, and hands. The success of these schools indicates the importance of harnessing the physical interests of the child.

If a teacher finds a child of the visual type, he should understand that this student will have less difficulty in subjects requiring him to use his eyes, such as geography. He will do better seeing, rather than listening to a lecture. This is a sample of the sort of insight into the problems of a particular child that a teacher should have. A teacher can get many other similar insights from his first look at a child.

In short, the ideal teacher has a sacred, fascinating task. He molds the minds of children, holding the future of mankind in his hands. But how shall we pass from the ideal to the actual? Envisioning

The Education of Children

educational ideals is not enough. We must find a method to implement them. Long ago, in Vienna, the present writer started out to find such a method, and the result was the establishment of advisory, or guidance, clinics in the schools (see *Guiding the Child*).

These clinics put the knowledge of modern psychology at the service of the educational system. A competent psychologist who understands not only psychology, but the life of the teachers and parents as well, joins the teachers to hold a consultation clinic on a certain day. On that day, the teachers meet to bring up their particular cases of problem children. They will be cases of lazy children, children who disrupt the class, children who steal, etc. The teacher describes his particular cases, the psychologist shares his own related experiences, then the discussion starts. What are the causes ? When did the situation develop? What should be done? The family life of the child and his whole psychological development are analyzed. With their combined knowledge, the group comes to a decision as to what should be done with a particular child.

At the next session, the child and the mother are both present. After the group has decided on the manner of influencing her, the mother is called in first. The mother listens to the explanation of why the child has failed. Then she tells her side of the story, and a discussion starts between the mother and the psychologist. Generally, the mother is quite happy to see all these signs of interest in her child's case, and is glad to cooperate. If she is unfriendly and antagonistic, then the teacher or the psychologist begins to speak about similar cases and other mothers until the resistance is overcome.

Finally, when the method of influencing the child is agreed on, he enters the room. He sees the teacher and the psychologist, and the psychologist talks to him, but not about his mistakes. The psychologist speaks as in a lecture, analyzing objectively—but in a way the child can grasp—the problems, reasons, and ideas responsible for the failure of children to develop properly. He shows the child why he felt discouraged, why he thought other children were preferred, how he came to despair of success, etc.

This method has been followed for nearly fifteen years. The teachers who have been trained in it are quite happy, and would not think of dropping the work they have been carrying on so successfully.

As for the children, they have gained doubly from this process. Those who were originally problem children have been made whole; they have learned courage and the spirit of cooperation. Others, who have not been called into the consultation clinics, have also benefited.

The Education of Children

When a situation that threatens to become a problem arises in the class, the teacher will propose that the children talk the matter out. Of course, the teacher directs the discussion, but the children participate and have full opportunity for expression. They begin to analyze the causes of a problem—say, laziness in the class. By the end, they will reach some conclusion, and the lazy child, who does not know that he is the intended target, will, nevertheless, learn a great deal from the discussion.

This summary account indicates the potential benefits of combining psychology and education. Psychology and education are two aspects of the same reality and the same problem. To influence the mind, we need to know how it works, and someone who knows the mind and how it works cannot help but use his knowledge to inspire others to higher and more universal goals.

Chapter XI

Influences From Outside

The broad psychological and educational outlook of Individual Psychology takes into consideration the "influences from outside." The old type of introspective psychology was so narrow that, in order to take care of what it had left out, Wundt invented a new science, Social Psychology. This is not necessary with Individual Psychology, which is both individual and social. It does not concentrate on the individual mind to the exclusion of the environment which stimulates the mind, or on the environment to the exclusion of its significance to particular minds.

No educator or teacher should believe that he is the only educator of a child. The waves of outside influence stream into the psyches of children and shape them directly or indirectly, by influencing the parents and bringing them to a certain state of mind which is transferred to the children. All this cannot he avoided, and it must therefore be taken into account.

First, the educator should consider economic circumstances. We must remember, for example, that some families live for generation after generation under very pressing circumstances, carrying on their struggle with a sense of bitterness and sorrow. They are so much affected by this sorrow and bitterness that they cannot educate a child to take a healthy, cooperative attitude. They live on the limits of human endurance, where people cannot work cooperatively because they are constantly worried and fearful.

Then, too, we must not forget that a long period of semi-starvation or bad economic circumstances influences the physical health of both parents and children, which in turn has an important psychological impact. We see this situation in the children born in postwar Europe. They are much more difficult to bring up than previous generations. Besides economic circumstances and their effect on child development, we must also remember the effect of parental ignorance of physical hygiene. This ignorance goes hand in hand with the timid, coddling attitude of parents. Parents want to pamper children and are afraid to cause them any pain. Sometimes they are careless, and they imagine, for example, that a curvature of the spine will be outgrown. They do not call for the doctor at the right time. Of course, this is a mistake, especially in cities where medical service is always available.

The Education of Children

If not corrected in time, a serious physical deficiency may lead to a severe and dangerous illness, which may leave bad psychological scars. All illness is a "dangerous corner" psychologically, and needs to be avoided as much as possible.

If these dangerous corners cannot be avoided, they can be made much less dangerous by developing the attitude of courage and social-mindedness in children. In fact, a child is psychologically affected by illness only to the degree that he is not social-minded. A child brought up in an environment where he feels a part of the whole will not be affected as much by a dangerous illness as a pampered child.

Case histories often show the beginning of psychological troubles after such diseases as whooping cough, encephalitis, chorea, etc. Although we may imagine that these illnesses cause psychological difficulties, they merely provide the occasions that bring out the hidden character flaws in a child. During his illness, a child feels his power, and discovers how he can rule the family. He has seen terror and anxiety on his parents' faces during the illness, and knows that it is all on his account. After the illness, he wants to stay at the center of attention, so he tries to dominate his parents with his whims and demands. Of course, this happens with a child who has never been socially trained and needs merely the opportunity to manifest his selfish strivings.

On the other hand, sometimes an illness may be the occasion of an improvement in a child's character. In the case of a second child of a schoolteacher, the teacher was very concerned about this boy, and did not know what to do with him. He sometimes ran away from home, and was the worst student in his class. One day, just as the father was about to send him away to a reformatory, doctors discovered the boy was suffering from tuberculosis of the hip. This disease requires the constant care of the parents over a long period. When the boy finally recovered, he became the best child in the family. All he needed was the extra attention from his parents which the illness provided. The reason he had been disobedient before was because he had felt overshadowed by a brilliant older brother. Because he could not be appreciated like his brother, he constantly rebelled. But the illness convinced him that he, too, could be appreciated by his parents in the way that his older brother was, so he learned to behave well.

Children's minds are often deeply impressed with the memory of illnesses they have gone through. Such things as dangerous illness and death surprise and astonish them. The mark left on their minds comes out later in life, when we find many people interested only in sickness and death. Some find a healthy way to harness their interest in sickness by becoming doctors or nurses. But many others live fearfully, and sickness becomes an obsession with them which stands in the way of their useful work. An examination of the biographies of more than a hundred girls revealed that nearly fifty per cent confess that the greatest fear they have in life is the thought of illness and death.

Parents should make sure that children are not too impressed by their childhood sicknesses. They should prepare their minds for such possibilities and spare them sudden shocks. They should teach them that life is limited, but long enough to be worthwhile.

Another "dangerous corner" of childhood life is meeting with strangers, acquaintances, or friends of the family. Mistakes are made in these encounters because these people are not really interested in what is best for the children. They like to amuse the children or do things which can influence them a great deal in a short time. They praise the children excessively, leading them to be conceited. In the short time they spend with them, they manage to pamper them, thus making trouble for their regular educators. All this should he avoided. No stranger should interfere in the educational methods of the parents.

Again, strangers often misunderstand the sex of a child, calling a boy "a pretty girl" or vice versa. This, too, should be avoided, for the reasons which we discuss in the chapter on adolescence.

The general home environment is naturally important because it gives children an indication of the extent to which the family takes part in social life. In other words, it give them the first impressions about co-operation. Children who grow up in an isolated family draw a sharp line between members of the family and outside people. They feel as if a chasm separates the home and the outside world, which of course they regard in a hostile light. An isolated family life does not promote social relationships and it inclines the children to be constantly suspicious, looking out only for their own interests. In this way, it handicaps the development of social-mindedness.

At the age of three, a child should already be prepared to join other children in games and should not be scared by the presence of strangers. Otherwise, he will later become bashful and self-conscious, taking a hostile attitude toward others. Generally, we find this trait among pampered children, who want to "exclude" others.

If a parent occupies himself early with the correction of such traits, he can be sure that the child will be spared a great deal of trouble later on. If a child has had good training in his first three or four years, if he has been taught to play with others and join in the community spirit, he will be spared not only bashfulness and selfishness, but also possible neurosis and insanity. Insanity and neuroses occur only in individuals who live in isolation, who have no interest in others, and who have no skill in cooperation.

While we are on the subject of family environment, we will mention the difficulties arising from a change in economic circumstances. If a family has once been rich, particularly when a child was very young, and then lost its money, this obviously presents a difficulty. Such a situation is hardest on a pampered child, for he is not prepared for circumstances under which he cannot get as much attention as before. He misses his past advantages and longs for them.

Suddenly becoming rich also brings difficulties for a family in the bringing up of children. Here the parents are not prepared for the proper use of their wealth, and they make mistakes especially in regard to the children. They want to give the children a good time; they want to pamper and spoil them because they feel they no longer need to restrain themselves on anything. As a result, we often find problem children among families that are newly rich. The son of a newly rich father is a notorious example of this type of problem child.

Such difficulties and even disasters can be avoided if a child is properly trained in cooperation. All these situations are like open doors through which a child can escape the necessary training in cooperation, so we must be especially watchful for this reason.

Not only are children influenced by abnormalities in material circumstances, such as poverty or sudden riches, but they are also influenced by abnormalities in psychological circumstances. Certain psychological prejudices may result from the family situation. These prejudices may arise from personal acts, for example, if the father or mother has done something socially disgraceful. In that case, the child's mind will be greatly affected. He will face the future in fear and trepidation. He will want to hide from his peers, afraid of being discovered as the child of such a parent.

The parents have a responsibility not only to provide an education in reading, writing, and arithmetic for their child, but also to give him the proper psychological basis of development so that he will not have to bear greater difficulties than others. Thus, if a father is an alcoholic, or if he is high-tempered, he must remember that it all affects the child. If the marriage is an unhappy one, if the husband and wife constantly quarrel, the child pays.

These childhood experiences are like living inscriptions in the soul of the child, which he cannot easily forget. He can, of course, overcome their effects if he has been trained in cooperation. But the

The Education of Children

very situations which create these difficulties for the child prevent him from getting that training from his parents. That is why a concerted movement has begun recently to organize child guidance clinics in the schools. If for some reason, the parent fails in his task, his work must be taken over by a psychologically trained teacher who can guide the child to a healthy life.

In addition to the prejudices arising from personal circumstances, some prejudices are related to nationality, race, and religion. These prejudices affect not merely the child, who is humiliated, but also the aggressive ones who do the humiliating. They become arrogant and conceited; they believe that they belong to a privileged group, and when they try to live up to the privilege which they have erected for themselves, they end up as failures.

The prejudices between nations and races are of course the basic causes of war, that great scourge of mankind which must be abolished, if progress and culture are to be saved. The teacher's task is to show war in its true light, and not give a child an easy, cheap opportunity to express his superiority striving by playing with guns and swords. These war games are not the proper preparation for a cultured life. Many boys join the army as a result of the military education of childhood, but besides those who join the army, a hundred times more are psychologically crippled for the rest of their life by their childhood warrior games. They go through life like warriors, with chips on their shoulders, never learning the art of getting along with their fellow men.

Around Christmas time and other seasons for toys, parents should keep an eye on the type of toys and games they put into children's hands. They should get rid of weapons and war games, as well as all books that worship war heroes and deeds of fighting.

Although a great deal can be said about the proper selection of toys, the principle is that we should select the type of toys that will stimulate a child to be cooperative and constructive in his activities. We can easily understand that games in which a child can work and build things are more worthwhile than ready-made or finished toys, which require a child merely to fondle a doll or an imitation dog, etc. Incidentally, in regard to animals, children should be instructed to treat an animal not as toy or a game, but as a companion. While he should not be afraid of animals, he also should not dominate them or be cruel to them. Whenever children exhibit cruelty to animals, we may suspect they have a desire to dominate and bully people weaker than themselves. If any animals, birds, dogs, or cats, are in the house, the children should be taught to regard them as living beings who feel and experience pain

The Education of Children

similar to human beings. Proper comradeship with animals may be regarded as a preparatory stage for social cooperation with people.

Relatives are part of the environment of children. First, we have to consider objectively the plight and situation of the grandparents, whose position is something of a tragedy in our culture. When people grow up, they should have room to develop further; they should have more occupations and interests. But just the reverse happens in our society. Old people feel shut out, so to speak, relegated to a corner, which is a pity. They could accomplish much more and be infinitely happier if they had more opportunity for working and striving. We should never advise a man at the age of 60, 70, or even 80 to retire from his business. Continuing in business is much easier than changing our whole way of life. But owing to our mistaken social customs, we put old people on the shelf while they are still full of activity. We give them no opportunity for continued self-expression. As a result, what happens? The children pay for the mistakes we make with the grandparents. We have put grandparents in the position of having to prove what they should not have to prove, that they are still alive and count in the world. In trying to prove their worth, they tend to interfere with the education of the grandchildren. They often pamper them terribly, in a disastrous attempt to prove that they still know how to bring up children.

We should avoid hurting the feelings of these good and kind old people. But while they should be given an opportunity for more activity, they should also be taught that children must grow up as independent human beings, not as the playthings of other people. They should not be exploited according to the exigencies of family politics. If the elderly have arguments with the parents, let them win or lose the arguments, but do not let them try to put the children on their side.

When we study the biographies of psychological patients, we often find that they were the favorites of their grandmothers or grandfathers. We immediately understand how this contributed to their childhood difficulties. Their favoritism either meant pampering, or stirring up rivalries and jealousies in relation to the other children. Also, many children say to themselves, "I was the favorite of my grandfather," then feel hurt if they are not the favorite of other people.

The "brilliant cousins" may also play a major role in a child's life, often as a great nuisance. Sometimes they are not only brilliant, but also beautiful, and we can readily see what trouble it creates for a child to be reminded that he has a brilliant or beautiful cousin. If he is courageous and social-minded, he will understand that to be bright means simply to be better trained, so he will look for a way to overtake the brilliant cousin. But if he believes, as most often happens, that brilliance is a blessing from nature—that people are born brilliant—then he will feel inferior and badly treated by fate. In this way, his whole development will be hindered. As for beauty, surely a gift of nature, but one constantly overvalued in our civilization, we can also see the mistakes in a child's style of life which may arise when the child smarts under the painful thought that he or she has a beautiful cousin. Even after twenty years, people still feel sharply the childhood envy of a beautiful cousin.

The only way to combat the ravages of this cult of beauty is to teach children that health and the ability to get along with our fellow beings are more important than beauty. Obviously, beauty has value, and a beautiful race of people is more desirable than an ugly race. But in any rational planning of things, one value cannot be isolated from the rest and held up as the supreme goal. This is what happens with beauty. We can conclude that beauty is not sufficient for a rational and good life by observing how many extremely handsome boys, as well as ugly ones, become criminals. We understand how these handsome boys may have become criminals. They knew they were handsome, so they thought everything would come their way. Therefore, they were not properly prepared for life. Later on, however, they found they could not solve their problems without effort, so they took the road of least resistance. As the poet Virgil said, "facilis descensus Averno," -- The descent to hell is easy.

A word should he said about reading matter for children. What kinds of books should be given to children? What should be done with fairy tales? How should a book like the Bible be read to them? The main point here is that we generally overlook that a child understands things in an entirely different way from an adult. We also overlook that each child grasps things along the line of his own particular type of interest. If he is a timid child, he will find in the Bible and in fairy tales stories that approve of his timidity and make him dread dangers. Fairy tales and Bible passages need to be commented on and interpreted, so that a child gets the intended meaning, not the one his subjective fancy dictates.

Of course, fairy tales are enjoyable reading, even for adults. But their sense of remoteness from particular times and places needs to be corrected. Children seldom understand the differences of time periods and cultures. When they read a fairy tale written in a totally different age, they do not make allowance for the difference in outlook. Most tales have a prince, who is always praised and decorated, and his whole character is presented in a very alluring fashion. Clearly, the circumstances described never existed, but they represent the fictional idealization relevant to a particular period when worshiping the prince was necessary. Children should be told about such things. They should be told about the make-believe behind the magic; otherwise, they may grow up looking for an easy way out of things, like a certain boy of twelve, who, when asked what he wanted to be, said, "I want to be a magician."

Fairy tales, when properly interpreted, can be used as a vehicle for instilling in children the sense of cooperation, as well as for enlarging their outlook. In regard to motion pictures, taking a one-year-old child to see a film holds no danger, but older children will misunderstand the pictures. They often misunderstand even plays based on fairy tales. Thus, a four-year-old child saw a certain fairy tale performed in a theatre. Years later, he still believed that there were women in the world who sell poisoned apples. Many children do not understand the theme correctly, or else they make sweeping generalizations. The parent's job is to explain things until he is sure they have understand properly.

One outside influence children can be spared is the reading of newspapers. Newspapers are written for adults and do not have the child's point of view. Some places have special children's newspapers, which is good. But the ordinary newspaper gives a distorted picture of life to the unprepared child. A child can easily believe that our whole life is full of murders, crimes, and accidents. Accident reports are specially depressing to young children. We can gather from remarks of adults how much they were afraid of fire during childhood, and how this fear has continued to obsess their minds.

These examples comprise merely a small selection of the outside influences which parents and educators should consider in the education of children. They are, however, the most important, and they illustrate the general principles involved. Again and again, the Individual Psychologist has to insist upon the watchwords, "Social Interest" and "Courage." Here, as in other problems, the same slogans hold true.

The Education of Children

Chapter XII

Adolescence and Sex Education

Whole libraries have been written about adolescence. The topic is indeed an important one, but for a different reason than most people imagine. Adolescents are not all alike; we find all varieties of children in this category: striving, clumsy, neat, dirty, etc. We also find adults and even old people who look and act like adolescents. From the point of view of Individual Psychology, this is not surprising, and it means that these adults have stopped at a certain stage of development. In fact, for Individual Psychology, adolescence is simply a stage of development through which all individuals must pass. We do not believe that any stage of development, or any situation, can change a person. But it does act as a test—as a new situation, which brings out the character traits developed in the past.

For example, in his early years, a child may be closely watched, not have much power, and not able to express what he wants. In the stage of adolescence, when he experiences rapid biological and psychological development, such a child will act as if he has lost his chains. He will go ahead quickly and his personality may develop in a rebellious direction. However, other children will begin to stop and look back, and by looking back toward the past, they will fail to find the right way in the present. They are not interested in life, and become very reserved. Their hesitation is a sign, in their case, not of energies held in leash in a repressed childhood and finding their release in adolescence, but rather of a pampered childhood which has deprived them of the proper preparation for life.

In adolescence, we are able to read a person's style of life better than ever before. The reason is, of course, that adolescence is nearer the front lines of life than childhood. We can now see better how he will behave toward others. We see whether he can make friends easily, whether he can be a fellowman who is socially interested in others.

Sometimes this social interest takes on an exaggerated expression, and some adolescents have lost the sense of balance, wanting only to sacrifice their lives for others. They overdo social contribution, which may also prove an obstacle to their development. We know that if a person really wants to be interested in others and work for the common cause, he must first take care of himself. He must have something to give of himself, if the giving is to mean anything.

191

On the other hand, we see many youths between fourteen and twenty who feel altogether lost socially. At fourteen, they have left school, losing touch with all their former companions; and it will take them a long time to form new ties. In the meantime, they feel entirely isolated.

Then we face the issue of occupation. Here again adolescence is revealing. It will reveal the attitude formed in the style of life. We will find some youths becoming independent and working marvelously. They will show that they are on the proper road to development. Others, however, will come to a stop in this period. They will not find the right occupation for themselves; they will constantly be changing—either changing jobs or changing schools. Or else they will be idle, not wanting to work at all.

None of these symptoms is created in adolescence; they are merely brought to the surface more clearly in this period. If a person really knows a particular child, he can predict how he will behave in the period of adolescence, when he is given opportunities to express himself more independently than in the period when he was watched, guarded, and restricted.

We turn to the third fundamental problem of life: love and marriage. What does the adolescent's answer to this problem reveal about his personality? Again we see no break with the pre-adolescent period, only a heightened psychological activity which makes the answers more clear-cut than before. Some adolescents have complete confidence about how to behave; they face the problem of love either romantically or courageously. In any case, they find the right norm of behavior toward the other sex.

At the other extreme, some become terribly shy about the problem of sex. Now that they are much nearer the front lines, so to speak, they show their lack of preparation. The personality indications derived from adolescence provide a reliable judgment as to the course of behavior in later life. We know what must be done, if we want to change the future.

If an adolescent seems antagonistic toward the other sex, we will find that he was probably a fighting child. Perhaps he felt depressed because another child was preferred. As a result, he now believes that he must prove his strength, be arrogant, and avoid displays of feeling. His attitude toward sex thus reflects his childhood experiences.

An adolescent may want to leave home, perhaps because he has never been satisfied with conditions there, and now aches for the first opportunity to break home ties. He does not want to be supported any more, although continuing the support is really in the best interests of both the child and parent. Otherwise, in case things go wrong for him, the parents' lack of help becomes an alibi for his failure.

Children who remain at home, but use every possible occasion to stay out at night, express the same tendency, to a smaller degree. Going out at night to seek amusement is, of course, much more appealing than staying quietly at home. It is also an implicit accusation against the home, and a sign that at home the child does not feel free, but guarded and watched. Thus, he has not had the opportunity to express himself and make his own mistakes. The period of adolescence is a dangerous time to make a beginning in this direction.

Many children also feel a sudden loss of appreciation more sharply in adolescence than they have felt before. Perhaps they had been good students at school and highly appreciated by their teachers; then they were suddenly transferred to a new school, to a new social environment, or to a new occupation. Then, too, we know that often the best students do not continue to be the best in adolescence. Although they seem to undergo a change, in reality they have not changed; the situation has changed. And the new situation reveals their character in ways the old one did not.

From all this, we can conclude that one of the best preventives for the troubles of adolescence is the cultivation of friendship. Children should be good friends with one another, with members of the family, as well as with people outside the family. The family should be a unit in which everyone trusts each other. The child should trust his parents and his teachers. Indeed, the only type of parent and teacher who can continue in his capacity as guide to the adolescent is one who has previously been a friend and sympathetic fellowman. A child will immediately shut out any other kind of parent or teacher during this period, not sharing any confidences with him, and even regarding him as a complete outsider or enemy.

At this time, girls may reveal their dislike of the feminine role, and try to imitate boys. Of course, they can more easily imitate boys in the adolescent vices, such as smoking, drinking, and joining gangs, than in the virtues of hard work. Also, the girls have the excuse that if they did not copy such behavior, the boys would not be interested in them.

If we analyze this masculine protest of the adolescent girl, we find that she never liked the feminine role from early childhood. However, her dislike was previously hidden, and emerges clearly only in adolescence. This is why observing the behavior of girls at this time is

The Education of Children

so important, for it is then that we find out how they stand in regard to their sex role of the future.

Boys at this age often like to play the role of a man who is extremely wise, brave, and self-confident. Others fear their problems, not trusting themselves to be really and completely men. If their education for the male role has been in any way deficient, this is the time when the defect will appear. They will seem effeminate, will like to behave like girls, and will even imitate the vices of girls: being coquettish, posing, etc.

Parallel with this feminine extreme, we also find boys who excel in the typically boyish traits, which may be carried to the extreme of vice. They will excel in drinking and sexual excesses. Sometimes they will even begin to commit crimes merely out of a desire to show off their manliness. Such vices are found among boys who want to be superior, to be leaders, and to astonish their comrades.

Behind the bravado and ambition of this type, however, often hides a secret trait of cowardice. Recently, we have had some notorious examples of this in America: types like Hickman, Leopold and Loeb. If we examine the careers of such people, we find that they were prepared for an easy life and always looked for easy successes. Such types are active but not courageous, just the right combination for criminality.

We often find children at the adolescent age striking their parents for the first time. If we do not look for the hidden unity behind their actions, we could imagine that these children have suddenly changed. But if we study what happened before, we realize that the individual is quite the same in character, only now he has more power and more possibilities for action.

Another aspect of adolescence is that every child, at some point, feels the need to prove that he is no longer a child. Of course, this is a treacherous feeling, for every time we feel the need to prove something, we usually go too far. And so the child also goes too far.

This is indeed the most significant symptom of adolescence. And the way to counteract it is by explaining to the youth that he does not have to convince us that he is no longer a child; we do not need proof. By telling him this, we may avoid the exaggerated features we have mentioned.

Among girls we often find a type inclined to exaggerate sexual relationships and become "boy-crazy." These girls constantly fight with their mothers and believe they are suppressed (and perhaps they really are suppressed); they have relationships with any man they meet in order to spite their mother. They are quite happy in the knowledge that their

The Education of Children

mother will be upset if she finds out. Many adolescent girls have had their first sexual relationship with a man after running out of the house because of a quarrel with their mother, or because their father was too severe.

It is ironic to think of girls being suppressed by their parents in order that they may be good girls, and then turning out bad because of the parents' lack of psychological insight. The fault in such cases does not lie with the girls but with the parents, because they have not properly prepared the girls for the situations they will face. They have sheltered the girls too much before adolescence; consequently, they have failed to develop in them the judgment and self-reliance necessary for confronting the pitfalls of adolescence.

Sometimes the difficulties appear not in adolescence but after it, in marriage. The principle is, however, the same. The girls were simply fortunate enough not to encounter an unfavorable situation in adolescence. But sooner or later, an unfavorable situation is bound to occur, and they must be prepared for it.

A single case history will be cited here to illustrate concretely the problem of the adolescent girl. The girl in this case was fifteen years old and came from a very poor family. Unfortunately, she had an older brother who was always sick and had to be nursed by the mother. The girl noticed the difference in attention from her early childhood. What complicated matters was that when she was born, her father was also sick, and her mother had to take care of both him and the brother. The girl had a double example of what it means to be nursed and get extra attention, so she wanted passionately to be cared for and appreciated by people. She could not find this appreciation in the family circle, especially as a younger sister was soon born into the family and deprived her of the modicum of attention that she still had. Now as fate would have it, when the younger sister was born the father got well, so that the baby got more attention than she herself had received during her infancy. Children notice these things.

The girl made up for her lack of attention at home by striving hard at school. She made herself the best student in her class, and because she was such a good student, she was given the opportunity to continue her studies and go through high school. But when she entered high school, a change took place. Her grades deteriorated, because her new teacher did not know her (and did not appreciate her). Still eager for appreciation, she now lacked it both at home and at school. She had to get her appreciation somewhere. And so she went out to look for a man who would appreciate her. She lived with the man for a fortnight.

Then the man got tired of her. We could have predicted what would happen; we could have predicted that she would realize that this is not the appreciation she wanted. In the meantime, the family became worried and started a search for her. Suddenly they received a letter from her, saying, "I have taken poison. Do not worry— I am happy." Suicide was obviously her next thought, after being defeated in her quest for happiness and appreciation. Nonetheless, she did not commit suicide; she used suicide to scare her parents into forgiveness. She continued to run around the streets, until her mother found her and brought her home.

If the girl had known, as we know, that her whole life was dominated by the striving to be appreciated, then all these things would not have happened. Also, if the teacher at the high school had realized that she had always done well in her studies and all she needed was some measure of appreciation, the tragedy would again not have taken place. At any point in the chain of circumstances, a proper handling of the girl could have prevented her going to ruin.

This brings up the matter of sex education, which has been frightfully exaggerated in recent times. Many people, if we may say so, seem to be insane on this subject. They want sex education at any and all ages, and they play up the dangers of sexual ignorance. But if we look into our own past and into the past of others, we do not see such great difficulties or such great dangers as they imagine.

The experience of Individual Psychology teaches that a child should be told at the age of two that he is a boy or a girl. At that time, it should also be explained to him that his sex can never be changed, and that boys grow up to be men and girls grow up to be women. If this is done, then the lack of other knowledge is not so dangerous. If he clearly understands that a girl will not be educated like a boy, or a boy like a girl, then the sex role will be fixed in his mind and he will be sure to develop and prepare for his role in a normal manner. However, if he believes that through some trick he can change his sex, then trouble will result. Trouble will also result if the parents express a desire to change the sex of a child. In *The Well of Loneliness,* we find an excellent literary presentation of this situation. Parents too often like to educate a girl like a boy, or vice versa. They photograph their children dressed in the clothes of the opposite sex. Also, sometimes a girl may look like a boy, then people in the environment begin talking to her as if she were a boy. This may start a great confusion, which can easily be avoided.

Any discussion about the sexes which tends to undervalue the female sex and regard boys as superior should be avoided. Children

The Education of Children

should be made to understand that both sexes are of equal worth. This is important not merely in order to prevent an inferiority complex on the part of the members of the undervalued sex, but also to prevent a negative effect on children of the male sex. If boys were not taught to think that they are the superior sex, they would not consider girls as mere objects of desire. Nor would they view the relationship between the sexes in an ugly light if they knew their future tasks.

In other words, the real problem of sex education is not merely explaining to children the physiology of sexual relationships; it involves the proper preparation of the whole attitude toward love and marriage. This is closely related to the question of social adjustment. If a person is not socially adjusted, he will make a joke out of the question of sex and look at things entirely from the point of view of self-indulgence. This happens of course all too often, reflecting the defects of our culture. Women have to suffer because in our culture, men play the leading role. But the man also suffers because by means of this fictitious superiority, he loses touch with the core sense of human values.

Children do not need the physical phase of sex education very early in life. We can wait until a child becomes curious, until he wants to find out certain things. When a mother and father are interested in a child, they will know the proper time to take the lead, if the child is too shy to ask questions. If he feels that his father and mother are friends, he will ask questions, and then the answers must be given in a manner proper to his understanding. We must avoid giving answers that stimulate the sex drive.

In this connection, we do not need to be alarmed by premature manifestations of the sex instinct. Sexual development begins very early, in fact in the first weeks of life. An infant experiences erogenous pleasures, and sometimes tries to stimulate the erogenous zones. We should not be frightened if we see signs of the beginning of certain behaviors, but we should do our best to hinder these practices without seeming to attach too much importance to them. If a child finds out that we are worried about these matters, he will continue his habits deliberately in order to gain attention. These actions make us think he is a victim of the sex drive, when he is really exploiting a habit as a tool for showing off. Generally, little children try to gain attention by playing with their genital organs because they know their parents are afraid of this practice. The psychology is similar to when children play sick, because they have noticed that when they are sick, they receive more attention and pampering.

Children should not be stimulated physically by too much kissing and embracing. It is cruel to the child, especially in the adolescent period. Nor should children be stimulated mentally on the subject of sex. Often, a child will discover some frivolous pictures in the father's library. We hear constantly of such cases in the psychological clinics. Children should not have access to books dealing with sexual matters on a level above their age. Nor should they be taken to see motion pictures that exploit sexuality.

If we avoid all such forms of premature stimulation, we have no need to fear. We need merely to speak at the right time in a few simple words, never upsetting the child and always giving answers in a true, clear manner. Above all, we must never lie to a child, if we want to retain his trust. If the child trusts the parent, he will discount the explanations he hears from his companions—perhaps ninety per cent of mankind get their sexual knowledge from companions—and will believe what the parent says. Such cooperation and camaraderie between child and parent are far more important than the various subterfuges used in the belief that they help the situation.

Children who experience too much of sex, or experience sex too early in life, generally shrink from sex later on. This is why parents should avoid having children notice their love-making. If possible, children should not sleep in the same room—and certainly not in the same bed—with the parents. Also, sisters and brothers should not sleep in the same room. Parents must be alert to see that children behave properly, and they should also be on the watch for outside influences.

These remarks sum up the most important items in the matter of sex education. We see here, as in all other phases of education, the primary importance of the sense of cooperation and friendliness within the family. With this cooperation, and with an early knowledge of the sex role and of the equality of men and women, a child is well prepared for any dangers he may face. And above all, he is well prepared for carrying on his work in a healthy manner.

The Education of Children

Chapter XIII

Pedagogical Mistakes

In raising children, a parent or teacher must never allow some things to discourage him. He must not despair because his efforts do not achieve immediate success; he must not anticipate defeat because the child is lethargic, apathetic, or extremely passive; nor must he permit himself to be influenced by the superstition that some children are gifted or ungifted. Individual Psychology claims that the effort should be made to stimulate the mental capacities of all children by giving them more courage, more faith in themselves, and the belief that difficulties are not insurmountable obstacles, but problems to face and conquer. These efforts will not guarantee success, but the many successful cases more than compensate for the less successful ones. In the following case, our efforts were successful.

A twelve-year-old boy was in his sixth year at elementary school. He was not in the least disturbed by his bad grades. He had an unusually unfortunate past history. Because of rickets, he could not walk until he was about three years old. At the end of his third year, he was able to speak only a few words. When he was four, his mother took him to a child psychologist who told her that the case was hopeless. The mother, however, did not believe this, and placed him in a child guidance institute. There, he developed slowly and without much help from the institute. When he was six, the institute authorities decided he was able to enter school. During the first two years at school, he received extra tutoring at home, so that he was able to pass his school examinations. He managed to get through the third grade and through the fourth as well.

At school, he attracted attention with his indolence; he complained that he could not concentrate or listen attentively. He did not get along well with his schoolmates, was teased by them, and appeared weaker than the others. Among all his schoolmates, he had only one friend whom he liked very much and with whom he went walking. He found the other children disagreeable and was unable to make contact with them. The teacher complained that the boy was weak in arithmetic and could not write, even though he was convinced that the boy was capable of accomplishing as much as the others.

In the light of the boy's past history and what he had already been able to do, his treatment had clearly been based on a mistaken diagnosis.

Here was a child suffering from an intense feeling of inferiority, in short, an inferiority complex. He had an older brother who got along very well. His parents claimed that the older brother was able to enter high school without ever studying. Parents like to say that their children do not have to study anything, then the children themselves like to boast about it. Obviously, learning without some sort of studying is impossible. This older brother probably trained himself to do most of his studying in the classroom by listening intently and retaining what he heard and saw at school. Children who do not pay so much attention in school have to do their studying at home.

What a difference between the two boys! Our child had to live constantly under the oppressive feeling that he was less capable than his brother, and that he was worth infinitely less than he. He probably heard this often enough from his mother when she was angry with him, or from his brother who used to call him a fool or an idiot. His mother said that the older brother often kicked the younger when the latter did not obey him. We had the result before us: a human being who believed that he was worth less than others. Life seemed to confirm his belief. His schoolmates laughed at him; his schoolwork was always faulty; he said he could not concentrate. Every difficulty frightened him. His teacher remarked from time to time that the child did not belong in that class or in that school. We can easily understand how the child believed he could not possibly avoid the situation into which he had fallen, and was convinced that the opinion others had of him was correct. It is pathetic when a child is so discouraged that he has no faith in the future.

We could easily see this child had lost his faith, not because he trembled and grew pale when we began to chat with him in a cheery fashion, but from a small sign which should always be noted. When we asked him how old he was (we knew that he was twelve), he answered: "Eleven years." Such an answer should never be considered an accident, because most children know exactly how old they are. We have often had occasion to determine that such mistakes have underlying reasons. When we consider what has happened in this child's life, then remember his answer, we get the impression that he is trying to recapture his past. He wants to return to the past, to the time when he was smaller, weaker, and even more in need of help than he is now.

We can reconstruct his system from the facts we already know. This child does not seek his salvation in the accomplishment of those tasks usually given to a child of his age; but he believes and behaves as if he were not as fully developed as others and could not compete with them. This state of feeling behind the others is expressed in the

The Education of Children

reduction of his years. He may possibly answer, "eleven years," and behave, under certain circumstances, like a child of five. He is so convinced of his inferiority that he attempts to adjust all his activities to this supposed state of being backward.

The child still wet himself in the daytime and was unable to control his bowel movements. These symptoms appear when a child believes, or wants to believe, that he is still a baby. They confirm our statement that this boy wanted to cling to the past, and return to it if possible.

A governess in the house had been there before the child was born. She was very attached to him, and took the mother's place whenever possible, acting as his support. We could draw further conclusions. We already know how the boy lived, we know that he did not like to get up early in the morning. A description of how long he took to get up was given to us with a gesture of disgust. Our conclusion was that he did not like to go to school. A boy who does not get along with his schoolmates, who feels oppressed, who does not believe that he is capable of accomplishing anything, cannot possibly want to go to school. As a result, he will not want to get up in time for school.

However, his governess said that he did want to go to school. In fact, when he was sick recently, he begged to be allowed to get up. This does not contradict in the least what we said. The question to be answered is, "How can the governess make such a mistake?" The circumstances were clear and amusing. When the boy was sick, he could permit himself to say that he wanted to go to school, because he knew positively that his governess would reply, "You cannot go because you are sick." His family, however, did not understand the seeming contradiction, and they were confused in their attempts to do something with the boy. We also had frequent opportunities to observe that the governess was incapable of understanding what was actually going on in the boy's mind.

Something else had developed which was the immediate cause of bringing the boy to us. He had taken money from the governess to buy candy. This also meant that he was behaving like a small child. To take money for candy is extremely childish. Very young children carry on in this fashion when they cannot control their greed for candy; they are the children who also cannot control their bodily functions. The psychological significance of this behavior is: "You must watch me; otherwise, I am capable of doing something naughty." The boy constantly tried to arrange situations that would make others occupy themselves with him because he had no confidence in himself. When we compared his situation at home and at school, the connection was clear. At home, he could get people to occupy themselves with him; in school, he could not. But who attempted to do something to correct the child's conduct?

Until the boy was brought to us, he was regarded as a backward, inferior child, and he did not in the least deserve this classification. He was a completely normal child who could accomplish as much as any of his schoolmates as soon as he regained faith in himself. He had always been inclined to view everything pessimistically, to accept defeat before he had made one step forward. His lack of self-confidence was expressed in every gesture and was confirmed in his teacher's report: "Cannot concentrate; weak memory; inattentive; has no friends; etc." His discouragement was so obvious that no one could overlook it, and circumstances were so much against him that changing his point of view would have been been difficult.

After our Individual Psychological questionnaire had been filled out, the consultation followed. We had to confer not only with the boy, but also with a whole group of people. First, we saw the mother, who had long since given him up as hopeless and only tried to keep him going so that he would eventually be able to do some sort of work. Second, we met with the older brother, who looked on the younger boy with contempt.

Our boy naturally had no answer to the question, "What do you want to be when you grow up?" This lack of response is unusually characteristic. We are always suspicious when a half-grown child really does not know what he wants to become. People do not generally land in the profession they chose as children, but that does not matter. They are, at least, led by an idea. In their earliest years, children want to become chauffeurs, watchmen, conductors, or whatever positions visible to them appear attractive to their childish opinions. But when a child has no material goal in view, we suspect that he wants to keep his eyes away from the future, to return to the past, or, in other words, to avoid the future and all problems connected with it.

This conclusion seems to contradict one of the basic claims of Individual Psychology. We have always spoken of the striving for superiority characteristic of children, and we have attempted to show that every child wants to develop himself, to become bigger than the others, to accomplish something. Suddenly, we have before us a child of whom the contrary can be said; a child who wants to go backwards, wants to be small and have others support him. How do we explain it? Movements in mental life are not always simple. They have a complicated

The Education of Children

background. Were we to draw naive conclusions in complicated cases, we would be mistaken. All these complications are tricky, and any dialectical attempt to make the opposite out of the thing itself, as for example, to say that the boy struggles in a backward direction because he appears in that way, the biggest, and in the safest position, is confusing unless we understand the whole picture completely. Actually, these children are correct in an amusing way. They can never be as strong or as dominating as when they are really quite small, weak, and helpless, and nothing is demanded of them. This child, who had no confidence in himself, was afraid he could not accomplish anything. Are we then to assume that he will willingly face a future which will expect something from him? He must avoid every situation in which his strength and abilities will be used to measure him as an individual. Nothing remains, therefore, but a greatly restricted sphere of activity where little will be asked of him. In this way, we can understand how merely a small portion remains of his striving for recognition, the recognition which he received as a tiny child dependent on others.

We had to confer not only with the boy's teacher, his mother, and older brother, but also with his father and with our colleagues. Such a string of conferences entails much work, and a great deal of labor could be saved if we could win the teacher over. This is not impossible, but it is not simple. Many teachers still cling fast to old methods and beliefs, regarding psychological examinations as something extraordinary. Many of them fear that a psychological examination indicates a loss of power, or else they regard it as an unwarranted interference. This is, of course, not so. Psychology is a science which cannot be learned all at once, but must be studied and practiced. It is, however, of little use when someone has the wrong point of view.

Tolerance is also a necessary quality, especially for a teacher, and having an open mind to new psychological ideas is wise, even when they seem to contradict the views we have previously held. As conditions exist to-day, we have no right to contradict flatly the opinion of the teacher. What are we to do in such a difficult situation? In our experience, nothing remains to be done in such cases but to take the child out of his difficult predicament, in other words, to remove him from that particular school. This procedure hurts no one. Practically no one knows what is going on, but a burden falls from the shoulders of the boy. He enters a different situation where everything is new to him. He can take care not to let other people think badly of him, not to let himself be held in contempt by others. How this is arranged is not easy to explain. Family circumstances have a great deal to do with it. Probably every case requires a slightly different handling. However, dealing with such children will be much easier when we have many teachers trained in Individual Psychology, who will regard such cases with understanding eyes and be able to help the children in school.

Chapter XIV

Educating the Parent

As we have frequently indicated, this book is addressed to parents and teachers, both of whom may profit equally from new psychological insight into the mental life of the child. In the last analysis, whether the education and development of the child take place primarily under the auspices of the parent or the teacher does not matter much, provided the child gets the proper education. We are referring of course to extra-curricular education, not the teaching of academic subjects, but the development of personality, which is the most important part of education. Now, although both the parent and the teacher can each contribute his share in this educational work, the parent correcting the deficiencies of the school, and the teacher correcting the deficiencies of the home, in our large cities and under modern social and economic conditions, the greater part of the responsibility falls on the teacher. On the whole, parents are not as open to new ideas as teachers, who have a professional interest in the education of children. The hope of Individual Psychology in preparing the children of tomorrow rests primarily on converting the schools and the teachers, although we, naturally, welcome the cooperation of parents.

In the course of the teacher's educational task, conflict with parents inevitably arises. Conflict is all the more inevitable in that the teacher's correctional work presupposes in some measure the failure of the parents. In a sense, it is an accusation of the parent, who often feels it as such. How should the teacher handle the parent in this type of situation?

The following remarks are addressed to this problem. They are written, of course, from the point of view of the teacher, who needs to handle the parent as a psychological problem. Unfortunately, some of the parents in question may find the following remarks uncomfortable to read.

Many teachers have remarked that approaching the parents of a problem child is often more difficult than approaching the child himself. Consequently, a teacher must always proceed tactfully. He must act on the assumption that the parents are not responsible for all the bad qualities the child shows. After all, parents are not trained educators, and they usually have only tradition to guide them. When they are summoned to school because of their children, they come feeling like accused criminals. Such a mood, revealing as it does some inward consciousness of guilt, demands the most tactful treatment from the teacher. Therefore, the teacher should try in such cases to change the parents' mood to a friendly, freer one, placing himself at the disposal of the parents as an assistant and relying on their good intentions.

The parents should never be reproached, even when there are just grounds. We can achieve much more when we succeed in establishing a sort of pact, when we persuade the parents to change their attitude and work with us according to our methods. Pointing out to them the faults in their past treatment does no good. Our aim should be to persuade them to try a new procedure. Telling them that they have done this or that incorrectly, only offends them and makes them unwilling to co-operate. As a rule, the deterioration of a child does not take place out of a clear sky; there is always a past history. The parents come to school in the belief that they have overlooked something. They should not be permitted to feel that we think so; they should not be spoken to condescendingly or harshly. Suggestions to parents should not be made in an authoritative manner. The sentences should always include "perhaps," "probably," "possibly," "you might try it this way." Even if we know exactly where the mistake is and how it should be corrected, we should never point it out to the parents bluntly, as if we want to force them. Needless to say, not every teacher has this much tact, nor can he acquire it suddenly. Interestingly, Benjamin Franklin expresses the same thoughts in his autobiography. He writes:

"A Quaker friend, having kindly informed me that I was generally thought proud, that my pride showed itself frequently in conversation, that I was not content with being in the right when discussing any point, but was overbearing and rather insolent, of which he convinced me by mentioning several instances, I determined to endeavor to cure myself,if I could, of this vice or folly among the rest, and I added Humility to my list, giving an extensive meaning to the word.

I cannot boast of much success in acquiring the reality of this virtue, but I had a good deal with regard to the appearance of it. I made it a rule to forbear all direct contradiction to the sentiments of others, and all positive assertion of my own. I even forbid myself the use of every word or expression in the language that imported a fixed opinion, such as certainly, undoubtedly, etc., and I adopted, instead of them, I conceive, I apprehend ,or I imagine a thing to be so or so, or so it appears to me at present. When another asserted something that I thought an error, I denied myself the pleasure of contradicting him abruptly and of showing

The Education of Children

immediately some absurdity in his proposition; and in answering I began by observing that in certain cases or circumstances his opinion would be right, but in the present case there appeared or seemed to me some difference, etc. I soon found the advantage of this change in my manner; the conversations I engaged in went on more pleasantly. The modest way in which I proposed my opinions procured them a readier reception and less contradiction; I had less mortification when I was found to be in the wrong, and I more easily prevailed with others to give up their mistakes and join with me when I happened to be in the right.

And this mode, which I at first put on with some violence to natural inclination, became at length so easy, and so habitual to me, that perhaps for these fifty years past no one has ever heard a dogmatic expression escape me. And to this habit (after my character of integrity), I think it principally owing that I had early so much weight with my fellow-citizens when I proposed new institutions, or alterations in the old, and so much influence in public councils when I became a member; for I was but a bad speaker, never eloquent, subject to much hesitation in my choice of words, hardly correct in language, and yet I generally carried my points.

In reality, there is, perhaps, no one of our natural passions so hard to subdue as pride. Disguise it, struggle with it, beat it down, stifle it, mortify it as much as one pleases, it is still alive, and will every now and then peep out and show itself; you will see it, perhaps, often in this history; for, even if I could conceive that I had completely overcome it, I should probably be proud of my humility."

Franklin's words probably do not fit every situation in life, which can neither be expected nor demanded. His attitude, nevertheless, shows us how unsuitable and unsuccessful aggressive opposition may be. No basic law in life suits every situation. Any rule goes only so far and then suddenly becomes unworkable. Certainly, at times a strong word may be appropriate. However, when we consider the situation between the teacher and the worried parents, who have already experienced humiliation and are prepared for further humiliation because of their child, and when we also consider that without the parents' cooperation we can do nothing, obviously, Franklin's method is the only logical one to adopt in order to help the child.

Under such circumstances, when proving we are right or superior is not important, but when we need to prepare the road we must follow to help the child, we naturally encounter difficulties. Many parents do not want to hear any suggestions. They are astonished or indignant, impatient and hostile, because the teacher has placed them and their child in such an unpleasant situation. Such parents have usually been trying for some time to close their eyes to their child's faults, to blind themselves to reality. Suddenly, their eyes are forcibly opened for them. The whole matter is most disagreeable, and we can understand how a teacher who approaches such parents harshly, or with little tact, loses all possibility of winning them over to his side. Many parents go even further. They meet the teacher with a verbal tide of indignation, making themselves unapproachable. In such cases, the teacher does better to show them that he needs their assistance; he must quiet them and bring them to the point of speaking in a friendly manner. We must remember that parents are often so entangled in the meshes of traditional, antiquated methods that they cannot free themselves quickly.

For example, when a father has discouraged his child badly by stern words and a sour facial expression, to suddenly assume a friendly expression and speak kindly to him, after ten years, is naturally hard. Furthermore, when a father suddenly changes his whole attitude toward his child, the latter will not believe at first that the change is a sincere one. He will regard it as a trick and will have to gain confidence slowly in his parent's changed demeanor. Highly intellectual people are no exception. In one case, a high school principal had driven his son almost to the point of breakdown by constant criticizing and nagging. The principal realized this in a conversation he had with us; then he went home and delivered a scathing sermon to his son. He had lost his temper again because his son had been lazy. Every time his son did something which did not please him, the father lost his temper and spoke cruelly. When this is possible with a man who considers himself an educator, we can imagine how it is with those parents who have grown up with the dogmatic idea that every child must be punished for his mistakes by a whipping. A teacher must use every device known to diplomatic art, every tactful phrase he can think of in his conversations with parents.

We must also remember that the custom of educating children with physical blows is widely spread in the poorer classes. Consequently, a child from this economic background, going home after a corrective conference with the teacher, often finds a continuation in the form of a whipping from his parents awaiting him. Sadly, our educational efforts are all too frequently rendered futile by the unwise parental treatment at home. In such cases, children are often punished twice for the same mistake, when we believe that once is enough.

We know the terrible results that sometimes follow such double punishment. Take the case of a child who must bring home a bad report card. Afraid of a whipping, he does not show it to his parents, and then

The Education of Children

afraid of punishment at school, he plays truant, or else he forges his parent's signature to the card. We must not overlook these facts, nor must we regard them lightly; we must regard the child in relation to the various elements in his environment. We must ask ourselves: What happens now when I take action? How will it affect this child? What assurance do I have that it will have a beneficial effect on him? Has the child reached a point where he can endure a failure, and will he be able to learn something constructive from it?

We know how differently children and adults react to difficulties. We must be most careful in reeducation and must be reasonably certain of results before we attempt to change a child's life style. Someone who has always proceeded with deliberation and objective judgment in the education and reeducation of children will be able to predict with greater accuracy the results of his efforts. Pedagogical work requires practice and courage, as well as the unshakable belief that no matter what the circumstances, we can always find a way to prevent a child from becoming discouraged. First, it is never too early to start. Someone who regards a human being as a unity and symptoms as part of that unity, will be able to understand and help a child far better than someones who seizes on a symptom and treats it according to some rigid scheme—such as a teacher who, when a child has failed to do his homework, immediately writes a note about it to the child's parents.

We are entering a period of new ideas, new methods, and new understanding in the education of children. Science is doing away with old, worn out customs and traditions. The knowledge we are gaining places more responsibility on the teacher, but as a compensation, it gives him far more understanding of the problems of childhood and with it far greater ability to help the children who pass through his hands. The important thing to remember is that a single behavior has no meaning when detached from the personality as a whole, and we can understand it only when we study it in connection with the rest of the human being.

Appendix I

An Individual Psychology Questionnaire

For the Understanding and Treatment of Problem-Children, Drawn up by the International Society of Individual Psychologists.

1. Since when has there been cause for complaint? What sort of situation (psychic or otherwise) did the child find himself in when his failings were first noticed?

> The following are important: change of environment, beginning of school life, births in the family, younger or older brothers and sisters, failures in school, changes of teachers or school, new friendships, illnesses of the child, divorce, new marriage, death of the parents.

2. Were any peculiarities noticed at an earlier age in regard to mental or physical weakness, timidity, carelessness, reserve, clumsiness, envy, jealousy, dependence on others when eating, dressing, washing or going to bed? Was the child afraid of being alone or of darkness? Does he understand his sexual role? Any primary, secondary or tertiary characteristics of gender? How does he regard the other sex? How far has he been enlightened on his sexual role? Is he a stepchild? Illegitimate? A foster child? Orphan? How did his foster parents treat him? Does he still have contact with them? Did he learn to speak and walk at the right time? Without difficulty? Was the teething normal? Noticeable difficulties in learning to read, draw, sing, swim? Is he particularly attached to either his father, his mother, his grandparents, or his nurse?

> We should notice any hostile attitude toward life, causes for the awakening of inferiority feelings, tendencies to exclude difficulties or people, and traits of selfishness, hypersensitivity, impatience, greediness, or excessive caution.

3. Does the child give much trouble? What and whom does he fear most ? Does he cry out at night? Does he wet the bed? Is he bossy toward weaker, or younger children? Does he show a strong desire to

The Education of Children

sleep in his parents' bed? Is he clumsy? Did he suffer from rickets? What about his intelligence? Is he teased and ridiculed? Is he vain about his appearance in regard to his hair, clothes, shoes, etc.? Does he bite his nails or pick his nose? Is he greedy when eating?

> These questions aim to clarify whether the child strives for significance with greater or lesser activity, and furthermore, whether defiance has prevented the adaptation of his impulses to the culture.

4. Does he make friends easily? Does he show tolerance toward people and animals, or does he molest and torment them? Is he fond of collecting or hoarding? What about avarice and covetousness? Does he lead others? Is he inclined to isolate himself?

> These questions relate to the child's ability to make contact and the degree of his discouragement.

5. With reference to all the above questions, what is the present position of the child? How does he conduct himself in school? Does he like school? Is he punctual ? Is he excited before going to school? Is he in a hurry? Does he lose his books, schoolbag, exercise books? Is he excited about his studies and before examinations? Does he forget to do his schoolwork, or does he refuse to do it? Does he waste his time? Is he lazy? Does he concentrate? Does he disturb the class? How does he regard the teacher? Is he critical, arrogant, or indifferent? Does he ask others to help him with his lessons, or does he wait until he is invited? Is he ambitious in gymnastics and sports? Does he consider himself comparatively untalented, or entirely so? Is he a great reader? What sort of literature does he prefer?

> These questions reveal the child's preparation for school, the result of the going-to-school "experiment," and his attitude toward difficulties.

6. Correct information about home circumstances: illness in the family, alcoholism, criminal tendencies, neurosis, disability, syphilis, epilepsy, the standard of living. Any deaths in the family, and how old was the child when they occurred ? Is he an orphan? Who is the dominating spirit of the family? Is the upbringing strict, nagging, or pampering? Are the

children made afraid of life? How is the supervision? Are there stepparents?

> From these questions, we see the child in his family position and can assess what impressions he received.

7. What is the child's position in regard to his place in the family constellation? Is he the eldest, youngest, only child, only boy, only girl? Is there rivalry, much crying, malicious laughter, a strong tendency to depreciate others?

> The above is significant for the character of the child and his attitude toward people in general.

8. Has the child formed any ideas about the choice of a profession? What does he think about marriage? What profession do the other members of the family follow? What about the married life of the parents?

> This information helps us determine whether the child has courage and confidence fin the future.

9. What are his favorite games, stories, characters in history and fiction? Does he like to spoil other children's games? Is he imaginative? Is he a coolheaded thinker? Does he indulge in daydreaming?

> These questions are in reference to a possible tendency to play the hero in life. A contrast in the child's behavior may be regarded as a sign of discouragement.

10. Earliest recollections? Impressive or periodical dreams about flying, falling, powerlessness, late arrival at railway station, or anxiety dreams?

> In this connection, we often find a tendency toward isolation, warnings to be careful, ambitious traits, and a preference for particular people, country life, etc.

11. In what respect is the child discouraged? Does he consider himself neglected? Does he respond readily to attention and praise? Does he have superstitious ideas? Does he avoid difficulties? Does he try his

The Education of Children

hand at various things only to give them up again? Is he uncertain about his future? Does he believe in the harmful effects of heredity? Was he systematically discouraged by those around him? Is his outlook on life pessimistic?

> Answers to these questions will help us prove that the child has lost confidence in himself and is now moving in a wrong direction.

12. Does he have further bad habits? Does he make faces? Does he act stupid, childish, or funny?

> These are not very courageous attempts to attract attention.

13. Does he have speech disabilities? Is he ugly? Clubfooted? Knock-kneed or bow-legged? Stunted? Abnormally stout or tall? Badly proportioned? Does he have physical abnormalities of the eye or ear? Is he mentally backward? Left-handed? Does he snore at night? Is he remarkably handsome?

> These questions refer to life difficulties which the child usually overrates, thus becoming discouraged. We also often see faulty development in the case of very pretty children who become obsessed with the idea that they should get anything they want without exerting themselves. Such children miss numerous opportunities to prepare themselves for life

14. Does he often talk of his incapacity, his "lack of talent" for school, for work, for life? Does he harbor suicidal thoughts? Do his failures and troubles connect in terms of timing? Does he overrate apparent success Is he servile, bigoted, or rebellious?

> Here we have manifestations of extreme discouragement, mostly apparent after vain efforts on the part of the child to get rid of his troubles. His failures are due partly to the ineffectiveness of his efforts, and partly to a lack of understanding from those around him. The symptoms are substitute satisfactions in a "Set "Sebenkriegsschatiplatz" ("secondary theater of operations": editor's note).

The Education of Children

15. Name the things in which the child is successful.

> Such "positive performances" give us important hints, for it is possible that the interests, inclinations, and preparations of the child point in a different direction from that which he has taken so far.

From answers to the above questions (which should never be put in rigid sequence or routinely, but casually and by way of conversation), we can form a correct notion of the uniqueness of the individual child. Although a child's failures are not justified, we will be able to understand them. The errors disclosed should always be explained in a patient and friendly way, without any threats.

The Education of Children

Appendix II

Five Case Histories With Commentaries
I
Case One

A boy, fifteen years old, is the only child of parents who have worked hard to achieve a modestly comfortable existence. They have been careful to see that he has everything necessary for physical health. In his early years, he was happy and healthy. His mother is a good woman, but she cries too easily. She makes her report about her son with much effort and many interruptions. We do not know the father, but the mother describes him as an honest, energetic man who loves his family and who has much confidence in himself. When the boy was very young and was disobedient, the father would remark, "It would be a fine state of affairs if I couldn't break his will." His idea of "breaking" was setting the boy a good example, not bothering to teach him much, but whipping him whenever he did something wrong. In early childhood, the boy expressed his rebelliousness by wanting to play master of the house, a desire frequently found in the spoiled. Only child. He showed early a striking inclination toward disobedience, developing the habit of refusing to obey as long as he did not feel the hand of his father.

When we stop here and ask what salient character trait will surely develop in this child, we must answer, "Lying." he will lie to escape his father's heavy hand. This is indeed the chief complaint with which the mother has come to us. Today the child is fifteen years old, and the parents never know whether he is lying or telling the truth. When we probe a little more deeply, we hear the following: The child was for a time in a parochial school, where his teachers also complained that he was disobedient and disturbed the class. For example, he would shout the answer to a question before he was asked, or he would ask a question in order to interrupt, or talk loudly to his classmates during class. He would write his homework in a most illegible hand; furthermore, he was left-handed. His conduct finally got beyond all bounds and his lying was noticeable, as soon as he feared punishment from his father. His parents at first decided to leave him in the school, but before long they had to take him out because his teacher concluded that nothing could be done with him.

The boy looked like a lively lad whose intelligence was recognized by all the teachers. He finished public school and had to take

The Education of Children

the entrance examinations for high school. His mother waited for him after the examination and he told her that he had passed the test. Everyone was very happy and they all went to the country for the summer. The boy frequently spoke of high school. Then the high school reopened. The boy packed his schoolbag, went to school, and came home each day for lunch. One day, however, the mother walked with him part of the way and as they crossed the street together, she heard a man say, "There's the boy who showed me the way to the station this morning." When his mother asked him what the man had meant and whether he had been to school that morning, the lad answered that school had ended at ten o'clock and he had walked with the man to the railroad station. Not satisfied with the explanation, the mother later spoke to the father about the matter. The father decided to accompany his son to school the following day. The next day on the way to school, the father learned, in answer to his insistent questioning, that the boy had failed in his entrance examinations, that he had never been to high school, and that he had loafed around the streets all this time.

His parents engaged a tutor and the boy was eventually able to pass the examinations, but his conduct did not improve. He still disrupted the classroom procedure, and one day he began to steal. He stole some money from his mother, lied violently about it, and confessed only when threatened with the police. And now we have before us a case of sad neglect. The father, whose pride was so great that he thought he could bend this twig, now gives his son up as hopeless. The boy is punished by being left alone with no one speaking to him or paying any attention to him. His parents also claim that they no longer beat him.

In answer to the question, "Since when has there been cause for complaint?" the mother replies, "Since his birth." When we receive such an answer, we assume that the mother wants to imply that the boy's bad conduct is inborn, because his parents have tried everything to straighten him out, and have been unsuccessful.

> *As a baby, the boy was extremely restless, he cried day and night. All the doctors, however, declared that he was quite normal and healthy.*

This is not as simple as it sounds. The crying of nursing infants is in no way remarkable. Many reasons may account for it, especially in the case of an only child where the mother has had no previous experience. Such children usually cry when they are wet, a condition which the mother is not always aware of. What did his mother do when he cried ? She took

The Education of Children

the baby in her arms, rocked him, and gave him something to drink. What she should have done was to find out the real cause of the crying, make the child comfortable, and then pay no more attention to him. The child would have stopped crying and would not now have this black spot in his past.

His mother says that he learned to talk and walk at a normal age without difficulty, and that his teeth developed normally. He had a habit of destroying his playthings soon after they were given to him. Such manifestations are often found without necessarily indicating a bad character. Worthy of note is the sentence, "It was impossible to make him occupy himself for any length of time with any one thing." We must ask here how should a mother train a child to play alone. There is only one way to do it. The child must be permitted to occupy himself without constant interruption by adults. We suspect that this mother did not do this and several remarks indicate it. For example, the boy always gave her a lot to do, always clung to her, etc. Here are the child's first attempts to induce his mother to pamper him, the oldest inscriptions on the scroll of his soul.

The child was never left alone.

The mother obviously says that in self-defense.

He was never alone, and to this day he does not like to be left alone even for an hour. Evenings he is never alone, and he has also never been left alone during the night hours.

This confirms how closely the child is tied to his mother and how he has been able to lean on her.

He was never afraid, and does not know fear today.

This statement challenges psychological common sense, because it does not agree with our findings. A closer examination of the facts gives us the explanation. The boy has never been left alone; therefore, he has had no need to be afraid, because children use fear to compel others to remain with them. Consequently, he had no use for fear, an emotion he would have manifested as soon as he was left alone. Now comes another seeming contradiction.

The Education of Children

> *He has a great fear of his father's cane.* (So he did have fear?) *When the whipping was over, however, he forgot it quickly and was lively again, even though he was sometimes spanked severely.*

    Here we see the unfortunate contrast: the mother yielding; the father stern, wanting to correct the mother's softness. And the child is driven more and more in the direction of his mother through his father's harshness. In other words, he turns toward the person who pampers him, and from whom he can get everything easily and cheaply.

    In the parochial school, at the age of six, he came under the supervision of the priests, and at that time the complaints began about his liveliness, restlessness, and inattentiveness. Complaints about his conduct were much more frequent than about his schoolwork. His restlessness was most noticeable. When a child wants to attract attention, what better method can he choose than restlessness? This child wants to be noticed. He has formed the habit of attracting his mother's attention, and now, in a larger circle, he wants the attention of the new members of the larger group at school. When the teacher does not understand the child's purpose, he attempts to correct the child's conduct by singling him out for scolding or for reprimanding, and the boy is then where he wants to be. He has to pay a big price for the attention he secures, but he is used to that. He received enough beatings at home and remained unchanged. Will the milder forms of punishment permitted at the school change him from his old ways? That is most improbable. When he condescended to go to school, he wanted to be the center of attention as a compensation.

    The parents tried to improve his behavior by pointing out to him that everyone needed to keep quiet for the good of the class. When we hear such futile admonitions, we become somewhat dubious about the common sense of the parents. The boy knows the difference between right and wrong as well as the adults. However, he is busy with quite another problem. He wants to be noticed and he cannot gain any attention in school by being quiet, neither can he easily gain attention by hard work. We see no riddle in his conduct, as soon as we are aware of the task he has set himself. Obviously, when the father comes along with his cane, the boy will he quiet for a while. But the mother says that as soon as the father goes away, the boy starts all over again, regarding the whippings and punishments as mere interruptions that disturb his progress for short periods, but not by any means achieving permanent change.

The Education of Children

But his temperament always broke through the restraint.

Children who want to attract attention must obviously do it by temperament. What we usually call temperament is nothing more than a convenient rhythm in which an individual fulfills tasks, and the form of that movement is determined by the goal. For example, if someone wants to lie quietly on the sofa, he does not need to develop such temperament. This temperament becomes a suspicious indication of what a person has in mind—in this case, to make himself conspicuous.

He formed the habit of taking all sorts of things from the house to school, exchanging them for money, and entertaining his companions with the proceeds. When his parents discovered this behavior, he was searched each day before leaving for school. He finally abandoned the practice, confining himself to playing jokes and making interruptions. This change was brought about only by severe punishment from his father.

We can understand his playing jokes; that activity reflects his desire to make others notice him, force his teacher to penalize him, and make himself superior to the school regulations.

His attempts to create disturbances gradually diminished, but returned periodically in full force and resulted in his being expelled from one school.

This confirms what we said before. Struggling to obtain recognition from others, this boy naturally meets obstacles and becomes aware of them. In addition, when we consider that he was left-headed, we have more insight into his mind. We can deduce that although he wanted to avoid difficulties, he managed to find them, then lacked the confidence to tackle them. But the less confidence he had in himself, the more he wanted to demonstrate that he was worthy of attention. He did not cease his mischief-making until the school could no longer tolerate him and expelled him. If we agree with the justifiable view that the school cannot permit one sinner to disturb the work of all the other students, then the only recourse is to expel the sinner. However, because we believe that the purpose of education is to correct shortcomings, expulsion is not the right method. It made getting attention from his mother easier, and he no longer had to exert himself in school.

The Education of Children

We should note here that, on the advice of one teacher, he was sent to a special home during the vacation period. There he was under more strict supervision than even at school and this experiment was also a failure. His parents, however, were still the chief supervisors. The child went home every Sunday, which pleased him very much. Yet, when he was not allowed to go home, he did not sulk. This is understandable. He wanted to play the great man and be regarded as such by others. He made no fuss about a whipping, did not permit himself to cry, nor in any way to behave in an unmanly fashion, no matter how disagreeable things were.

His school report cards were never very bad; he always had tutoring at home.

We conclude from this information that he was not independent. The teacher had told the parents that the boy could learn much better, if only he were somewhat quieter. We are convinced that the boy can learn because all children, except for the feeble-minded, can learn.

He has no talent for drawing.

Significantly, this deficiency may indicate that he has not entirely overcome the clumsiness of his right hand.

One of the best in the gymnasium, he learned to swim quickly and has no fear of danger.

This strength shows that he is not completely discouraged, but that he has been using his courage for unimportant things, which he could do easily and with certainty of success.

He is a stranger to shyness and tells everyone what he thinks, no matter whether it happens to be the janitor or director of the school, in spite of his being admonished repeatedly not to be forward.

We already know that he pays no attention when he is forbidden to do this or that, and we cannot therefore accept his lack of shyness as evidence of courage. We know that many children are well aware of the distance that separates them from the teachers and officials of the school. This boy who does not fear being whipped by his father is naturally not

The Education of Children

afraid of the principal, and speaks impudently in order to make himself important; in this way, he actually achieves his goal.

He is not quite certain about his sex, but says frequently that he wouldn't like to be a girl.

We see no definite indications about his opinion of his own sex, but we always find in boys of such mischievous character the tendency to degrade girls. They derive a sense of their own superiority from the degradation of the girls.

He has no real friends.

This is quite understandable, because other children do not like to constantly give him the role of leader.

His parents have not yet explained sexual matters to him. His behavior always expresses a desire to rule.

He himself knows the facts which we have to get about him with so much effort. In other words, he knows well what he wants, but he unquestionably does not know the connection between his unconscious goal and his behavior. He does not understand the extent and origin of this intense desire to rule. He wants to rule because he sees his father ruling, and the more he wants to rule, the weaker he really is, because he has to depend on others; while his father, whom he has taken as a model, rules in a self-contained manner. In other words, his ambition feeds on his weakness.

He always wants to start something, even with those stronger than he is.

These stronger people are, however, weaker because they take their duties seriously. The boy only trusts himself when he can be impudent. Incidentally, we cannot easily rid him of this rudeness because he has no faith in his ability to learn anything; therefore, he must hide behind his impudence.

He is not selfish; he gives freely.

If we assumed that generosity were a sign of goodness, we would have difficulty connecting it with the rest of his character. However, we know that a person can show superiority by being generous. Seeing how this trait fits in with a lust for power is important. He feels this generosity as a personal elevation. He has probably learned from his father this trick of showing off by being generous.

He still makes a lot of trouble. He is afraid first of all of his father, then, of his mother. He is ready to get up at any hour and is not particularly vain.

This last statement concerns outer vanity, whereas his inner vanity is extraordinarily great.

He has given up the old habit of picking his nose. He is a stubborn child, fussy about food, does not like vegetables or fats. He is not completely unfriendly, but prefers those children with whom he can do anything, and likes animals and flowers very much.

In the background of a liking for animals, sometimes we find a striving for superiority, a desire to dominate. Such a liking is usually not objectionable, if it leads toward a union with all living creatures. With some children where it is expressed as a desire to dominate, it gives the mother more to pay attention to.

He manifested a great desire for leadership, to be sure not for intellectual leadership. He developed a tendency to collect things, but not possessing sufficient patience, no collection was ever completed.

The tragedy of such individuals is that they leave everything unfinished because they fear the responsibility of a completed result.

On the whole, his behavior has improved since the age of ten. It was impossible formerly to keep him in the house because he always wanted to play the hero on the streets. His improvement has been brought about at the cost of great effort.

To confine him to the narrow limits of the house proved in reality the best means of satisfying his strong desire for self-assertion. Small wonder that he does more mischief within these narrow confines. He should have been left on the street under proper supervision.

The Education of Children

When he comes home he turns to his school work, shows no desire for leaving the house, but finds ways for wasting his time.

We shall always be confronted with distraction and time-wasting when we confine a child to such a narrow sphere that he has to work under constant supervision. He must be given an opportunity for activity, in order to play a role among his peers.

He used to go gladly to school.

This suggests that his teacher was not severe. In this way, he was easily able to play the part of a hero.

He used to lose most of his schoolbooks. He was not afraid of examinations; he always believed that he could do everything brilliantly.

We find here a rather common trait. Optimism under all circumstances shows that a person does not believe in himself. Such people are certainly pessimists, but they manage to do violence to logic, taking refuge in a dream world where they can attain everything; they show no signs of surprise when they face defeat. They have a feeling of predestination enabling them to appear as optimists.

He suffers from a great lack of concentration. He is liked by some teachers and greatly disliked by others.

In any case he seems to be liked by the milder teachers who are pleased with his manners. He also disturbs them less, because no difficult tasks are assigned to him. Like most spoiled children, he lacks either the inclination or the habit of concentration. Up to the age of six, he felt no need for this, since his mother took care of everything. Everything in life had been prearranged, as if he were enclosed in a cage. His lack of preparation appeared as soon as he was confronted with difficulties. He had acquired no means for coping with difficulties; he had no interest in others enabling him to cooperate with them. He had neither the desire nor the self-confidence necessary to accomplish something independently. What he possessed was the desire for prominence, the desire to get to the front without any effort. But he failed to disrupt the peace of the school; he failed to get attention, and this made his character worse.

The Education of Children

He always wanted to take everything easily, and get everything in the easiest way without regard for other people. This had become the dominant motif of his life, which was expressed in all his specific acts, such as thefts and lies.

The mistake underlying the development of his life style is obvious. His mother, to be sure, supplied him with a stimulus for developing his social feeling, but neither his mother nor his stern father succeeded in determining what to do next. These social feelings were confined to the world of his mother. In her presence, he felt he was the center of attention.

His striving for superiority was thus no longer directed toward the useful side of life, but toward the vanity of his own person. In order to bring him to the useful side of life, we must begin the development of his character anew. We must gain his confidence, so he will gladly listen to us. At the same time, we must widen the sphere of his social relationships, accomplishing what the mother failed to do with her only child. He will have to be reconciled with his father. His education has to proceed step by step, until he understands the mistake of his past life style in the same way that we understand it. Since his interest will no longer be focused on a single person, his independence and courage will grow and he will direct his superiority striving toward the useful side of life.

Case Two

This is a case of a ten-year-old boy.

The school complains that his work is poor and he is three terms behind.

Ten years old and three terms behind—we suspect that he may be feeble-minded.

He is now in 3B. His I.Q. is 101.

Therefore, he cannot be feeble-minded. What can be the cause of his backwardness? Why does he disrupt the class? We see striving and activity on his part, but all on the useless side. He wants to be creative, active, and the center of attention, but in the wrong way. We can also see that he fights the school. He is a fighter. He is an enemy to the

The Education of Children

school, so we understand why he is behind; the routine of the school is difficult for such a fighter.

He is slow to obey commands.

This is obvious. He acts intelligently; in other words, there is a method in his madness. If he is a fighter, then he has to resist commands. He fights with other boys; he brings toys to school. He wants to make his own school.

He is bad in oral arithmetic.

This means that he lacks social-mindedness and the social logic that goes with it (See Chapter VII).

He has a speech defect and goes to a speech class once a week.

This speech defect is not based on an organic deficiency. This is a symptom of a lack of social cooperation, which shows itself in his impeded speech. Language is an attitude of cooperation; the individual has to connect himself with another person. As things are, the boy uses this speech defect as a tool for his combativeness. We do not wonder why he does not seek to remedy this speech defect, for to remedy it means to give up this tool for attracting attention.

When the teacher talks to him, he moves his body from side to side.

He seems to prepare for an attack. He does not enjoy having the teacher speak to him because he is not the center of attention. The teacher is the conqueror if she speaks and he has to listen.

The mother (to be exact, the stepmother, since the mother died in his infancy) complains only that he is nervous.

This mysterious idea of nervousness covers a multitude of sins.

He was brought up by two grandmothers.

One grandmother is bad enough; we know that grandmothers usually pamper children terribly. In considering why they do it, our

The Education of Children

culture is at fault for having no place for older women. They rebel against this treatment and want to be treated properly, which is only right. A grandmother wants to prove the importance of her existence, which she does by pampering the children and getting them to cling to her. In this way, she asserts her right to be recognized as a worthwhile individual. If we hear about two grandmothers, than most likely a terrible competition is going on. One will want to prove that the children like her more than the other. Naturally, in this competition for his favor, the child finds himself in a sort of paradise where he gets everything he wants. All he needs to say is, "The other grandmother gave me this," and the other will want to outbid her rival. At home, this child is the center of attention, and we can see how he makes this attention his goal. Now he is in school where he does not have two grandmothers, only one teacher and many children. The only way he can be the center of attention here is by fighting.

During the time he was living with the grandmothers, he did not get good grades at school.

The school was not the right place for him. He was not prepared for it. The school was a test of his ability to cooperate, and he was not trained for it. A mother is the one who can best develop this ability for cooperation.

The father remarried a year and a half ago and the child lives with the father and stepmother.

Here we find, of course, a difficult situation. The trouble begins or the trouble is increased when a stepmother or stepfather enters the situation. The problem of stepparents is traditional and has not yet been improved; the child especially suffers. Stepmothers, even of the best kind, generally have trouble. The problem of stepparents is not insoluble, but it can be solved only in a certain manner. Stepmothers and stepfathers should not expect appreciation as their right, but they should try their best to win appreciation. With two grandmothers to complicate the situation, the stepmother's difficulty with the child is increased.

The stepmother tried to be affectionate when she first came into the family. She did all she could to win the boy. An older brother is also a problem.

The Education of Children

Another fighter in the family, and think of the terrible rivalry between the two brothers, increasing the general combativeness.

The child fears the father and obeys him, but he does not obey the mother. Therefore, she reports him to the father.

This is really a confession that the mother cannot educate the child, so she leaves the problem to the man. When the mother reports to the father what the children do and do not do, when she menaces them with the words, "I will tell your father," the children understand that she cannot manage them and has given up the job. So they look for opportunities to dominate her. When the mother speaks and acts in this way, she expresses her inferiority complex.

Mother will take him out to places and buy him things, if he promises to behave.

The mother is in a difficult situation. Why? Because the grandmother overshadows her, as the children think the grandmother is more important.

The grandmother sees him only occasionally.

Someone who comes for only a few hours can easily interfere with the children and leave all the trouble for the mother.

No one in the family seems to really love the child.

They do not seem to like him any more. After spoiling him by pampering, even the grandmother now dislikes him.

The father whips him.

The whipping does not help, however. The child likes praise and if praised, he is entirely contented. But he does not know how to earn praise by acting properly. He prefers to demand praise from the teacher without earning it.

He works better if he receives praise.

The Education of Children

This is of course the case with all children who want to be the center of attention.

Teachers do not like him because he is sullen.

This is the best means he could use, because he is a fighter.

The child suffers from enuresis.

This also expresses his desire to be the center of attention. He does not fight in a direct way, but in an indirect way. How can such a child fight his mother in an indirect way? By wetting the bed and making her get up in the middle of the night; by screaming out in the night; by reading in bed instead of going to sleep; by not getting up in the morning; by bad eating habits. In short, he constantly has some means to keep his mother preoccupied with him, both in the daytime and at night. With the two weapons of enuresis and a speech defect, he fights the environment.

The mother has tried to rid him of this habit by waking him several times in the night.

The mother is therefore with him several times at night. Thus, even in this way, he attains his goal.

Children are not fond of the boy because he wants to boss them. A few weak ones try to imitate him.

A weak and discouraged person, he does not want to carry on in a courageous manner. The weak children in school like to imitate him because this is how weak children gain attention.

On the other hand, he is not redly disliked, and "the other children are glad to think that he has improved whenever his work is chosen as the best."

The children are glad when he improves. Their good will reflects well on the teacher. The teacher really understands how to make the cooperative spirit live in the children.

The boy likes to play ball on the street with other children.

The Education of Children

He has relationships with others when he is sure to succeed and conquer.

The case was discussed with the mother and we explained to her that she was in a difficult situation with the child and the grandmothers. We also explained to her that the boy is jealous of the older brother and fears that he may be left behind. During the interview, the boy did not speak a word although he was told that we were all his friends at the clinic. Speech for this boy would mean cooperation. He wants to fight, so he refrains from speaking. We saw the same lack of social-mindedness expressed in his refusal to do anything about his speech defect.

This may seem astonishing, but we often find even adults who act this way in social life; they fight by not speaking. A couple once had a violent quarrel. The husband screamed loudly and said to his wife, "Now you are silent!" She replied, "I am not silent; I just do not speak!"

In the case of this boy he, too, "just does not speak." When the interview was over, we told him he could go, but he did not seem to want to leave. He was irritated. We told him the discussion was over, and still he did not go. He was told to come again with his father next week.

In the meantime, we said to him, "You acted quite correctly in not speaking because you always do the opposite of what's required. If you are told to speak, you are silent; when you should be silent in school, you disrupt the class by talking. You believe that this makes you a hero. If we told you, "Don't speak at all!" then you would speak. We merely need to lead you on and ask the opposite of what we want."

The child obviously could be made to speak because he would need to answer questions. Thus, he would cooperate with speech and language. Later, when the situation is explained to him and he understands his mistakes, he could gradually improve.

In connection with his case, we should remember that as long as such a child remains in his familiar situation, he has no incentive to change. The mother, father, grandmothers, teachers, comrades—all fit into his accustomed life style. His attitudes are fixed in respect to them. But the clinic confronts him with an entirely new situation. We must even try to make his new situation as new as possible, a totally new environment, so that he will better reveal the character traits belonging to the old situation for which he is trained. We would do well to tell him, "You must not speak at all!" Whereupon he will say, "I will speak!" In

The Education of Children

this way, nobody has entered into conversation with him directly, and he is not on guard with his inhibitions.

At the clinic, the children generally stand before a large audience, which impresses them greatly. It is a new situation, giving the impression that they are not only connected with their own small environment, but that others are also interested, and that they are thus part of a larger whole. All this makes them want to be more a part of the whole than before, especially if they are asked to come again. They know what will happen; they will be questioned and asked how they are getting on. Some come once a week and some come every day, depending on the nature of the case. They are trained to improve their behavior toward the teacher. They know they will not be accused, reproached or criticized, but that everything will be judged as if through an open window. This always impresses people. If a couple have a quarrel and someone opens a window, the quarrel stops, and it becomes an entirely different situation. When a window is open and they can be heard, people do not want to reveal their mistaken character traits. This is one step forward, and this step occurs when children come to the clinic. Making their behavior public helps them improve.

Case Three

This is the case of an oldest child, thirteen and a half years old.

At the age of eleven, he had an I. Q. of 140.

We might say, therefore, that this is a bright child.

Since he entered the second term of high school, he has made very little progress.

From experience we know that if a child believes he is bright, he often expects everything without effort; consequently, he may come to a standstill. For instance, in adolescence, these children feel they are much more grown up than they really are. They want to prove that they are not children any more. The more they attempt to express themselves, the more they meet the difficulties of real life. They then begin to doubt whether they really are as clever as they previously thought they were. Telling a child he is bright or that he has an I.Q. of 140 is not advisable. Children should never know their I.Q. and neither should the parents.

The Education of Children

All this explains why such a bright child may fail later on. This situation is fraught with danger. An ambitious child who is unsure of how to succeed in a positive way will look for how to succeed in a negative one. Some of these negative ways include: becoming lazy or wasting time, becoming neurotic, committing crimes, or committing suicide. Children use a hundred varieties of alibis in order to feel successful in a useless, negative way.

Favorite subject is science. Associates with boys younger than himself.

We know that children join with younger children in order to have things easier, in order to be superior and be the leader. Liking to associate with younger children is a suspicious sign, although not necessarily so—sometimes the attitude is fatherly. But some weakness is usually present, because the expression of a paternal instinct involves the exclusion of play with older children. This exclusion is a conscious act.

Likes football and baseball.

We can assume, therefore, that he excels in these games. Probably we shall hear that he does quite well in certain directions, but shows no interest in others. Wherever he can be sure of success, he will be active; wherever he is not sure of success, he refuses to participate. Of course, this is not the correct way to act.

Plays cards.

That means wasting time.

This seems to take his attention away from the usual routine of going to bed early and doing his homework at the proper time.

Now we are coming to real complaints, all focused on the same point. He cannot succeed in his studies, so he simply wastes time.

As an infant he developed slowly. After two years, he began to develop rapidly.

The Education of Children

We do not know why he developed slowly in his first two years. He was probably pampered and what we have now is the result of a pampered childhood. The slow development might have been due to this pampering. We see pampered children who do not want to speak, move, or function because they like being helped too much, and they are thus not stimulated to develop. But after two years, this boy must have encountered a stimulus which led to his rapid development. Some strong stimulus probably made him a bright and intelligent child.

Outstanding features are honesty and stubbornness.

While his honesty is a nice asset, it is not enough for us. We do not know if he uses it to criticize others, or to boast. Because we know that he likes to lead and boss others, his honesty could be an expression of his superiority striving. We are not sure whether he would continue to be honest if he were in an unfavorable situation. As for his stubbornness, he really wants his own way and likes to be different, not led by others.

He bullies his younger brother.

This statement confirms our judgment. He wants to be a leader and because his younger brother does not obey, he bullies him. This is not very honest and we will find, if we really know him, that he is something of a liar. When he boasts, we see his feeling of superiority. His outward expression of a superiority complex clearly shows that he suffers inwardly from a sense of inferiority. He undervalues himself because he is overvalued by others, and because he undervalues himself, he has to make up for it by boasting. Praising a child too much is not wise because then he gets the idea that much is expected of him. When he cannot easily meet expectations, he begins to tremble and be afraid; consequently, he organizes his life so that his weakness will not be discovered. Ergo, he bullies his brother. This is his style of life. He does not feel strong or confident enough to solve the problems of life independently and properly. Hence, his passion for playing cards. When he plays cards, nobody can discover his inferiority, even if he has bad report cards. His parents would say his bad grades are because of his card-playing, thus saving his pride and vanity. He comes to believe: "Yes, because I like cards I am not a good student; if I did not play cards, I would be the best student. But, I play cards." Satisfied, he has the comfortable feeling that he could be the best. As long as this boy does not understand the logic of his own psychology, he can wail to himself

The Education of Children

and hide his feeling of inferiority both from himself and from others. And as long as he can do this, he will not change. Therefore, in a very friendly manner, we must reveal to him the springs of his character and show him that he really acts like a person who does not feel strong enough to accomplish his work. He feels strong enough only to hide his feeling of weakness, his feeling of inferiority. As we have said, this must be done gently, with constant encouragement. We should not constantly praise him and wave his high I.Q. before him; this frequent reminder probably made him afraid that he might not always be successful. We know quite well that later in life the I.Q. is not very important; all good experimental psychologists know that an I.Q. can merely show a present situation as revealed in the test, and that life is too complicated for a test to show anyone's capacity for successful problem-solving. A high I.Q. does not prove that a child is really able to solve all the complex problems of life.

The boy's real difficulty is his lack of social-mindedness and his feeling of inferiority. And this must be explained to him.

Case Four

This case of an eight and a half-year-old boy illustrates how children are pampered. Criminal and neurotic types spring chiefly from the class of pampered children. The great need of our age is that we stop pampering children. This does not mean that we have to stop liking them, but it means that we have to stop indulging them. We should treat them like friends and equals. This case is valuable for the way it portrays the features of a pampered child.

Present problem: Repeated every grade in school and is now only in the second grade.

A child who repeats grades in the first years of school may well be suspected of feeble-mindedness. We must keep that possibility in mind in our analysis. On the other hand, with a child who starts out well and then slumps, feeble-mindedness may be ruled out.

Talks baby talk.

He wants to be pampered, so he imitates a baby. But this means that he must have a purpose and goal in mind, since he considers acting like a baby to be an advantage. The existence of a rational, conscious plan in this case rules out feeble-mindedness. He does not like schoolwork because he was not prepared for school. And so, instead of developing along social lines in school, he expresses his striving by antagonizing and fighting the environment. Of course, he pays for this attitude of antagonism by being held back in every grade.

Disobeys and fights badly with his older brother.

Hence, we see that the older brother is a hindrance for him, probably because the older brother is a good student. The only way he can compete with his older brother is by being bad. Also, in his dream life he imagines he would he ahead of his brother if he were a baby.

Walked at twenty-two months.

He probably suffered from rickets. If he did not walk until twenty-two months, then he was probably constantly watched, and his mother was continually with him during this time. We can see how this organic imperfection has been a stimulus for the mother to watch him more and pamper him.

He talked early.

Now we are sure that he is not feeble-minded. Difficulty in learning to speak is a major expression of feeble-mindedness.

He always talks baby talk. The father is very affectionate.

He also pampers him.

He prefers the mother. There are two boys in the family. Mother says the older boy is clever. The two boys fight a great deal.

Rivalry between the children is present in most families, especially between the first two children, but any two children who grow up together often become rivals. The psychology of the situation is that when another child comes along, the first is dethroned, and as we have seen (Chap.8) rivalry can be prevented only if children are properly prepared for cooperation.

The Education of Children

He does poorly in arithmetic.

The greatest difficulty in school for the pampered child is usually arithmetic, for arithmetic involves a certain social logic which pampered children do not have.

There must be something wrong with his head.

We cannot find it. He acts quite intelligently.

The mother and teacher believe that he masturbates.

He may. Most children do masturbate.

The mother says he has dark rings under his eyes.

We cannot properly conclude that masturbation is responsible for the rings under his eyes, although people generally suspect it.

He is very finicky in eating.

We see how he wants to keep his mother preoccupied, even in connection with his eating.

He is afraid of the dark.

Being afraid of the dark is also a sign of a pampered childhood.

The child's mother says he has a lot of friends.

We believe they are the ones he can boss.

He is interested in music.

Examining the external ear of musical individuals is instructive. We find that the ear of a musical person has better developed curves. When we saw this boy, we were positive he had a fine and sensitive ear. This sensitivity may express itself in a liking for harmony, and a greater capacity for musical training.

He likes to sing, but he has ear trouble.

The Education of Children

Such people cannot easily endure our noisy life. Their tendency to ear infections is greater than among others. The formation of the auditory organ is inherited, explaining why both musical talent and ear trouble are passed on from generation to generation. This boy is suffering from ear trouble, and some very musical people are in his family.

The proper course of treatment for the boy is to try to make him more independent and self-reliant. At present he is not self-reliant, but believes that his mother must always occupy herself with him and never leave him alone. He constantly wants extra help from his mother, and mothers are, usually, only too glad to give this help. He is now free to do what he wants, free to make mistakes. For only by making mistakes can he learn self-reliance. He must learn not to compete with his brother for his mother's favor. At present, each brother feels the other is preferred, and each one is therefore needlessly jealous of the other.

Making the boy courageous enough to face the problems of school life is especially necessary. Think what will happen if he does not continue at school. The moment he drops out of school, he will have detoured to the useless side of life. One day he will play hookey from school, another day he will stop school altogether, disappear from home and join a gang. An ounce of prevention is worth a pound of cure; we would do better to adjust him now to school life than to deal later with a juvenile delinquent. School is the crucial test. At present, because he is not prepared to solve problems in a social way, he has difficulties at school. But the school's task is to give him new courage. Of course, the school has its own problems: perhaps the classes are overcrowded, and perhaps the teachers he has come across are not well prepared for this work of psychological encouragement. That is the tragedy of things. But if this boy can find a single teacher who can nurture and encourage him properly, then he will be saved.

Case Five

A case history of a ten-year-old girl.

Referred to the clinic from school because of difficulties with arithmetic and spelling.

The Education of Children

Arithmetic is usually a difficult subject for a pampered child. Although pampered children are not necessarily poor in arithmetic, we have often found this to be our experience. We know that left-handed children frequently have difficulties in spelling because they are trained to look from the right to the left side, and when they read, they read from the right to the left. They read and spell correctly, but in reverse, which hardly anyone understands. They know only that they cannot read and they will say they cannot read or spell correctly. Thus, we suspect that the girl may be left-handed. Perhaps, she has difficulties in spelling for another reason. In New York, we must consider the possibility that she may be from another country, and therefore does not understand English properly. In Europe, we do not have to consider such a possibility.

Important points in past history: The family lost most of its money in Germany.

We do not know when they came from Germany. This girl may have experienced good times which suddenly came to an end, presenting her with a new situation, like a test. This new situation will reveal whether she has been properly trained for cooperation, social adjustment, and courage. It will also reveal whether she can bear the burden of being poor—which means in other words, whether she can cooperate. She seems unable to cooperate properly.

She was eight years old and a good student when she left Germany.

That was two years ago.

She does not get along well in school here because the spelling is difficult and arithmetic is not taught in the same way as in Germany.

The teacher does not always make allowances for these differences.

Pampered by her mother, to whom she is very much attached. Likes both parents the same.

If you ask children the question "Whom do you prefer, your mother or your father?" they will generally give the answer, "I like them both the same!" They are taught to give this answer to such a question.

The truth of this answer can be tested in many ways. For instance, we can put the child between the two parents and when we speak to the parents, she will move toward the one to whom she feels most attached. We can see the same thing when the parents are in a room and the child enters. Again, she will go to the one to whom she feels most attached. She has a few girl friends of her own age, but not many.

Earliest remembrances: At the age of eight, she was in the country with her parents and used to play with a dog in the grass. They also had a carriage at this time.

She remembers her riches, the grass, the dog and the carriage. It is the same as with a man who was formerly rich and always looks back to the days when he had a car, horses, a fine house, servants, etc. We can understand that she does not feel contented.

Dreams about Christmas and what Santa Claus will bring her.

Her dream life expresses the same outlook as her waking life. She constantly wants more because she feels deprived and wants to regain what she had in the past.

Leans on the mother.

This dependency is a sign of her discouragement and her difficulties at school. We explained to her that things were harder for her than for the other children and that she could learn by studying more and being courageous.

She came to the clinic again, without her mother. She is getting along a little better in school and has been doing everything alone at home.

She was advised to be independent, rather than depend on her mother, and do everything alone.

She cooked breakfast for her father.

This is a sign of a sense of developing cooperation.

The Education of Children

She believes she is more courageous, and seemed to be more at ease in this interview.

She is to return and bring her mother.

She returned with her mother, who came for the first time. The mother had been working hard and could not get away before. She reports that the girl is a foster child, adopted when two years old, who does not know she is a foster child. In her first two years, she was in six different places.

This is not a pleasant past. This girl seems to have suffered greatly in her first two years. Thus, we are dealing with a child who was probably once hated and neglected, then came to this woman who takes good care of her. The child wants to cling to this favorable situation because of the unconscious impression in her mind of her early bad experiences. In two years, a child can be greatly impressed.

When the mother took the child, she was told that she must be very strict as the child's family was not a good one.

The person who gave this advice was poisoned with the idea of heredity. If she were strict and the girl became a problem child, then the judge could say, "You see, I am right!" He would not know that he is the guilty one.

The mother was bad and the foster mother feels a greater responsibility for the girl because she is not her own child. She sometimes hits the girl.

The situation is not as favorable as before. Sometimes the pampering stops and she is punished instead.

The father pampers the girl and gives her whatever she wants. If she wants something, she will not say, "please" or "thank you." She says "You are not my mother."

Either the child knows the fact or uses a phrase which hits the right spot. We know of a boy of twenty, who does not believe his mother is his real

The Education of Children

mother, yet the parents swear the boy could not know it. Evidently, he has such a feeling. Children form conclusions out of very small things. "The child does not know she is adopted," but sometimes they feel it.

She says this to the mother, but not to the father.

The father does not give her a chance to attack him in that way because he gives her everything.

The mother cannot understand the change at the new school. Now she has a bad report card and she has had to hit her.

The poor child has a bad report card, she is humiliated and feels inferior, then the mother spanks her; it is too much. Even one of these things would be too much—either to be spanked or to get a bad school report. Teachers should consider that when they give children bad school reports, it begins more trouble at home. A wise teacher would avoid giving bad school reports, if she knew that these reports provide the mother with an opportunity to spank the child.

The child says that she sometimes forgets herself and has an outburst of temper. She is excited at school and disrupts the class. She believes she must always be the first.

We can understand this desire in an only child trained by her father to get everything she wants. We can understand how she likes to be the first. We know that in the past she had the country fields, etc., and that she feels deprived of her past advantages. Now her superiority striving is much stronger, but as she has no channels for its expression, she forgets herself and makes trouble.

We explained to her that she must learn to cooperate. We told her that she gets excited in order to be the center of attention, and that her outbursts of temper are only an excuse to get everybody to look at her. She does not work in school because her mother is angry about her grades and she fights her mother.

Dreams that Santa Claus brought her many things. Then she awakes and finds nothing.

Here again she arouses the feelings and emotions of having everything she wants and "awakes and finds nothing." We must not

The Education of Children

overlook the snake in the grass. If we arouse such feelings and emotions in a dream and awake and see nothing, then we will naturally feel disappointed. Yet the dream arouses only the feelings which agree with the attitude after awakening. In other words, the emotional goal of the dreams is not the arousing of marvelous feelings of possessing everything; the emotional goal is precisely to be disappointed. The dreams are created for this purpose until the goal is satisfied and the disappointment takes place. In depression, people have marvelous dreams, but awake and find things quite the contrary. We can understand why this girl wants to be disappointed. She wants to accuse her mother because her present life must appear to her in very dark colors. She feels she has nothing and her mother does not give her anything. "She spanks me; only father gives me things."

Summing up this case, we can see that the child constantly wants to be disappointed so that she can accuse her mother. She fights her mother and if we want to stop this fighting, we must be able to convince her that her behavior at home, her dreams, and her behavior at school all belong to the same mistaken pattern. Her mistaken style of life results primarily from her having been in America only a short time, and not being well trained in the English language. Therefore, we must convince her these difficulties could be easily overcome, but she deliberately uses them as a weapon with which to fight her mother. We must also influence the mother to stop spanking the child, so as not to give her an excuse for fighting. The girl must be brought to realize that "I am not attentive and forget myself, and have outbursts of temper because I want to have trouble with my mother." If she knows this, then she can stop her bad behavior. Before she knew the meaning of all the experiences and impressions in her home and school life and in her dreams, a change of character was, of course, out of the question.

And so we see what psychology is—to understand the use a person makes of his impressions and experiences. Or, in other words, psychology means to understand the scheme of apperception by which a child acts and by which he reacts to stimuli, to understand how he interprets certain stimuli, how he responds to them, and how he uses them for his own purposes.

Index

A

above 8, 20, 55, 156, 162, 198, 211, 212, 214
accusation 47, 48, 193, 205
   accuse 241
achievement 70, 73, 126, 149
activity. 16, 18, 54, 91, 101, 102, 103, 107, 109, 111, 122, 124, 128, 129, 148, 188, 192, 203, 211, 219, 223, 224
   active 10, 23, 24, 92, 123, 155, 156, 194, 224, 231
adapt 2, 80, 116, 167
   adaptation 211
adjustment 31, 102, 122, 151, 152, 158, 162, 197, 237
adolescence 177, 185, 191, 192, 193, 194, 195, 230
affect 56, 62, 87, 111, 139, 172, 187, 209
affection 8, 47, 73, 74, 96, 102, 143, 168
alcohol ....
   alcoholism 9, 18, 147, 211
alibi 133, 193
ambition 86, 87, 102, 116, 117, 118, 120, 121, 124, 125, 127, 145, 146, 156, 194, 221
   ambitious 86, 117, 119, 120, 136, 146, 162, 211, 212, 231
anger 10, 12, 87, 101, 116, 124
antithesis ....
   antithetical 162
anxiety 43, 105, 136, 145, 184, 212
anxiety ....
   anxious 118, 145
apperception 32, 113, 158, 162, 241
archetype 102
arrangement 73, 119
art 9, 20, 28, 104, 105, 122, 131, 154, 172, 187, 208
art
   artist 19, 101
   artists 120, 143, 163
as if ... 6, 18, 23, 25, 31, 32, 46, 53, 57, 59, 65, 66, 68, 75, 76, 79, 80, 81, 84, 85, 86, 103, 108, 109, 113, 121, 139, 185, 191, 196, 200, 206, 223, 230
assertion 156, 206
assumption 25, 71, 78, 80, 109, 127, 169, 205
attention. 7, 11, 14, 15, 17, 31, 35, 46, 48, 49, 53, 68, 73, 75, 76, 77, 78, 79, 86, 93, 101, 109, 110, 112, 122, 123, 124, 125, 128, 131, 132, 133, 134, 143, 144, 145, 146, 167, 184, 186, 195, 197, 199, 200, 212, 213, 216, 217, 218, 219, 220, 222, 223, 224, 225, 226, 228, 231, 240
attitude 5, 6, 12, 14, 17, 24, 25, 28, 34, 36, 39, 40, 47, 48, 60, 74, 79, 80, 85, 87, 95, 106, 107, 110, 111, 112, 116, 127, 134, 135, 138, 139, 140, 145, 146, 148, 154, 157, 158, 163, 164, 165, 166, 171, 172, 173, 183, 184, 185, 192, 197, 206, 207, 208, 210, 211, 212, 225, 231, 234, 241
avarice 211
avoiding 33, 103, 169
awareness 3, 14
awkward 27, 72, 119

B

bashfulness 185
beauty 72, 73, 142, 169, 189

Index

becoming................6, 9, 14, 25, 36, 38, 72, 74, 96, 111, 185, 186, 192, 209, 213, 231
being.... 6, 8, 9, 10, 11, 12, 15, 17, 18, 19, 22, 23, 24, 26, 27, 32, 33, 35, 36, 37, 39, 40, 41, 42, 44, 45, 46, 47, 60, 64, 65, 66, 68, 69, 72, 73, 75, 76, 78, 81, 84, 89, 90, 91, 92, 94, 96, 101, 104, 106, 107, 112, 114, 115, 116, 118, 119, 121, 122, 127, 128, 129, 131, 133, 134, 135, 136, 137, 138, 140, 143, 150, 152, 153, 155, 157, 160, 167, 174, 177, 179, 186, 194, 195, 196, 200, 201, 206, 209, 210, 216, 218, 219, 220, 222, 232, 234, 237, 238, 241
belief..................... 22, 33, 47, 49, 122, 150, 154, 155, 157, 176, 198, 199, 200, 206, 209
belonging.. 8, 137, 170, 229
below..39, 55, 119, 162
biting...81
blind..19, 28, 208
blushing...130
body... 101, 139, 142, 169, 225

C

case.. 9, 11, 12, 14, 15, 20, 24, 25, 28, 30, 31, 35, 36, 37, 39, 40, 57, 58, 62, 65, 67, 71, 84, 86, 95, 100, 101, 102, 105, 106, 109, 113, 114, 125, 127, 128, 129, 131, 133, 135, 136, 138, 144, 147, 152, 160, 161, 163, 165, 166, 169, 170, 172, 176, 178, 181, 184, 186, 191, 192, 193, 195, 199, 204, 207, 208, 213, 216, 219, 223, 224, 228, 229, 230, 233, 234, 236, 241
case...
    cases....5, 6, 7, 18, 28, 30, 31, 38, 39, 43, 60, 64, 65, 70, 71, 75, 85, 86, 87, 104, 105, 117, 119, 136, 138, 139, 140, 142, 147, 150, 156, 161, 173, 181, 195, 198, 199, 203, 206, 207, 208
causality.. 111, 112
caution..60, 210
change 15, 18, 24, 28, 31, 44, 52, 75, 82, 85, 86, 89, 90, 95, 97, 121, 122, 128, 135, 136, 139, 159, 167, 173, 176, 178, 186, 191, 192, 193, 195, 196, 206, 207, 208, 209, 210, 218, 219, 229, 233, 240, 241
character.....36, 38, 49, 56, 61, 86, 89, 103, 105, 109, 111, 116, 121, 135, 138, 141, 148, 159, 160, 161, 162, 164, 176, 184, 189, 191, 193, 194, 207, 212, 215, 217, 221, 222, 223, 224, 229, 230, 233, 241
character..
    character traits..................... 38, 86, 103, 105, 116, 135, 138, 141, 161, 162, 164, 191, 229, 230
    characteristics.. 32, 70, 78, 92, 115, 138, 156, 158, 169, 210
child... 5, 6, 7, 8, 9, 10, 11, 14, 15, 16, 17, 18, 19, 20, 21, 22, 23, 24, 25, 26, 27, 28, 29, 30, 31, 32, 33, 35, 37, 38, 39, 40, 41, 42, 43, 44, 45, 46, 47, 48, 51, 52, 53, 54, 55, 56, 59, 60, 61, 62, 63, 64, 66, 67, 68, 69, 71, 72, 73, 74, 75, 76, 78, 80, 82, 83, 85, 86, 87, 88, 89, 90, 91, 94, 97, 100, 101, 102, 103, 104, 105, 108, 109, 110, 111, 113, 114, 116, 117, 118, 119, 120, 121, 122, 123, 125, 126, 127, 128, 129, 130, 131, 132, 133, 135, 136, 137, 138, 139, 140, 141, 142, 143, 144, 145, 146, 147, 148, 149, 151, 152, 154, 155, 156, 157, 158, 159, 160, 161, 162, 163, 164, 165, 166, 167, 168, 169, 170, 172, 173, 174, 175, 176, 177, 178, 179, 180, 181, 182, 183, 184, 185, 186, 187, 188, 189, 190, 191, 192, 193, 194, 196, 197, 198, 199, 200, 201, 202, 203, 205, 206, 207, 208, 209, 210, 211, 212, 213, 214, 215, 217, 218, 220, 222, 223, 226, 227, 228, 229, 230, 232, 233, 234, 235, 237, 238, 239, 240, 241
child...
    children...2, 3, 4, 5, 6, 7, 8, 10, 14, 15, 16, 17, 19, 20, 23, 24, 25, 27, 28, 30, 31, 32, 33, 35, 36, 37, 38, 41, 42, 43, 44, 45, 48, 54, 55, 57, 61, 62, 64, 65, 68, 69, 73, 74, 75, 76, 77, 78, 79, 81, 82, 83, 85, 86, 88, 89, 91, 92, 93, 94, 95, 100, 102, 103, 104, 105, 109, 110, 114, 115, 116, 117, 118, 119, 120, 121, 122, 123, 124, 125, 126, 127, 128, 129, 131, 132, 133, 134, 135, 136, 137, 138, 139, 140, 141, 142, 143, 144, 145, 146, 147, 148, 149, 150, 151, 152, 154, 155, 156, 157, 159, 160, 161, 162, 163, 164, 165, 167, 168, 169, 170, 172, 173, 174, 175, 176, 177, 178, 179, 180, 181, 183, 184, 185, 186, 187, 188, 189, 190, 191, 193, 194, 196, 197, 198, 199, 200, 201, 202, 204, 205, 208, 209, 210, 212, 213, 216, 217, 220, 221, 222, 223, 225, 227, 228, 230, 231, 232, 233, 234, 235, 237, 238, 240
child guidance.. 125, 187, 199

Index

choice 25, 44, 58, 68, 69, 136, 148, 158, 207, 212
clean 55
    cleaning 66
    cleanliness 43
common sense 54, 57, 58, 65, 112, 152, 153, 159, 163, 166, 170, 217, 218
community 8, 15, 23, 34, 79, 107, 126, 151, 152, 153, 185
community ....
    communal 103, 107, 126, 152, 153
    communal life 126, 152, 153
comparison 58, 147
compensation 20, 102, 104, 115, 142, 149, 150, 162, 209, 218
compensation ....
    compensatory 102, 136
competition 175, 226
complex 61, 109, 110, 114, 233
compulsion ....
    compulsive 168
concentrate 12, 80, 123, 143, 146, 172, 173, 183, 199, 200, 202, 211
    concentration 7, 80, 223
concept 14
    conception 49, 107, 137
conflict 108, 113, 136, 205
conscience 137
conscious 23, 54, 74, 106, 131, 173, 185, 231, 234
conscious ....
    consciousness 23, 108, 143, 206
constitution 168
contact 16, 34, 84, 85, 104, 118, 123, 129, 130, 137, 138, 147, 152, 153, 199, 210, 211
contempt 202, 203
contribution 9, 191
cooperate 4, 7, 81, 97, 180, 181, 223, 226, 229, 237, 240
cooperate ....
    cooperation 2, 84, 137, 172, 181, 186, 188, 190, 198, 205, 207, 225, 226, 229, 234, 237, 238
cosmos 126
courage . 8, 9, 18, 19, 20, 21, 25, 27, 32, 33, 40, 41, 42, 48, 49, 50, 60, 65, 68, 76, 81, 92, 108, 119, 120, 121, 128, 130, 132, 133, 134, 136, 138, 142, 145, 146, 147, 148, 154, 163, 167, 179, 181, 184, 199, 209, 212, 220, 224, 236, 237
    courageous 65, 120, 122, 138, 139, 140, 188, 194, 213, 228, 236, 238, 239
covetousness 211
coward 78, 135
    cowardice 18, 41, 104, 135, 194
creative 17, 20, 22, 24, 224
creative ....
    creative power 17, 20
crime 124, 177
    criminal 18, 103, 116, 125, 147, 154, 211
    criminality 9, 18, 33, 69, 124, 168, 194
critical 3, 12, 39, 47, 48, 91, 135, 211
cruel 170, 177, 187, 198
cruel ....
    cruelty 145, 170, 187
cry 47, 52, 89, 128, 145, 210, 216, 220
cry

Index

crying..28, 58, 84, 88, 91, 97, 128, 212, 216
culture..20, 23, 81, 95, 144, 187, 188, 197, 211, 226
cure..123, 128, 135, 155, 206, 236
curse..62

D

Darwin, Charles..53, 150
daydream..41, 54, 162
deaf..129, 142, 152
deaf..
    deaf-mutism..129
    deafness..142
death..35, 38, 40, 41, 44, 49, 62, 147, 162, 184, 210
defeat..60, 117, 120, 124, 133, 136, 141, 146, 157, 199, 202, 223
defense..69, 150, 217
defiance..68, 81, 211
defiance..
    defiant..7, 81, 116
deficiency..20, 81, 139, 154, 166, 184, 220, 225
delinquency..33
    delinquent..236
delusion..58, 74
democracy..
    democratic..122
Demosthenes..94
dependence..105, 110, 150, 210
    dependency..34, 238
depreciation..96, 115
depreciation..
    depreciation tendency..96
depression..241
depression..
    depressed..19, 39, 40, 74, 83, 154, 192
depth..111
desire to dominate..187, 222
despair..133, 177, 181, 199
dethronement..112
detour..123, 163
development...2, 4, 5, 15, 16, 21, 31, 35, 37, 39, 58, 64, 67, 68, 69, 85, 91, 92, 100, 101, 102, 103, 104, 108, 109, 111, 114, 115, 117, 120, 122, 129, 138, 139, 141, 143, 144, 149, 151, 152, 153, 154, 159, 164, 168, 169, 170, 172, 176, 179, 181, 183, 185, 186, 189, 191, 192, 197, 205, 213, 224, 232
diagnosis..64, 199
difficulty.. 20, 89, 100, 102, 110, 119, 124, 125, 129, 131, 135, 142, 143, 147, 152, 158, 159, 166, 175, 180, 186, 200, 210, 217, 222, 226, 233, 235
    difficulties...6, 7, 8, 17, 20, 21, 25, 40, 45, 54, 56, 57, 63, 94, 96, 118, 119, 120, 125, 129, 131, 140, 142, 143, 147, 148, 155, 156, 157, 163, 172, 173, 176, 177, 178, 184, 186, 187, 188, 195, 196, 199, 207, 209, 210, 211, 212, 213, 219, 223, 230, 236, 237, 238, 241
discipline..28, 35, 38, 81, 161
discouraged 18, 21, 32, 33, 43, 80, 81, 104, 117, 133, 136, 137, 139, 143, 145, 149, 152, 156, 157, 161, 181, 200, 208, 209, 212, 213, 220, 228
    discouragement......27, 30, 89, 106, 120, 125, 130, 133, 136, 145, 179, 202, 211, 212, 213, 238
disease..105, 141, 147, 184
disorderly..155, 167

Index

disposition ... 48
distance ... 81, 84, 137, 138, 163, 220
distraction ... 223
division of labor ... 106
dog ... 115, 187, 238
dog ...
    dogs ... 187
dominance ...
    dominant ... 113, 121, 224
doubt ... 43, 48, 78, 82, 169, 230
doubt ...
    doubtful ... 22
    doubting ... 40
dream ... 38, 40, 41, 49, 56, 57, 58, 59, 60, 61, 62, 63, 64, 79, 80, 223, 234, 238, 241
dreams ... 19, 40, 41, 49, 53, 55, 56, 57, 59, 60, 61, 65, 68, 117, 148, 212, 241
drive ... 110, 117, 147, 197
drive ...
    drives ... 14, 15, 16, 17, 23, 125

E

early memories ... 26
eating ... 11, 19, 73, 144, 210, 211, 228, 235
economy ...
    economic ... 35, 147, 183, 186, 205, 208
education ... 5, 14, 100, 104, 105, 109, 120, 122, 126, 135, 136, 141, 151, 152, 158, 159, 163, 164, 175, 176, 179, 180, 182, 186, 187, 188, 190, 194, 196, 197, 198, 205, 209, 219, 224
education ...
    educator ... 105, 122, 125, 126, 134, 135, 136, 139, 176, 183, 208
    educators ... 3, 125, 143, 144, 159, 170, 185, 190, 205
ego ... 106, 127, 128, 136, 137
ego ...
    egotism ... 103
emotion ... 56, 170, 217
    emotional ... 22, 241
empathy ... 66, 69
empathy ...
    empathize ... 66, 68
encourage ... 77, 78, 97, 122, 134, 163, 177, 236
encourage ...
    encouragement ... 78, 131, 140, 148, 233, 236
enemy ... 78, 135, 193, 224
enemy ...
    enemies ... 6, 39, 105, 151
energy ... 30, 40, 68
    energetic ... 215
enuresis ... 131, 144, 228
environment ... 10, 36, 66, 67, 75, 82, 84, 92, 93, 100, 104, 110, 124, 128, 129, 130, 133, 134, 136, 140, 141, 144, 145, 148, 149, 154, 155, 157, 158, 159, 160, 161, 165, 167, 168, 177, 183, 184, 185, 186, 188, 193, 196, 209, 210, 228, 229, 230, 234
envy ... 105, 116, 118, 135, 140, 189, 210
epileptic ...
    epilepsy ... 30, 47, 147, 211
equal ... 22, 63, 71, 72, 97, 158, 197
    equality ... 97, 116, 198

246

Index

equilibrium 14
error 32, 107, 109, 176, 206
Esau 75
escape 6, 16, 17, 29, 50, 61, 123, 128, 176, 177, 186, 207, 215
ethics 153
evil 116, 122, 154, 170
examination 22, 25, 49, 83, 86, 105, 106, 108, 128, 130, 136, 146, 160, 174, 185, 203, 216, 217
    examinations 136, 173, 199, 203, 211, 216, 223
exclusion 123, 134, 183, 231
excuse 88, 124, 132, 157, 193, 240, 241
excuse ....
    excuses 124, 132, 157
expectation ....
    expecting 6, 33
experience 20, 23, 27, 28, 29, 30, 32, 39, 40, 53, 54, 61, 76, 85, 117, 123, 147, 148, 155, 156, 158, 160, 161, 170, 174, 187, 196, 198, 203, 216, 230, 237

F
failure 6, 18, 30, 39, 104, 111, 120, 142, 166, 167, 168, 181, 193, 205, 209, 220
failure ....
    failures 7, 84, 101, 163, 187, 210, 213, 214
fairy tale 131, 146, 156, 170, 189, 190
family 5, 14, 15, 25, 28, 30, 44, 53, 54, 58, 68, 71, 73, 87, 89, 104, 111, 119, 122, 123, 125, 129, 130, 131, 132, 134, 138, 142, 143, 144, 147, 148, 150, 155, 156, 157, 158, 159, 160, 165, 167, 170, 172, 173, 176, 178, 181, 184, 185, 186, 188, 193, 195, 196, 198, 201, 210, 211, 212, 215, 226, 227, 234, 236, 237, 239
family constellation 111, 130, 134, 148, 155, 156, 159, 212
fantasy 40, 41, 42, 54, 65, 82, 96, 161, 162, 163, 170
fate 46, 122, 157, 174, 189, 195
father 9, 11, 12, 18, 26, 27, 28, 31, 35, 38, 39, 40, 42, 47, 49, 52, 62, 63, 69, 73, 74, 76, 77, 78, 96, 110, 130, 138, 142, 147, 148, 156, 168, 170, 173, 177, 184, 186, 195, 197, 198, 203, 208, 210, 215, 216, 218, 219, 220, 221, 222, 224, 226, 227, 229, 234, 237, 238, 239, 240, 241
fatigue 31, 86, 87
favoritism 188
fear 6, 33, 40, 43, 47, 48, 57, 60, 68, 88, 101, 116, 121, 129, 130, 135, 138, 143, 145, 148, 176, 177, 185, 186, 190, 194, 198, 203, 210, 217, 218, 220, 222
feeble-mindedness 114, 139, 165, 167, 233, 234
feeling 3, 6, 8, 9, 11, 12, 15, 16, 17, 19, 21, 22, 23, 27, 32, 35, 36, 37, 39, 40, 41, 43, 44, 46, 49, 51, 52, 55, 56, 57, 58, 60, 61, 65, 66, 67, 68, 69, 71, 72, 73, 74, 75, 76, 77, 78, 79, 80, 83, 84, 88, 95, 102, 103, 104, 107, 108, 115, 116, 117, 119, 123, 126, 128, 129, 130, 133, 135, 137, 138, 139, 140, 141, 143, 145, 147, 148, 149, 150, 151, 152, 153, 154, 155, 158, 161, 162, 165, 166, 167, 168, 169, 192, 194, 200, 205, 223, 224, 232, 233, 240
feeling ....
    feeling of inferiority 3, 21, 22, 51, 52, 55, 60, 71, 72, 77, 102, 108, 115, 117, 130, 133, 137, 138, 139, 141, 143, 149, 155, 162, 200, 233
    feeling of superiority 55, 232
    feeling of worth 108
fellow man 107
female 39, 74, 96, 157, 168, 196
female ....
    feminine 158, 168, 169, 193, 194
fiction 157, 212
fiction ....
    fictional 189

Index

fictitious..................197
   fictitious superiority..................197
firstborn..................31, 37, 38, 44
forget..................56, 58, 64, 79, 124, 162, 163, 177, 183, 186, 211, 241
forget..................
   forgetting..................114, 124, 176
form........20, 25, 32, 57, 76, 80, 89, 95, 96, 105, 108, 121, 124, 129, 142, 146, 149, 150, 154, 158, 161, 165, 177, 192, 208, 214, 219, 240
freedom..................104, 130, 141
Freud..................49
friendship..................69, 79, 95, 106, 193
future......46, 48, 49, 56, 62, 64, 82, 97, 98, 111, 116, 120, 122, 124, 132, 136, 141, 159, 164, 167, 180, 186, 192, 194, 197, 200, 202, 203, 212, 213

G

game..................79, 118, 187
   games..................55, 117, 179, 185, 187, 212, 231
genital..................197
glance..................2, 137
glands..................31, 139
goal.... 7, 10, 15, 16, 17, 23, 26, 32, 33, 36, 41, 44, 50, 54, 59, 61, 65, 66, 72, 86, 87, 97, 101, 102, 107, 108, 111, 112, 113, 122, 128, 133, 143, 151, 152, 156, 165, 166, 189, 202, 219, 221, 226, 228, 233, 241
goal..................
   goal of perfection..................143
God..................116
Goethe..................49
greed..................145, 201
group..................79, 80, 105, 128, 150, 151, 178, 181, 187, 202, 218
guidance..................100, 113, 125, 181
guilt..................206

H

habit..............23, 24, 43, 81, 116, 124, 130, 132, 167, 197, 207, 215, 217, 218, 219, 222, 223, 228
hallucination..................166
handwriting..................20, 45, 63, 120
happy..................29, 33, 40, 46, 50, 52, 56, 57, 62, 63, 64, 105, 156, 165, 181, 194, 196, 215, 216
happy..................
   happiness..................19, 107, 126, 196
hate..................165
hate..................
   hated child..................102
hate;hatred..................105, 157
headache..................
   headaches..................86, 87, 118
heart..................5, 23, 35, 69, 86, 146, 180
heredity..................164, 176, 177, 213, 239
hero..................64, 66, 95, 123, 170, 212, 222, 223, 229
homosexuality..................
   homosexual..................40
horizontal..................22
hostility..................83, 98
   hostile..................10, 67, 74, 75, 86, 93, 137, 138, 140, 145, 164, 171, 185, 207, 210

Index

human....... 3, 5, 6, 8, 9, 15, 17, 22, 23, 27, 34, 36, 56, 60, 68, 69, 87, 100, 101, 102, 106, 110, 111, 112, 115, 116, 118, 126, 129, 133, 135, 137, 143, 150, 151, 152, 153, 159, 170, 177, 183, 188, 197, 200, 209
human nature... 3, 5, 8, 87, 110, 115, 150, 170
humiliation.. 145, 207
humility...207
hunger.. 56
hurting..188
hypersensitivity..210
hypothesis.. 14, 106, 129

I

idea.....6, 14, 36, 48, 49, 53, 54, 55, 84, 96, 116, 121, 127, 139, 143, 151, 152, 158, 162, 169, 170, 175, 177, 202, 208, 213, 215, 225, 232, 239
ideal..9, 16, 17, 35, 36, 73, 103, 104, 108, 122, 162, 169, 170, 175, 180
illness..30, 31, 35, 38, 67, 141, 184, 211
image...41, 103, 164
image..
    images...59
imagination... 38, 102, 116, 162, 163
imagination..
    imaginary...116
imitation..187
impatience..146, 210
impatience...
    impatient...207
imperfection...234
imperfection..
    imperfect...101, 102
inborn...8, 15, 115, 216
incomplete...169
independence..36, 88, 89, 125, 144, 224
    independent.................25, 35, 53, 77, 89, 90, 109, 118, 122, 131, 134, 188, 192, 220, 236, 238
Individual Psychology... 1, 2, 3, 4, 8, 9, 16, 17, 33, 34, 37, 50, 53, 55, 56, 66, 70, 82, 83, 100, 101, 103, 104, 105, 107, 108, 109, 111, 114, 121, 137, 155, 169, 174, 176, 178, 183, 191, 196, 199, 202, 204, 205, 210
individuality..159
indolence..168, 199
inertia..176
infantile...49
inferiority. 15, 22, 102, 104, 115, 120, 124, 133, 134, 136, 138, 139, 141, 143, 152, 168, 197, 200, 201, 210, 227, 232
inferiority..
    inferiority complex... 133, 134, 136, 138, 141, 197, 200, 227
    inferiority feeling..116, 143, 210
insane..196
insecurity...15, 87, 95, 143
insight... 3, 16, 36, 53, 87, 114, 180, 195, 205, 219
instinct..14, 197, 231
intelligence...36, 64, 82, 121, 141, 144, 173, 174, 176, 211, 215
    intelligent... 10, 12, 110, 153, 232
intention...14
    intentions.. 105, 206

Index

interest......5, 6, 7, 8, 9, 16, 19, 21, 36, 37, 38, 40, 43, 44, 45, 46, 48, 54, 63, 67, 68, 69, 70, 71, 72, 80, 81, 83, 100, 126, 134, 142, 143, 152, 172, 173, 175, 180, 181, 184, 186, 189, 205, 223, 224, 231
intolerance..................39
irritability.................130
   irritable................130, 145, 147
isolation................83, 186, 212

J

Jacob..................75
jealousy................38, 46, 111, 131, 159, 210
   jealous................46, 118, 159, 160, 229, 236
joke..................197
   jokes..................219
joy 30, 46, 50, 64, 76, 107, 129, 156, 168

K

Kramer, Josef..................48

L

language................9, 34, 84, 91, 153, 171, 206, 207, 229, 241
laughter..................212
law................34, 104, 125, 159, 207
law................
   laws................18, 108, 151, 157, 170
laziness................21, 76, 127, 128, 146, 182
   lazy................7, 21, 75, 76, 110, 127, 128, 137, 146, 157, 181, 182, 208, 211, 231
leadership..................222
   leader................75, 130, 145, 221, 231, 232
learning................31, 74, 75, 77, 88, 91, 94, 142, 143, 187, 200, 210, 234
left-handedness................20, 45, 77, 119, 120
Lichtenberg, George..................49
life plan................15, 16
life style (see also style of life)................148, 209, 224, 229
liveliness..................218
logic................50, 56, 57, 58, 59, 61, 107, 114, 126, 148, 150, 152, 159, 223, 225, 232, 235
love................4, 6, 9, 17, 39, 45, 55, 67, 70, 79, 80, 105, 107, 131, 140, 165, 192, 197, 198, 227
loyalty..................106
lying................46, 68, 155, 166, 215

M

maladjustment..................163
male................168, 194, 197
mankind................106, 107, 137, 151, 154, 163, 168, 180, 187, 198
marriage................9, 17, 35, 67, 96, 107, 149, 158, 186, 192, 195, 197, 210, 212
marry................40, 61, 65, 158
masculine protest................169, 193
masculinity................
   masculine................39, 95, 157, 168, 169, 193
masturbation..................235
mathematics................77, 139, 142, 153
maturity................29, 151
memory................38, 39, 40, 41, 43, 44, 45, 59, 69, 125, 173, 184, 202
mental disorder..................147
mental health..................126
metaphor................58, 84

Index

mind... 9, 11, 24, 50, 74, 75, 103, 114, 121, 122, 137, 142, 147, 153, 154, 172, 174, 176, 177, 182, 183, 186, 196, 201, 203, 219, 233, 239
misinterpretation 124, 159
mood 50, 56, 57, 59, 60, 61, 62, 65, 83, 87, 115, 125, 206
morality 23, 36
mother.. 6, 7, 9, 10, 11, 12, 13, 15, 18, 19, 24, 25, 26, 27, 28, 29, 30, 33, 35, 36, 38, 39, 42, 45, 46, 47, 48, 51, 52, 54, 62, 63, 64, 65, 67, 68, 69, 71, 72, 73, 74, 75, 85, 90, 91, 92, 93, 96, 110, 112, 113, 114, 130, 131, 134, 138, 143, 144, 148, 161, 163, 167, 170, 173, 177, 181, 186, 194, 195, 196, 197, 199, 200, 201, 202, 203, 210, 215, 216, 217, 218, 219, 222, 223, 224, 225, 226, 227, 228, 229, 234, 235, 236, 237, 238, 239, 240, 241
motives 47
movement 17, 26, 44, 53, 55, 79, 124, 131, 137, 141, 144, 187, 219
murder 58, 88
murderer 18, 58
music 23, 45, 142, 149, 179, 235
musical 235, 236

N

nagging 47, 135, 143, 146, 152, 208, 211
nation 5
need....5, 6, 14, 17, 19, 28, 36, 40, 44, 47, 56, 62, 69, 74, 79, 83, 93, 103, 104, 105, 118, 119, 123, 125, 127, 143, 145, 148, 151, 152, 154, 155, 163, 165, 178, 182, 186, 189, 194, 197, 198, 200, 207, 217, 219, 223, 229, 233
neglect 38, 110, 122, 176, 216
neglect ....
    neglected child 24, 32, 33, 39, 68, 69
neurosis 18, 116, 126, 136, 186, 211
    neuroses 4, 9, 57, 69, 147, 186
    neurotic 133, 231, 233
nightmare 103
    nightmares 61, 144
normal 4, 20, 29, 36, 72, 102, 103, 104, 105, 113, 117, 118, 134, 137, 139, 141, 155, 172, 176, 196, 202, 210, 216, 217
normality 103

O

obedience 28, 145, 169
objective 9, 82, 101, 102, 103, 106, 107, 108, 111, 127, 141, 147, 153, 209
obstacle 100, 120, 124, 142, 178, 191
occupation 68, 106, 136, 148, 192, 193
only child 35, 36, 46, 75, 85, 110, 134, 148, 155, 157, 160, 212, 215, 216, 224, 240
opinion 3, 40, 75, 89, 119, 137, 138, 146, 200, 203, 206, 221
optimism 9, 40, 74, 135
optimistic 18, 22, 33, 176
oral 225
orator 142
organ 19, 33, 38, 101, 102, 119, 133, 137, 180, 232, 236
organ ....
    organ inferiority 19, 133
orientation 111
overcoming 6, 41, 44, 57

P

pain 89, 134, 138, 152, 183, 187
painter 20

Index

palpitation 146
palpitation ....
    palpitations 87
pampering 7, 8, 15, 31, 38, 63, 85, 91, 102, 143, 148, 188, 197, 211, 226, 227, 232, 233, 239
pampering ....
    pampered 6, 7, 8, 10, 12, 15, 16, 25, 26, 30, 31, 32, 35, 36, 38, 46, 51, 67, 68, 75, 77, 80, 82, 83, 85, 86, 88, 89, 91, 92, 102, 105, 110, 113, 123, 129, 131, 144, 146, 157, 167, 172, 173, 184, 185, 186, 191, 232, 233, 235, 237
paralysis 130
parent 41, 87, 100, 103, 106, 109, 125, 126, 134, 135, 185, 186, 187, 190, 193, 198, 199, 205, 208, 209
    parents 2, 3, 4, 8, 10, 12, 14, 26, 28, 29, 30, 31, 35, 36, 39, 41, 44, 45, 46, 58, 62, 63, 64, 65, 67, 72, 73, 75, 82, 92, 104, 105, 107, 110, 112, 113, 123, 125, 127, 129, 132, 138, 142, 144, 147, 148, 149, 151, 152, 157, 160, 162, 164, 165, 167, 170, 172, 174, 176, 177, 179, 181, 183, 184, 185, 186, 187, 188, 190, 193, 194, 195, 196, 197, 198, 200, 205, 206, 207, 208, 209, 210, 211, 212, 215, 216, 218, 219, 220, 221, 230, 232, 237, 238, 240
passivity ....
    passive 123, 130, 140, 146, 199
patient 53, 90, 106, 214
pattern 6, 31, 53, 95, 101, 109, 111, 112, 121, 122, 127, 133, 139, 159, 165, 241
peace 97, 103, 110, 125, 223
perception 46, 49, 98, 101, 139
perfection 101
personal superiority 57
personality 5, 23, 86, 100, 101, 105, 106, 107, 109, 110, 112, 113, 114, 115, 118, 121, 139, 145, 161, 164, 174, 191, 192, 205, 209
perspective 35, 43, 59, 165
perverse 163
perversion 9
pessimism 48, 141
philosophy 16, 65, 153, 162, 163
physician 38, 44
pity 89, 188
Plato 153
play 7, 11, 14, 29, 32, 43, 54, 60, 67, 72, 79, 81, 84, 95, 111, 117, 118, 143, 158, 161, 174, 179, 185, 188, 194, 196, 197, 212, 215, 217, 220, 222, 223, 228, 231, 232, 236, 238
    pleasure 10, 45, 76, 206
poet 189
politics 188
possession 157
poverty 30, 36, 186
power 16, 47, 48, 58, 92, 107, 112, 113, 114, 116, 124, 140, 142, 146, 151, 157, 160, 161, 184, 191, 194, 203, 222
practical 3, 4, 100, 154, 174
praise 118, 123, 128, 135, 155, 185, 212, 227, 233
predestination 223
preparation ... 6, 7, 9, 17, 19, 22, 67, 77, 82, 136, 148, 158, 169, 172, 173, 174, 175, 179, 187, 191, 192, 197, 211, 223
prestige 133, 135, 136, 161
pride 72, 206, 207, 216, 232
primitive 153, 156
private intelligence 163

Index

problem.... 3, 4, 5, 6, 9, 14, 15, 18, 20, 21, 22, 25, 28, 30, 31, 40, 41, 49, 50, 54, 56, 57, 59, 61, 65, 66, 69, 70, 81, 90, 96, 100, 104, 106, 107, 108, 109, 111, 118, 120, 124, 126, 127, 135, 137, 139, 148, 149, 151, 160, 165, 171, 177, 178, 180, 181, 182, 186, 192, 195, 197, 205, 218, 226, 227, 233, 239
    problem child 4, 5, 9, 14, 18, 21, 28, 30, 31, 66, 69, 70, 104, 111, 118, 126, 139, 160, 165, 171, 181, 186, 205, 239
profession 148, 158, 172, 177, 202, 212
proof 34, 63, 66, 88, 130, 139, 148, 194
prophesy 135
prostitution 18, 69
protection 18, 63, 95, 133, 151, 163
psyche 34, 38, 56, 71, 100, 111
psychic 4, 109, 111, 112, 139, 147, 210
psychology 3, 8, 14, 23, 24, 100, 109, 112, 152, 181, 182, 183, 197, 232, 234, 241
psychology ....
    psychological 7, 16, 49, 57, 63, 79, 100, 101, 102, 103, 104, 105, 109, 113, 114, 115, 123, 125, 127, 128, 133, 139, 150, 161, 166, 172, 173, 176, 178, 179, 181, 183, 184, 186, 188, 191, 192, 195, 198, 201, 203, 205, 217, 236
punishment 7, 15, 20, 26, 33, 36, 67, 68, 84, 105, 109, 124, 128, 144, 165, 177, 208, 215, 218, 219
purpose 3, 50, 151, 174, 179, 218, 219, 233, 241
purposeful 59

R

race 31, 44, 65, 73, 74, 75, 89, 90, 91, 92, 113, 151, 179, 187, 189
rage 39, 71
rational 100, 189, 234
readiness 116
reality... 57, 59, 60, 65, 101, 102, 103, 106, 108, 112, 117, 136, 141, 146, 153, 161, 162, 163, 174, 182, 193, 206, 207, 208, 222
reason. 3, 12, 15, 30, 33, 37, 50, 59, 61, 72, 80, 82, 83, 90, 101, 107, 111, 112, 119, 120, 146, 148, 153, 156, 157, 159, 165, 168, 184, 186, 187, 191, 237
reasoning 17
rebellion 165
recollection 24, 37, 38, 39, 43, 44, 45, 47, 48, 51, 52
rejection 121
religion 34, 78, 187
religion ....
    religious 9, 78, 122
repression ....
    repressed 191
resentment 169
resistance 181, 189
responsibility 14, 122, 125, 146, 173, 176, 186, 205, 209, 222, 239
responsibility ....
    responsible 85, 102, 125, 133, 177, 181, 205, 235
restlessness 218
retreat 121
revenge 12, 125
ridicule 134, 135, 145
rigid 105, 209, 214
role. 5, 14, 15, 23, 39, 43, 53, 54, 55, 60, 66, 67, 72, 79, 91, 93, 95, 96, 97, 98, 111, 117, 122, 134, 138, 143, 147, 154, 158, 161, 168, 188, 193, 194, 196, 197, 198, 210, 221, 223
role ....
    role-playing 23

Index

Rousseau, Jean-Jacques..76
rule... 89, 91, 111, 145, 157, 159, 160, 163, 178, 184, 206, 207, 221
    rules.. 7, 17, 28, 34, 38, 79, 125, 151, 155, 159, 169, 170, 221, 234
S
salvation... 114, 174, 200
Saul.. 156
scheme... 105, 113, 114, 137, 162, 165, 209, 241
school.....2, 3, 4, 5, 6, 7, 9, 14, 15, 17, 18, 20, 23, 24, 26, 27, 28, 29, 30, 31, 32, 33, 35, 36, 39, 40,
    45, 46, 48, 52, 53, 61, 62, 64, 67, 69, 71, 72, 73, 74, 75, 77, 79, 80, 81, 82, 83, 84, 85, 86, 90,
    92, 94, 95, 96, 103, 104, 109, 110, 112, 113, 114, 117, 119, 121, 122, 123, 124, 125, 128, 130,
    134, 136, 138, 140, 142, 145, 146, 147, 153, 156, 160, 161, 164, 166, 167, 172, 173, 174, 175,
    176, 177, 178, 179, 180, 181, 187, 192, 193, 195, 196, 199, 200, 201, 202, 203, 205, 206, 208,
    209, 210, 211, 213, 215, 218, 219, 220, 223, 224, 225, 226, 228, 229, 230, 233, 234, 235, 236,
    237, 238, 240, 241
Schumann, Clara.. 142
science...46, 49, 77, 105, 162, 176, 183, 203, 231
second child.. 31, 37, 38, 44, 75, 79, 89, 92, 111, 184
security..46, 143, 153
self....21, 22, 23, 25, 26, 27, 39, 40, 50, 57, 58, 76, 78, 89, 100, 106, 110, 116, 117, 120, 122, 124,
    134, 135, 136, 137, 150, 154, 169, 175, 185, 188, 194, 195, 197, 202, 217, 221, 222, 223, 236
self..
    self-assertion..116, 117, 222
    self-centeredness.. 21
    self-confidence... 22, 39, 50, 57, 123, 154, 202, 223
    self-esteem...23, 25, 26, 27, 78
    self-evaluation.. 22, 76, 136
    self-preservation.. 150
sensation... 66
sense organ..180
sensitive.. 73, 142, 143, 161, 235
sex........................... 39, 95, 107, 157, 167, 168, 169, 180, 185, 192, 194, 196, 197, 198, 210, 221
sexual..... 9, 18, 23, 33, 49, 69, 76, 97, 120, 124, 146, 147, 168, 169, 180, 194, 196, 197, 198, 210,
    221
sexuality... 147, 180, 198
shame... 116
shock.. 147, 167
shyness..220
sickness... 147, 184
significance...................... 4, 5, 26, 37, 39, 48, 49, 52, 109, 110, 127, 128, 134, 177, 183, 201, 211
significant......... 19, 38, 48, 49, 54, 55, 67, 75, 86, 95, 130, 133, 148, 153, 155, 166, 173, 194, 212
simile..60
simplicity... 153
skin...52
sleep.. 47, 57, 68, 73, 91, 93, 144, 166, 198, 211, 228
sleep;sleeping..18, 68, 166
smell..115
smoking...193
social....6, 8, 9, 11, 12, 14, 15, 16, 17, 19, 27, 28, 32, 34, 36, 37, 39, 40, 41, 44, 46, 65, 67, 68, 69,
    73, 74, 75, 78, 79, 80, 83, 103, 104, 106, 107, 108, 114, 122, 125, 126, 129, 130, 135, 137,
    139, 145, 148, 149, 150, 151, 152, 153, 154, 158, 166, 168, 177, 178, 183, 184, 185, 188, 191,
    193, 197, 205, 224, 225, 229, 233, 234, 235, 236, 237
social context... 15, 34
social interest... 69, 80, 191

Index

social usefulness............107
socially useful............34, 166
society............5, 9, 14, 15, 16, 17, 18, 28, 33, 34, 80, 81, 104, 114, 122, 125, 137, 138, 151, 188
Socrates............110
sorrow............183
soul............68, 75, 101, 103, 137, 186, 217
speech............91, 92, 94, 129, 131, 142, 149, 152, 213, 225, 228, 229
stature............166
status............176
stealing............26
stomach............64, 68, 90
striving............7, 9, 17, 18, 23, 27, 42, 44, 59, 60, 76, 89, 96, 100, 102, 107, 111, 115, 117, 121, 122, 124, 126, 127, 129, 130, 133, 134, 136, 137, 139, 145, 150, 154, 155, 156, 161, 166, 167, 168, 188, 191, 195, 196, 202, 222, 224, 234
striving............
    striving for significance............44
    striving for success............133
stupi;stupidity............121, 139
stupid............124, 135, 136, 147, 153, 154, 162, 213
stuttering............84, 85, 129, 130, 131, 132, 133, 134
style of life............101, 107, 108, 114, 144, 149, 158, 161, 173, 178, 189, 191, 192, 232, 241
subjective............101, 107, 112, 159, 175, 189
submission............115
success............33, 68, 76, 81, 83, 97, 104, 110, 115, 118, 119, 120, 122, 124, 128, 129, 143, 161, 167, 180, 181, 199, 206, 213, 220, 231
suffering............3, 19, 30, 31, 57, 152, 157, 161, 170, 184, 200, 236
suicide............9, 65, 69, 133, 146, 168, 177, 196, 231
suicide............
    suicides............21, 120
superiority 17, 23, 33, 44, 49, 59, 60, 61, 88, 89, 101, 102, 104, 111, 115, 116, 117, 121, 122, 124, 126, 127, 129, 130, 133, 134, 137, 145, 150, 154, 155, 157, 160, 161, 167, 168, 169, 175, 187, 202, 221, 222, 224, 232, 240
    superior............17, 44, 72, 74, 76, 87, 95, 96, 97, 140, 150, 161, 162, 169, 194, 196, 207, 219, 231
    superiority complex............232
    superiority striving............115, 129, 137, 150, 161, 187, 224, 232, 240
superstition............24, 120, 147, 176, 199
suspicion............47, 135, 137, 142
syle............101, 107, 108, 114, 144, 149, 158, 161, 173, 174, 178, 189, 191, 192, 232, 241
sympathy............58, 105, 132, 134, 145, 170, 177
    sympathetic............58, 106, 113, 134, 193
symptom............91, 104, 131, 144, 194, 209, 225
symptoms............16, 84, 86, 87, 105, 111, 121, 124, 131, 135, 144, 168, 169, 192, 201, 209, 213

T

tardiness............121
teacher..6, 7, 8, 18, 24, 25, 29, 30, 31, 33, 38, 49, 52, 58, 64, 67, 73, 76, 80, 84, 88, 106, 109, 113, 120, 123, 125, 128, 130, 134, 136, 138, 146, 149, 165, 166, 167, 168, 172, 173, 174, 175, 176, 177, 178, 179, 180, 181, 182, 183, 184, 187, 193, 195, 196, 199, 200, 202, 203, 205, 206, 207, 208, 209, 211, 215, 218, 219, 220, 223, 225, 226, 227, 228, 230, 235, 236, 237, 240
teacher............
    teachers.2, 3, 18, 28, 33, 67, 84, 87, 95, 107, 117, 121, 125, 146, 173, 174, 175, 176, 177, 178, 181, 193, 203, 204, 205, 210, 215, 220, 223, 229, 236
teeth............217
temper............164, 165, 177, 208, 240, 241

255

Index

temper..
    temper tantrums... 164, 165
temperament... 169, 219
tension.. 66, 86, 87, 88, 110, 117, 128, 130, 131, 147, 166
the question............... 9, 29, 45, 67, 72, 100, 106, 107, 128, 149, 161, 167, 197, 202, 216, 237, 241
theoretical.. 3, 4, 174
thinking............................... 12, 43, 49, 54, 64, 68, 74, 77, 79, 93, 96, 101, 110, 137, 153, 154, 162
thought....... 11, 25, 29, 40, 41, 48, 54, 58, 62, 74, 96, 113, 143, 147, 152, 153, 166, 168, 176, 178, 181, 185, 189, 196, 206, 216, 230
time 3, 5, 9, 11, 12, 14, 19, 20, 22, 23, 31, 32, 33, 38, 40, 42, 44, 46, 49, 52, 61, 62, 66, 75, 76, 78, 80, 81, 82, 83, 85, 88, 90, 92, 94, 95, 97, 103, 104, 110, 111, 114, 117, 118, 122, 123, 124, 126, 128, 129, 130, 132, 133, 134, 136, 138, 139, 141, 142, 148, 151, 152, 153, 154, 155, 156, 158, 161, 164, 165, 167, 170, 172, 179, 183, 185, 186, 187, 189, 192, 193, 194, 196, 197, 198, 200, 201, 208, 210, 211, 215, 216, 217, 218, 223, 224, 226, 231, 234, 238, 239, 241
timidity.. 89, 138, 189, 210
training.... 8, 20, 23, 33, 41, 53, 69, 83, 104, 120, 122, 139, 159, 176, 179, 180, 185, 186, 187, 235
trait... 121, 137, 157, 185, 194, 215, 222, 223
trait..
    traits.......... 39, 45, 60, 69, 100, 102, 105, 110, 116, 118, 125, 158, 168, 169, 185, 194, 210, 212
trap... 76, 84, 113, 158
treatment..... 8, 27, 39, 47, 57, 74, 114, 121, 129, 130, 134, 149, 165, 170, 199, 206, 208, 226, 236
truancy.. 124
truth... 17, 58, 118, 150, 153, 215, 238
truth;truthfulness.. 106

U

ugliness.. 167
uncertainty... 49, 115, 121, 157
unconscious... 23, 24, 27, 53, 54, 69, 76, 106, 159, 221, 239
understanding. 4, 7, 9, 16, 22, 28, 49, 60, 66, 81, 82, 83, 84, 90, 100, 101, 104, 106, 108, 110, 121, 148, 152, 154, 159, 170, 177, 197, 201, 204, 209, 213
unhappy.. 141, 149, 156, 186
unhappy...
    unhappiness... 123, 148
unique... 8, 53, 67, 101, 114, 115, 150, 155
uniqueness.. 28, 64, 116, 159, 214
unity... 16, 17, 22, 25, 37, 43, 100, 101, 108, 109, 114, 115, 164, 194, 209
unruliness.. 168
upward striving.. 108

V

vain... 66, 211, 213, 222
value... 16, 18, 93, 111, 116, 127, 153, 174, 176, 189
    values.. 126, 162, 197
vanity.. 222, 224, 232
vertical... 22, 101
virtue.. 117, 123, 143, 206

W

war... 57, 60, 156, 187
wasting time.. 231
weakness.... 15, 41, 95, 104, 115, 116, 133, 135, 138, 140, 145, 146, 149, 151, 167, 169, 210, 221, 231, 232
weapon... 84, 132, 133, 144, 241
Wild.. 14, 110

Index

wisdom 100
wish 8, 49, 54, 58, 62, 129, 168, 174
withdrawal 163
woman 33, 45, 64, 97, 98, 101, 110, 122, 158, 162, 168, 169, 170, 215, 239
work ... 2, 3, 7, 19, 20, 24, 30, 31, 33, 35, 40, 46, 48, 56, 63, 67, 69, 74, 76, 77, 86, 92, 94, 97, 110, 113, 122, 123, 128, 130, 133, 134, 136, 137, 144, 145, 146, 153, 168, 169, 173, 176, 177, 179, 181, 183, 185, 187, 191, 192, 193, 198, 202, 203, 205, 206, 209, 213, 218, 219, 223, 224, 228, 233, 236, 240
world 2, 15, 32, 34, 37, 40, 41, 49, 54, 56, 57, 101, 102, 103, 119, 133, 135, 137, 138, 141, 148, 151, 158, 161, 162, 163, 171, 185, 188, 190, 223, 224
worthlessness 116

Y

younger 11, 14, 38, 71, 72, 73, 74, 75, 78, 79, 89, 91, 94, 95, 111, 130, 131, 134, 140, 155, 156, 157, 159, 195, 200, 202, 210, 231, 232
youngest 148, 155, 156, 212
youngest ....
    youngest child 148, 155, 156

Appendix A

Appendix A:

Basic Principles of Classical Adlerian Psychology

Henry T. Stein, Ph.D.[8]

Alfred Adler (1870-1937) developed the first holistic theory of personality, psychopathology, and psychotherapy that was intimately connected to humanistic philosophy of living. His lectures and books for the general public are characterized by a crystal clear common sense. His clinical books and journal articles reveal an uncommon understanding of mental disorder, a deep insight into the art of healing, and a great inspiration for encouraging optimal human development. Adler's essential principles are as follows.

Unity of the Individual

Thinking, feeling, emotion, and behavior can only be understood as subordinated to the individual's style of life, or consistent pattern of dealing with life. The individual is not internally divided or the battleground of conflicting forces. Each aspect of the personality points in the same direction.

Goal Orientation

There is one central personality dynamic derived from the growth and forward movement of life itself. It is a future-oriented striving toward a goal of significance, superiority, or success. In mental health, it is a realistic goal of socially useful significance or superiority over general difficulties; in mental disorder, it is an unrealistic goal of exaggerated significance or superiority over others. The early childhood feeling of inferiority, for which one aims to compensate, leads to the creation of a fictional final goal which subjectively seems to promise

---

[8] This brief overview was first published in 1997 on the Classical Adlerian Psychology web site at http://go.ourworld.nu/hstein/principl.htm. A more comprehensive exposition of principles, "Classical Adlerian Theory and Practice," may be found in Volume 1 of *The Collected Clinical Works of Alfred Adler*, or on the web at http://go.ourworld.nu/hstein/theoprac.htm.

Appendix A

future security and success. The depth of the inferiority feeling usually determines the height of the goal which then becomes the "final cause" of behavior patterns.

Self-Determination and Uniqueness

The goal may be influenced by hereditary and cultural factors, but it ultimately springs from the creative power of the individual, and is consequently unique. Usually, individuals are not fully aware of their goal. Through the analysis of birth order, repeated coping patterns, and earliest memories, the psychotherapist infers the goal as a working hypothesis.

Social Context

As an indivisible whole, a system, the human being is also a part of larger wholes or systems--the family, the community, all of humanity, our planet, the cosmos. In these contexts, we meet the three important life tasks: occupation, love and sex, and our relationship with other people--all social challenges. Our way of responding to our first social system, the family constellation, may become the prototype of our world view and attitude toward life.

The Feeling of Community

Each human being has the capacity for learning to live in harmony with society. This is an innate potential for social connectedness which has to be consciously developed. Social interest and feeling imply "social improvement," quite different from conformity, leaving room for social innovation even through cultural resistance or rebellion. The feeling of genuine security is rooted in a deep sense of belonging and embeddedness within the stream of social evolution.

Mental Health

A feeling of human connectedness, and a willingness to develop oneself fully and contribute to the welfare of others, are the main criteria of mental health. When these qualities are underdeveloped, feelings of

Appendix A

inferiority may haunt an individual, or an attitude of superiority may antagonize others. Consequently, the unconscious fictional goal will be self-centered and emotionally or materially exploitive of other people. When the feeling of connectedness and the willingness to contribute are stronger, a feeling of equality emerges, and the individual's goal will be self-transcending and beneficial to others.

Treatment

Adlerian individual psychotherapy, brief therapy, couple therapy, and family therapy follow parallel paths. Clients are encouraged to overcome their feelings of insecurity, develop deeper feelings of connectedness, and to redirect their striving for significance into more socially beneficial directions. Through a respectful Socratic dialogue, they are challenged to correct mistaken assumptions, attitudes, behaviors and feelings about themselves and the world. Constant encouragement stimulates clients to attempt what was previously felt as impossible. The growth of confidence, pride, and gratification leads to a greater desire and ability to cooperate. The objective of therapy is to replace exaggerated self-protection, self-enhancement, and self-indulgence with courageous social contribution.